EDUCATION AND CLASS: CHINESE IN BRITAIN AND THE UNITED STATES

To Mum and Dad

Education and Class: Chinese in Britain and the United States

YUAN CHENG
Nuffield College
University of Oxford

Avebury

Aldershot · Brookfield USA · Hong Kong · Singapore · Sydney

Published by
Avebury
Ashgate Publishing Limited
Gower House
Croft Road
Aldershot
Hants GU11 3HR
England

Ashgate Publishing Company
Old Post Road
Brookfield
Vermont 05036
USA

British Library Cataloguing in Publication Data

Cheng, Yuan
  Education and Class: Chinese in Britain
  and the US
  I. Title
  371.97951
ISBN 1 85628 652 5

Library of Congress Cataloging-in-Publication Data

Cheng, Yuan,   1964–
  Education and class : Chinese in Britain and the United States /
  Yuan Cheng
    p. cm.
  Includes bibliographical references (p.) and index.
  ISBN 1-85628-652-5 : $59.95
  1. Chinese students-- Education--Great Britain. 2. Chinese
  students--Education--United States. 3. Chinese--Great Britain-
  -Social conditions. 4. Chinese--United States--Social conditions.
  5. Chinese--Employment--Great Britain. 6. Chinese--Employment-
  -United States. I. Title
  LC3085.G7C44   1994
  371.97'951041--dc20
                                                        94-8724
                                                         CIP
Printed and Bound in Great Britain by
Athenaeum Press Ltd, Newcastle upon Tyne.

Contents

Figures

Tables

Acknowledgements

I would like to thank Anthony Heath for his inspiration and encouragement throughout this project. I owe thanks to him for his constructive academic advice, solid statistical assistance and for his insisting, on several occasions, that I should "just try it one more time", from which I have benefited tremendously in preparing this book. I would also like to thank John Goldthorpe for his inspired discussions and rigorous criticism. My thanks also go to Ceri Peach for his generosity in offering both academic advice and moral support. Thanks are also due to the following individuals for useful discussions and helpful comments: David Cox, Duncan Gallie, Chelly Halsey, Clive Payne, Joan Payne, Terry Ranger, Byron Shafer and Tariq Madood. For practical help, I am indebted to Jane Roberts for spending much time and energy on preparing my data. Finally, I would like to thank Lianmao Peng for his patience, understanding and support.

Introduction

Research goals

In this book, I shall compare the relative chances of occupational success of Chinese in Great Britain and Chinese in the United States in the 1980s.[1] Using existing large scale governmental sample surveys, I shall study the ethnic occupational attainment process. The focus is on the effect of education in determining occupational attainments.

Since the 1960s, there has been much research on Chinese in the U.S. Guided by liberal concern about racial and ethnic equality, many studies examined the effects of formal schooling and labour market experience on ethnic occupational attainments. Research of this kind primarily used secondary analysis of nationally representative sample data. Very often, comparisons were made between different ethnic groups. Findings concerning Chinese have generally reached a consensus that Chinese are relatively successful in obtaining professional occupations through extraordinary educational achievements.[2]

---

[1] This book studies Chinese who reported to be in work or unemployed. Therefore, it does not include illegal immigrants and those within working age but not in the labour force.

[2] More recently, studies of Chinese occupational attainments have shown that formal schooling has enabled Chinese to enter high paying occupations and industries. Yet within these occupations and industries, Chinese earn less than their white counterparts. This is because Chinese are under-represented in high paying positions, such as managerial positions. See Harriet Duleep, *Economic Status of Americans with Asian Descent: An Exploratory Investigation* (Washington: The United States Commission of Civil Rights, 1988).

1

Earlier studies of the ethnic occupational attainment process in Britain, however, paid scant attention to Chinese immigrants and their descendants.[3] The limited number of published studies on Chinese are predominantly case studies, emphasizing the concentration of Chinese in the catering industry and their low social profile as a consequence of occupational encapsulation.

It is noticeable that most of the case studies from which these findings were obtained, were conducted in areas with large Chinese concentrations, for instance, Chinatown, where the traditional Chinese business of restaurants and take-aways prevails. The research findings are therefore relevant only to the catering Chinese community. They cannot be applied to the whole working Chinese population in Britain.

In this book, my first aim is to do an empirical study of the relative occupational attainments of Chinese in Britain. It is to draw an objective occupational profile for the working Chinese as a whole against the broader background of the British society. This suggests that findings on Chinese will be obtained through comparisons with other ethnic groups in Britain.

My second aim is to compare the relative chances of occupational success of Chinese in Britain with those of Chinese in the U.S. I want to see whether the occupational success of Chinese in the U.S is an exceptional case, or whether it can also be applied to other western industrial societies, such as Britain.

This comparison is important because of two related factors. First, the common perception is that Chinese are more occupationally successful in the U.S than they are in Britain. Does this reflect the true relative situations of Chinese in these countries or simply our limited knowledge of them? Secondly, on the basis of this commonly held perception, inferences about American exceptionalism are often made. Is it true that America is exceptional among western societies in allowing Chinese immigrants and their children to rise to the higher levels of the occupational structure? Do Chinese encounter more restrictive chances in Britain? Without making comparative results available, none of these questions can be answered.

This study also aims at answering a broader sociological question concerning the relative chance of occupational attainments for the same ethnic minority in two different industrial societies, i.e. Chinese in Britain and the U.S. The comparison will show whether the ascriptive penalty or advantage associated with ethnicity is the same in Britain and America, or whether it is true that America is exceptional in allowing ethnic minorities to succeed occupationally.

---

[3] Home Affairs Committee. *The House of Commons Second Report from the Home Affairs Committee (Session 1984-1985): Chinese in Britain* (1985) 1.

Theories and hypotheses

Traditionally, discussions on ethnic occupational attainments are often centred around the theory of industrialism.[4] According to this theory, industrialization requires more efficient use of human talents. Therefore, people of all classes should be given an equal chance to realize their own potential. As a result, occupational position should be increasingly legitimized by achieved status such as education and work experience, and not by ascriptive characteristics, such as ethnicity.

In spite of these suppositions about industrialism, previous studies have shown that ethnicity, often, still accounts for occupational disparity between majority whites and ethnic minorities.[5] This is largely due to the fact that, given the same amount of education and seniority, some ethnic minorities do not achieve the same occupational level as their white counterparts. That is to say, minority members of all educational backgrounds suffer disadvantage in transforming their qualifications into commensurate occupational levels, although the degree of ethnic penalty may vary from one minority group to another. Because of this, the positive role of education in the advancement of ethnic minorities, which is implied by the human capital argument, is not generally supported.

Thus, the first hypothesis to test is whether the effect of ethnicity in general, Chinese in particular, is significant in Britain and America, once educational level and age are held constant. Can higher Chinese achievements in America be explained by higher educational attainments? Or are ethnic penalties simply greater in Britain?

The null hypothesis is that Chinese with the same qualifications as whites and other non-white minorities, enjoy the same chance of occupational success. Ethnicity in general, Chinese in particular, makes no difference in occupational outcome for those possessing the same

---

[4] See Clark Kerr, *Industrialism and Industrial Man* (New York: Oxford University Press, 1964); Peter Blau and O.D.Duncan, *The American Occupational Structure* (New York: John Wiley & Son, Inc., 1967).

[5] According to Blau and Duncan, ethnic minority members have to cross three hurdles in the process of occupational attainment. American Blacks, for instance, have lower social origins which entail lower levels of education than whites. Thus they are handicapped at the first hurdle. Secondly, even given the same educational qualifications, Blacks enter the job market at lower levels. Finally, given the same education and career beginnings, the income of Blacks is lower than that of whites. Thus, the authors consider the socioeconomic disadvantage of American Blacks to be a result of multiple handicaps. See Peter Blau and Otis Dudley Duncan, *The American Occupational Structure* (New York: John Wiley and Sons, Inc. Press, 1964); Otis Dudley Duncan, "Inheritance of Poverty or Inheritance of Race," *On Understanding of Poverty: Perspectives from the Social Sciences*, ed. D.P.Moynihan (New York: Basic Books, Inc. Press, 1965).

3

educational backgrounds. The level of occupational attainments may vary from one ethnic group to another, but for all ethnic groups, given the same educational qualification and age, the level of occupational success should be the same.

The ethnic assimilation theory asserts that the longer an ethnic group stays, the more it assimilates to the host society. Structural assimilation in education and occupation is considered essential because of its positive role in helping immigrants and their children to be acculturated and subsequently assimilated.[6] Occupational integration is expected to reach a higher level among native-born ethnic minority members than among foreign-born immigrants. Thus, the effect of ethnicity is expected to be weaker in accounting for occupational differentials among the second and subsequent generations of ethnic minorities. With regard to Chinese, the question is whether, given the same education and age, British or American-born Chinese display less disparity in occupation than Chinese immigrants, when compared with other ethnic groups. This is the second hypothesis to test.

In addition to the above theories on the role of education in determining ethnic occupational success (i.e. industrialism and human capital), a new theory on ethnic enclave economy has recently been developed. It argues that the enclave may provide no worse chances for occupational success than the outside labour market.[7] In New York City, positive effects of occupational returns to college education and labour market experiences are found for Chinese working both inside and outside the Chinese catering industry.[8] Thus, the third hypothesis to test is whether the enclave effect on Chinese occupational success persists after education and age are held constant.

All three hypotheses concerning ethnic occupational attainments will be tested for male and female Chinese separately in Britain and the U.S. To study ethnic effects on occupation, comparisons are made between Chinese and majority whites and major ethnic minorities in each country. In the British case, Chinese are compared with British whites, Indians, Pakistanis, African Asians, West Indians and Irish. In the American case, Chinese are

[6] Milton Gordon, *Assimilation in American Life: The Role of Race, Religion and National Origin* (New York: Oxford University Press, 1964).

[7] See Portes et al. "Immigrant Enclaves: An Analysis of the Labour Market Experiences of Cubans in Miami," *American Journal of Sociology* 86 (1980): 295-319; "Unwelcomed Immigrants: the Labour Market Experiences of 1980 (Mariel) Cuban and Haitian Refugees in South Florida," *American Sociological Review* 50 (1985): 494-514.

[8] Min Zhou and J. Logan, "Returns to Human Capital in Ethnic Enclaves: New York City's Chinatown," *American Sociological Review* 54 (1989): 809-820. Note, "returns" refer to earnings.

compared with American whites, Japanese, Koreans, Filipinos, Indians, Vietnamese, Hispanics, and Blacks.

The last comparative hypothesis concerns national differences in the relative chances of Chinese occupational success. The null hypothesis says, that after controlling for education, age, ethnicity, and national differences in occupational distribution and education, being Chinese in Britain entails the same propensity to succeed occupationally as being Chinese in the USA. This is to say, Chinese Americans are not more successful than British Chinese. It follows that America is not exceptional in providing avenues for Chinese immigrants to rise to the higher levels of occupational structure.

Although Chinese form the centre of statistical analysis, sociological discussion of the results does not apply only to Chinese. Prompted by the theoretical propositions behind hypothesis testing, the discussion will also address the relative occupational positions of other non-white ethnic minorities. The purpose is to try to understand (on a speculative level) the larger social forces which form the occupational situation of ethnic minorities in industrial societies.

To summarize, in this book I shall study the relative occupational position of Chinese in Britain and America. By studying Chinese in relation to majority whites and major ethnic minorities, I shall extend my discussion to include all non-white ethnic minorities. The conclusions with regard to ethnic occupational returns to education and ethnic assimilation will also apply to all ethnic minorities. By drawing comparisons between the relative occupational levels of Chinese in Britain and the U.S, I hope to make some inferences about the degrees of openness in the two societies.

Chapter descriptions

Theory

I first review previous work by American and British researchers on Chinese occupational attainments. I also discuss the research questions of this book in the light of existing literature. Then, I lay out the theoretical foundations of the major analysis to follow. The aim is to guide future discussion on ethnic occupational attainment process. Therefore, the rest of this chapter considers concepts relevant to ethnic occupational attainments: industrialism, human capital, enclave economy and American exceptionalism.

Data and methodology

In this chapter, I first describe the data sets I use in the analysis. In brief, I use a pooled data set of British national Labour Force Surveys 1983-1989 for the analysis of Chinese in Britain, and the 1980 United States Census of Population and Housing Public Use Microdata Sample A for the analysis of Chinese in the U.S. Secondly, I discuss the statistical techniques used in each chapter of data analysis: cross-tabular analysis in Chapters Three, Four and Six and the logistic regression analysis in Chapters Five, Seven and Eight. I also illustrate how to understand the logit models. Explanations are given for measures of goodness of fit, such as G-square (G^2), degrees of freedom (d.f), change in G-square (ΔG^2), change in degrees of freedom ($\Delta d.f$), significance (p-value), percentage reduction in G^2 (rG^2) and index of dissimilarity, known as the percentage of misclassified cases (ID). In addition, I explain how to understand the parameter estimates and their transformations from fitted log odds ratios into fitted probabilities. Included in this chapter is a list of variables used in the logistic regression equations, with notes on how they are coded and the grounds for including them.

Demographic profile of Chinese in Britain

This answers simple questions about Chinese in Britain, who they are, where they come from, when they enter the country, and where they live. Thus, I look at a series of demographic variables, such as ethnic origin, country of birth, sex, age, year of arrival and region of residence. The analysis is guided by the belief that certain demographic characteristics may contribute positively to the subsequent occupational success of an ethnic group. Thus, the aim of this chapter is also to find out the relative demographic potential Chinese possess as compared with British whites, Indians, Pakistanis, African Asians, West Indians, and Irish.

Educational attainments of Chinese in Britain

In this chapter, I present secondary historical material on imperial China to show that, in spite of traditional Chinese culture placing high value on learning for its own sake, the belief that education would eventually lead to upward social mobility may also motivate the pursuit of learning. Similar evidence is also available for urban and rural Hong Kong, where the majority of Chinese population in Britain originate. Next, I examine the educational level of Chinese in Britain, as compared with other ethnic groups. To test the strength of ethnic effects on education, I fit multinomial logit models in which education is a function of age and ethnic origin for men and women separately.

Occupational attainments of Chinese in Britain

This chapter focuses on the occupational attainment process of Chinese in Britain. First, I look at the occupational distribution of Chinese in comparison with other ethnic groups. Then, I test hypotheses concerning occupational returns to education as well as sector difference in occupational returns to education. The hypotheses relate to industrialism, human capital and the ethnic enclave economy. These hypotheses are tested separately for male and female immigrants.

Demographic profile of Chinese in the United States

In this chapter, which is a comparison to Chapter Three, I explore a series of demographic variables on sex, age, year of arrival, region of residence, and level of English speaking[9] for all ethnic groups in the U.S. The purpose is to see how, given their demographic potentials, Chinese are likely to fare occupationally, in comparison with American whites, Blacks, Hispanics, Japanese, Koreans, Filipinos, Indians, and Vietnamese.

Educational and occupational attainments of Chinese in the United States

This long chapter correspond to Chapters 4 and 5.[10] I start by looking at the educational distribution of all ethnic groups in the U.S. As in Chapter Four, I test the strength of the relationship between ethnic origin and the highest educational level by fitting multinomial logit models, in which the highest grade is a function of ethnicity and age. Next, as in Chapter Five, I test the hypotheses concerning ethnic occupational attainments. Again, the same hypotheses are tested separately for male immigrants, female immigrants, native-born males, and native-born females.

---

[9] The information on level of English speaking is available only in the American data set. Similar information is not available in the British data set.

[10] This chapter is not split up into two chapters, with separate ones on education and occupation, because historical materials presented in Chapter Three "Educational Attainments: Chinese in Britain" are applicable to the Chinese in the U.S.. The empirical analysis on education is fairly short and can hardly form a chapter on its own. Thus, it is simply combined with the analysis on occupation.

This chapter compares the relative chances of Chinese occupational success. The purpose is to see if being Chinese in Britain entails different relative chances of occupational success from being Chinese in the U.S. To draw a comparison between two nations, I first make response and explanatory variables comparable. Then, I fit a logit model where occupational attainment is a function of age, education, ethnicity, country, education by country and ethnicity by country. The interaction of ethnicity by country is the key effect, showing ethnic differences in relative occupational success across countries.

Conclusion

In this chapter, I summarize the major findings from previous analysis, first on Chinese in Britain and Chinese in the U.S. separately, then on the comparison between Chinese in these countries. At the end, I discuss possible policy implications, especially with regard to Chinese in Britain.

1 Literature review

Chinese occupational attainments

Chinese in the United States

In the past three decades, much research has been done on Chinese occupational attainments in the U.S. Primarily using survey data, researchers studied, among other things, the level of socio-economic achievements of Chinese.[1] The research indicated a noticeable presence of immigrant professionals and technicians of Chinese origin, the proportion of which among occupationally active immigrants consistently exceeded the average among the U.S. workers. These immigrants were considered a positively self-selected group aspiring for occupational and economic success through hard work.[2]

In this section, I shall examine the major research findings since the 1960s in chronological order. The purpose is to see, from existing literature, how Chinese immigrants and their American born children have fared occupationally, in comparison with other ethnic groups in contemporary America.

The idea of Chinese being a successful minority was first introduced to the American public by the popular press in the 1960s.[3] A feature article carried by the U.S. News and World Report in 1966 stated that the nation's 30,000 Chinese Americans were achieving substantial economic

---

[1] Studies on Chinese socio-economic achievements are often discussed in relation to and referred to as socio-economic achievements of Asian Americans.

[2] Portes Alejandro and Ruben G. Rumbaut, *Immigrant America: A Portrait* (Berkeley: University of California Press, 1990) 10-11.

[3] USCCR, *Success of Asian Americans: Fact or Fiction ?* (Claring House Publication 64, 1980) 1.

success by "dint of ... hard work".[4]   Throughout the 1960s and 1970s, such a model minority image was also applied to Japanese and Koreans.[5] Each story contained a common theme, that is Asian Americans presented an example of diligence and success for other Americans to emulate.

The popular views have their basis in social science literature during this time. Several studies of the 1960 U.S. census concluded that Asian Americans had attained a high level of occupational success. Although much was written on the success story of Japanese,[6] Chinese were also considered to be reaching parity with Japanese in education and upward occupational mobility.[7] In the 1970s, a number of researchers published results which continued to stress the theme of success.[8] The success of Chinese was said even to "challenge conventional wisdom regarding the consequences of racial discrimination".[9]

The positive image of Asian Americans was enhanced by mass media coverage and helped form commonly held perceptions of Asian Americans, including Chinese, as success stories. Starting from the late 1970s, however, a change in the emphasis of research, from Chinese occupational attainments to their continued economic disadvantage, is noticeable. A research report based on a consultation of Asian Americans civil rights issues, sponsored by the USCCR in 1980, denied the overall success of Asian Americans and suggested substantial differentiation among the Asian American groups.[10]

With regard to intra-group differentiation, which also applies to Chinese, the Commissions suggested the following:

---

[4] U.S. News and World Report, "Success Story of One Minority Group in U.S.," *U.S. News and World Report* (Dec 26, 1966) 73-76.

[5] William Petersen, "Success Story: Japanese American Style," *New York Times Magazine* (January 9, 1966) 38.; "Success Story: Outwhiting the Whites," *Newsweek* (June 21, 1971) 24.; Sandra G. Boodman, "Korean Americans: In Pursuit of Economic Success," *Washington Post* (July 13, 1978) Md.1.

[6] Barbara F. Varon, "The Japanese Americans: Comparative Occupational Status" in *Demography* 3 (1967); William Petersen, *Japanese Americans*. New York: Random House, 1971.

[7] Calvin Schmid and Charles Nobbe, "Socioeconomic Differentials Among Nonwhite Races," *American Sociological Review* (December, 1965) 909-922.;   B. L. Sung. *Mountain of Gold: The Story of the Chinese in America* (New York: MacMillan Co., 1967).

[8] Stanford Lyman, *Chinese Americans* (New School for Social Research, 1974); Wen H. Kuo, "On the Study of Asian Americans: Its Current State and Agenda" in *Sociological Quarterly* 20 (1979) 279-290.

[9] B.R.Chiswick, "An Analysis of the Earnings and the Employment of Asian American Men," *Journal of Labour Economics* 1 (1983) 197.

[10] USCCR, (1980) 1-28.

The stereotype of success focuses on those Asian Americans who are doing well, but it ignores the large number who are not. The percentage of college graduates, for instance, is high among many groups of Asian Americans. On the other hand, the adults with fewer than 5 years of schooling is also high when compared with majority Americans. Although many Asian Americans are in high paying occupations, a disproportionately large number are also in low paying jobs.[11]

This is confirmed by another report released eight years later. High levels of poverty were found among several groups of recent Asian immigrants, Chinese included.[12]

With regard to inter-group differentiation, especially between white and non-white ethnic groups, the Commission confirmed a general consensus of Asian American's lower income levels relative to their high educational attainments, based on a series of earlier studies.[13] It concluded that the desire to be successful manifested in the high educational attainment of many members of Asian groups had apparently not been rewarded by a commensurate income.[14] The patterns emerging from research in this period may be best summarized by Hirschman in a review paper entitled "America's Melting Pot Reconsidered",

Asian Americans, especially those of Chinese and Japanese origin have made significant strides towards socioeconomic equality with the majority population. The gains are more

---

[11] Ibid., 17.

[12] USCCR, *Voices Across America: Roundtable Discussions of Asian Civil Rights Issues* (1988).

[13] These studies include: U.S. Department of Health, Education and Welfare, Office of Special Concerns, *A Study of Selected Socio-Economic Characteristics of Ethnic Minorities Based on the 1970 Census, Vol. II: Asian Americans* (1974); R.M.Jiobu, "Earning Differentials Between Whites and Ethnic Minorities: the Cases of Asian Americans, Blacks and Chicanos," in *Sociology and Social Research* 61 (1976) 24-38.; Amado Y. Cabezas. "Disadvantaged Employment Status of Asian and Pacific Americans," *Civil Rights Issues of Asian and Pacific Americans: Myths and Realities, a Consultation Sponsored by the U.S. Commission on Civil Rights* (1979); Harold Wong. *The Relative Economic Status of Chinese, Japanese, Black, and White Men in California.* (Ph.D. Thesis, University of California, Berkeley, 1980).

[14] USCCR, *Success of Asian Americans: Fact or Fiction.* Clearing House Publication 64, 1980.

evident in education and occupational levels than in earnings.[15]

The updated research findings instantly became the object of new governmental investigations, especially by such organization as the United States Commission on Civil Rights. Since its first Asian-USCCR Hearings held in Washington D.C. in 1979, the organization has published many results, culminating in the releasing of Harriet Duleep's report on *The Economic Status of Americans with Asian Descent: An Exploratory Investigation in 1988.*[16]

The most important findings of this report suggest that, adjusting for broad occupational and industrial categories, American-born Asian men with high levels of schooling earn less than comparable non-Hispanic white men. It appeared that extensive formal schooling enabled Asians to enter high paying occupations and industries. Yet within these occupations and industries, Asians are under-represented in higher paying positions. Further evidence in support of this conclusion shows that American-born Asian men are less likely to be in managerial positions than their white counterparts.

To summarize, the above research findings concerning the level of socio-economic success of Chinese in the U.S. have shown that, although Chinese Americans have not yet reached economic parity with majority whites, they have been able to obtain high occupational positions through investment in formal schooling. Given this newly discovered economic handicap, Chinese Americans cannot be seen as a success minority. Yet, in so far as occupation is concerned, they may still be considered relatively successful, because their level of occupational returns to education is already equitable to that of whites.[17]

Methodologically, these findings have suggested that survey based studies are able to provide evidence about the whole Chinese population in the U.S.. In other words, results obtained from such studies are nationally

---

[15] Charles Hirschman, "American's Melting Pot Reconsidered" in *Annual Review of Sociology* 9 (1983) 397-423.

[16] In the following year, three USCCR sponsored roundtable conferences were held in Houston, Texas, New York City and San Francisco. For more details, read the summary and transcript of roundtable conferences entitled *Voices Across America: Round Table Discussions of Asian Civil Rights Issues* (USCCR, 1989).

[17] In this thesis, I will not look at the income level of the Chinese, but will focus on the level of occupational attainments. The indicator for occupational attainment will be derived from occupation category and employment status within occupation, following Goldthorpe's Class Schema. Thus, it is different from the occupational attainments normally discussed in American literature.

representative. In addition, the statistical technique of multiple regression analysis has been applied to data analysis in many studies. It provides a powerful means of understanding the occupational attainment process by disentangling the effects of possible explanatory variables on the outcome of occupational success.

Unfortunately, such methods remain largely unfamiliar to British researchers working on the Chinese community. As a result, nationally representative quantified findings concerning occupational attainments are not yet available for Chinese in Britain.

Chinese in Britain

Chinese, with an estimated population exceeding 100,000 in the 1980s, form the third largest non-white ethnic minority in Britain.[18] However, "Chinese have hitherto figured very little in discussion concerning race relations and ethnic minorities in Britain".[19] In this section, I shall review the limited number of existing studies related to Chinese occupational attainments in Britain.

The House of Commons Second Report From the Home Affairs Committee (Session 1984-1985): Chinese in Britain is the most recent governmental investigation of Chinese in Britain. Covering areas such as language and education, finance and funding, social services, housing, immigration and nationality, and careers and employment, the report is by far the most complete study concerning Chinese in this country. With regard to employment, the Committee suggests the following:

> Employment is predominantly in catering. Estimates of the proportion so engaged are generally about 90%, though sometimes more. Others would put it slightly lower because of the industries such as importing and wholesaling to serve the Chinese catering trade. A large proportion of catering families-perhaps 60%-now run take-aways (including fish and chip shops) rather than restaurants. The number of Chinese professionals is growing, but it remains as yet tiny in percentage terms possibly as 2 or 3 percent.[20]

---

[18] Runnymede Trust Report, "The Chinese Community in Britain (Background Paper)," *Runnymede Trust Bulletin* 178 (April,1985) 5.

[19] Home Affairs Committee, *The House of Commons Second Report From the Home Affairs Committee (Session 1984-1985): Chinese in Britain* (1985) 1.

[20] Ibid., p.16.

With regard to the effects of such occupational distribution over the Chinese community in Britain, the report continues:

> The concentration on catering has had immense consequences for the community's development in Britain, particularly in shielding the Chinese from the wider society through its long and unsocial hours and its ability, at least until recently, to absorb all available Chinese labour.[21]

The report encountered much criticism from the Chinese community after its publication in 1985.[22] An underlying theme running through all criticism seems to be alleged in accuracy of the information on which the conclusions about Chinese are drawn, including a whole range of descriptive statistics, from the actual number of Chinese in Britain to a true percentage of unemployed. This is blamed on inaccurate estimation by the councils at local levels. Hence, there is a lack of reliable information at national level.[23] As a result, considerable doubts have been cast upon the credibility of the report as a whole. In fact, concern has been expressed about the report being taken as "definitive and authoritative" in the absence of other materials on Chinese, and about the danger that British people would read it without true knowledge and understanding of the Chinese community.[24]

Academic research, too, has failed to provide reliable information on the occupational profile of Chinese in Britain. A great deal of emphasis has been laid on the catering Chinese and little effort has been made to include employment aspects of all working Chinese. Existing studies, most of which were conducted by researchers of Chinese origin, are restricted to case studies at local level of the catering Chinese, typically in metropolitan areas with relatively large Chinese concentrations.[25]

---

[21] Ibid.

[22] A conference on "Chinese Community in Britain" was held at Conway Hall, London on March 30, 1985. It was organized by the Chinese Information and Advice Centre, a GLC funded voluntary organization, to discuss the HAC report on *The Chinese in Britain*. At this conference, limitations of the report are summarized. For this, see Chinese Information and Advice Centre, *Chinese Community in Britain: Conference Report* (1985) 5-9.

[23] The Runnymede Trust, *The Chinese Community in Britain: The Home Affairs Committee Report in Context* (1986) 5, 12.

[24] Ibid., 1.

[25] For examples: Yeuk Lin Linda Lai, *Chinese Families in London: A Study into Their Social Needs* (M.A. Thesis in Public and Social Administration, Brunell University, 1975); Chuen-hing William Cheung, *The Chinese Way: A Social Study of the Chinese Community in a Yorkshire City* (Thesis in Social Administration and Social Work,

Although these studies apply to Chinese in the catering industry only, the findings do provide interesting insights into employment among the majority of the working Chinese. They also indicate differences in Chinese occupational distribution and occupational prospects caused by gender and generation.

Most catering Chinese in Britain work in family business, where kinship plays an important role in economic life. In an early study of catering Chinese in London, Ng pointed out three major functions of kinship network in determining one's employment status. Kinship helps bring workers from overseas to Britain, secures employment for the immigrants and provide opportunities for job mobility.[26] These patterns are better illustrated by later researchers.

An estimated majority of 80% of Chinese in Britain have their origin in Hong Kong, the rest from Southeast Asia, mainland China, Taiwan and elsewhere.[27] The most recent wave of migration from Hong Kong started in the 1950s. This flow of Chinese was related directly to the take-off of the Chinese restaurant business after WWII. The migration itself was undertaken through family efforts:

> Many Hong Kong Chinese who came in the 50s and 60s relied on contacts already established in Britain to find employment. These contacts were often brothers, uncles, cousins, fellow villagers or friends. In a sense, the foothold established by these relatives and friends facilitated the passage of the newcomers.[28]

Some researchers have pointed out that the Chinese chain migration from Hong Kong and employment concentration in the catering trade are heavily shaped by the admission requirements imposed by the

---

University of York, 1975); Lynn Irene Loh, *The Chinese Community in Liverpool* (Merseyside Area Profile Group, 1982).

[26] Kwee Choo Ng, *The Chinese in London* (London: Oxford University Press, 1968) 44.

[27] Anthony Shang, *The Chinese in Britain* (London: Batsford Academic and Educational, 1988) 20.

[28] Ibid., 14. For detailed information on this migration, especially its effects on the sending community, see James L. Watson, "The Chinese: Hong Kong Villagers in the British Catering Trade," *Between Two Cultures: Migrants and Minorities in Britain* (Oxford: Basil Blackwell, 1977); James L. Watson, "Chinese Emigrant Ties to the Home Community," *New Community* 5 (1976/7); James L. Watson, *Emigration and the Chinese Lineage: The Mans in Hong Kong and London* (Berkeley: University of California Press, 1975).

15

Commonwealth Immigration Act in 1962. The Chinese came under the work voucher system, which demanded that the prospective immigrant be issued with an employment voucher for a specific job for a single named employer in Britain.[29] It was a time when a big number of Chinese immigrants already in Britain moved into the catering industry, boosted by the changing diets and conventions about eating out in Britain.[30] Thus, the second function of the kinship network is to provide jobs for new immigrants. This probably explains why new Chinese immigrants worked in a variety of positions in Chinese restaurants, as cooks, waiters, counter workers and kitchen helpers.

The third function of the family oriented catering business, with regard to personal job prospect, is to provide job mobility, both geographically and in terms of employment status. Kin folks normally help each other in pooling financial resources to start new businesses elsewhere in the U.K. or even in continental Europe.[31] Within the firm itself, preferential promotion of kinsmen is also noticeable.[32] More recently, family firms are also said to curb unemployment by absorbing additional members into their own business even when it is not economically viable, as it is considered shameful to register as unemployed.[33]

The family orientation of the Chinese catering firms determines a well defined order of subordination, based on the idea of paternalism. There were those who governed and there were those who were governed, each according to his ability, but all having an equal interest in the success of the firm. The normal pattern is one with father as the entrepreneur, whose business is inherited by male heirs after he relinquished control over the firm.[34]

In a system like this, the subordination of women is to be expected from their employment relationship to their husband, who is the boss of the firm. A woman normally works side by side with her husband and contributes the same number of hours to the family business.[35] Yet, her economic role does not depend so much on her contribution to the family

---

[29] Susan C. C. Baxter. *A political Economy of the Ethnic Chinese Catering Industry* (Ph.D Thesis, University of Aston, 1988) 102.

[30] Anthony Shang, p.14.

[31] Ng, p. 44.

[32] Siu-lun Wong, "The Chinese Family Firm: A Model," *British Journal of Sociology* 36 (1985) 58.

[33] The Runnymede Trust, *The Chinese Community in Britain: The Home Affairs Committee Report in Context* (1986) 12.

[34] Siu-lun Wong, 1985. p. 64.

[35] Ng, p. 55.

business.[36] A majority of Chinese take-away shops were registered in the sole name of the male head of the household, and in virtually all cases, no wages or salaries were received by women.[37] The economic role of the women was consistently subsumed within their roles as mothers, wives and keepers of the house.[38]

Women are by no means the only group to feel frustrated by their occupational prospects within the catering trade. Apart from the benefits associated with the enclave economy, negative effects such as long, unsocial hours, low pay, normally unpleasant working conditions, and above all, limited and insular career prospects encourage Chinese youths to break away from the traditional catering trade.

In a survey study of the employment prospects of Chinese youths in London and Edinburgh, Chan discovered that Chinese youngsters generally dislike working in the catering business.[39] Most of them have what they call the dream of "san-si", meaning, they dream of joining the three top professions, medicine, law and accountancy.[40] He also found evidence of encouragement in parental attitudes to his interviewees. Most parents thought that they themselves were obliged to continue their present occupations in the catering and allied trades. Yet they hoped that their children could have career jobs. Though material success was emphasized, job prestige and social status were also considered important.[41]

In spite of expressed desires for occupational mobility among the second generation, researchers found that Chinese children faced serious difficulties turning their dreams into reality. To name a few, blocked job opportunities caused by poor English and poor academic performance.[42]

---

[36] Susan, C. C. Baxter, *The Chinese and Vietnamese in Birmingham* (Research Commissioned by Race Relations and Equal Opportunities Unit, Birmingham City Council, 1986) 24.

[37] The question arising from this observation is how to define women's employment status in a survey. When family owned and controlled firms are in fact husband owned and controlled firms, should women, the underpaid or non-paid family workers be counted as employees or co-employers? This should be kept in mind in later analysis and discussion.

[38] Susan S.C.C. Baxter, *A Political Economy of the Ethnic Chinese Catering Industry.* p. 147.

[39] Alfred Chan, *Employment Prospects of Chinese Youths in Britain.* Commission for Racial Equality, 1986. p.8.

[40] Ibid., p.6.

[41] Ibid., p.6.

[42] Several researchers have pointed out the practice of Chinese immigrants sending their children back to Hong Kong to receive elementary education, out of fear that their British born children will lose touch with Chinese culture. This explains poor English proficiency when the children rejoin their parents in Britain. Poor academic work may be partially accounted for by the fact that children in catering families have to help with

Thus the Home Affairs Committee warned in their report of the danger that Chinese concentration on catering, with all its attendant problems, might be perpetuated by a new generation which has not willingly chosen it.[43] This supposition we shall test in later analysis.

It should also be mentioned that the relatively recent arrival of refugees from Vietnam has provided Chinese restaurateurs with an alternative source of cheap labour, in addition to family members.[44] Since the fall of Saigon in 1975, Britain has admitted nearly 20,000 Vietnamese refugees, the majority of whom are of Chinese origin.[45] Because of a relatively non-selective system of admittance, few of the British Vietnamese intake possessed transferrable skills or knowledge of fluent English.[46] As a result, a few are employed casually on a part-time basis within the Chinese catering business, or consigned to other areas of menial work. This entails low pay and minimal employment rights.[47] Most of them remain unemployed due to ineffective governmental resettlement policies.[48]

In spite of the above findings of detailed micro-level study, two shortcomings are obvious in existing literature on Chinese in Britain: lack of knowledge about Chinese outside the catering industry and lack of knowledge about Chinese as a whole in comparison with other ethnic groups in Britain. This is because British studies of Chinese occupational attainments are largely ethnographic, unlike American studies.

It has been indicated by previous research that apart from the catering Chinese, there exists a group of Chinese professionals. Its number is to said to be growing,[49] but it has been little studied.[50] Many of these

---

the business for long hours after school and that their parents, themselves poorly educated and speaking little English, are normally not effective in helping their children to adjust and achieve at British schools. For more details, see Anne Garvey and Brian Jackson, *Chinese Children in Britain: Research and Action Project into the Needs of Chinese Children* (Cambridge: National Education Research and Development Trust, 1975); John Derek Michael Freeborne. *The Chinese Communities in Britain: with Special Reference to Housing and Education* (Ph.D. Thesis, University of London), 1980.

[43] Runnymede Trust, 1986. p.13.

[44] Baxter, 1988. p.153.

[45] Commission for Racial Equality, *Vietnamese Refugees in Britain* (1983). In later analysis, those who claim themselves to be born in Vietnam but whose ethnic origin is Chinese, will be counted as Chinese.

[46] P. Jones, *Vietnamese Refugees: A Study of Their Reception and Resettlement in the U.K.* (Home Office, 1982).

[47] Baxter, 1988. p.153.

[48] A.H.Halsey, *British Social Trend Since 1900: A Guide to the Changing Social Structure of Britain* (Oxford: MacMillan, 1988).

[49] Home Affairs Committee, 1985. p.16.

[50] James Watson, 1974. p.194-195.

professionals are said to have come from urban Hong Kong,[51] a few from Southeast Asia.[52] They had western education and spoke good English. To some extent, they had been directly recruited into the British expanding service professions.[53] Although they offered professional assistance to the Chinese community, they had little in common with Chinese in traditional jobs. They might be regarded as a separate and distinct class.[54]

Nevertheless, the author sees no reason to exclude these Chinese professionals from any study concerning Chinese immigrants in Britain, given the self-evident fact that they are Chinese and migrants. Moreover, the predicted inflow of thousands of skilled office workers and professionals from Hong Kong after 1997 will rapidly increase this segment of the Chinese population. This may imply not only a substantial boost to Britain's economy, but also a profound break with the traditional immigration of dominantly catering workers.[55] Hence, no far-sighted research can afford to ignore the potential of the Chinese middle class in Britain.

Another point concerns the relative position of Chinese within the British occupational structure. Until now, little comparative work has been done to compare the level of occupational attainments of Chinese with that of majority whites. Nor has there been work on comparisons of Chinese with other non-white ethnic minorities in that respect. This leaves the common perceptions on Chinese unchecked.

Many factors may have contributed to the lack of comparative information about Chinese in this country, the obvious one being that in several existing comparative studies on ethnic occupational attainments, Chinese have not been included.[56] Lack of nationally representative data

---

[51] Ibid.

[52] Baxter, 1986. p.28.

[53] Ibid.

[54] Private communication with Anthony Shang, author of *The Chinese in Britain*. (London: Batsford Academic and Educational, 1984).

[55] Economist. "The Chinese in Britain: A Chequered History," *Economist* (April 28, 1990).

[56] For major existing national studies on ethnic socio-economic success, see: R. McNabb and G. Psacharopoulos, *Racial Earning Differentials in the U.K*, Centre for Labour Economics, LSE. Discussion Paper No.76, 1980.; Mark B. Stewart, *Racial Discrimination and Occupational Attainments in Britain*, Centre for Labour Economics, LSE. Discussion Paper No 145, 1982.; Colin Brown, *Black and White Britain: The Third PSI Survey* (Gower: Policy Studies Institute, 1985); J. Brennan and P. McGeevor, *Employment of Graduates from Ethnic Minorities* (Council for National Academic Award, 1987); *Ethnic Minorities and the Graduate Labour Market*, 1990; Anthony Heath and Ridge, John. "Social Mobility of Ethnic Minorities," *Journal of Bioscience Supplement* 8 (1983) 169-184.

on ethnic minorities with sufficiently large sample sizes may have made it impossible or difficult to distinguish all culturally distinctive ethnic minorities. But the view that Chinese can take care of themselves, and therefore pose less of a problem than other ethnic minority communities, seems to be hidden under the initial decisions on data collection and subsequent technical difficulties in data analysis.

Theories on occupational attainments of ethnic minorities

Assimilation

Assimilationists are concerned with the role of occupational achievements in the process of assimilation. In Park's race relations cycle, immigrants, after coming into contact with the host society, compete for scarce resources, including jobs, with the native population. This is considered a necessary step for all immigrants before accommodation with the members of the host society and assimilation into the host society.[57]

Later, Gordon produced a more sophisticated seven dimensional paradigm to explain the process of ethnic assimilation-cultural, structural, marital, identificational, attitude receptional, behaviour receptional, and civic. Although cultural assimilation is likely to occur first, Gordon asserts that structural assimilation, defined as large scale entrance into the institutions of the host society, is the "keystone of the arch of assimilation". This is because, after structural assimilation, all the other types of assimilation follow one after another. In its relation to cultural assimilation, structural assimilation definitely produces acculturation, although the opposite does not necessarily hold.[58]

Gordon's suppositions on structural assimilation have been tested by later researchers who study the role of educational and occupational integration in assimilation. The results are normally obtained from studies of more than one generation.

In his study of three generations of Japanese Americans, for instance, Montero looked at the link between socioeconomic mobility and four aspects of assimilation, relating to daily social contacts and intermarriage.

---

[57] Robert Park and Ernest W. Burgess, *Introduction to the Science of Sociology.* (Chicago: The University of Chicago Press, 1924) 734-784. Race relations cycles remain controversial. Researchers such as Lipset (1950) and Lyman (1986) have questioned the sequence and inevitability of the cycles. They argue, by giving the example of American Blacks, that not all minority groups can reach accommodation, let alone final assimilation.

[58] Milton Gordon, *Assimilation in American Life: The Role of Race, Religion and National Origin* (New York: Oxford University Press, 1964) 71-81.

He found that occupational status goes hand in hand with educational achievements, and in most cases, both are related to indicators on assimilation. The rate of assimilation becomes greater with succeeding generation.[59] The effect of education on the level of assimilation was also discovered by Kuo and Lin's study of the Chinese community in Washington D.C..[60]

It is not the major concern of this thesis to study the process of ethnic assimilation. But given the importance of occupational integration for subsequent stages of assimilation, knowledge about the level of occupational attainments might be helpful in predicting the possible direction of future assimilation for ethnic minorities in general and the Chinese in particular.

Industrialism and diminishing ethnic effects

The logic of industrialism asserts universalistic principles, which discourage the assignment of individuals to occupations or jobs by ascribed attributes, such as "by traditional caste, by racial groups, by sex or by family status".[61] The rationale behind this is the liberal argument that the potential of society's human resources can be more fully exploited in a fluid class structure with a high degree of mobility than in a rigid social system. Class lines that restrict mobility and prevent men born into the lower strata from even discovering what their capabilities might be constitute a serious waste of human talent.[62]

If, in traditional societies, this waste of human talent was unavoidable from the perspective of social order, and only regrettable for the individuals concerned, as there were normally more people qualified for high positions than there were such positions, this waste is nevertheless regarded as being detrimental to the efficiency of modern industrialized societies. This is because technical progress has created a need for advanced knowledge and skills on the part of a large proportion of the labour force, not merely a small professional elite. Under these conditions,

[59] D. Montero, "The Japanese Americans: Changing Patterns of Assimilation Over Three Generations," *American Sociological Review* 46 (1981) 829-39.

[60] W.H.Kuo and Nan Lin, "Assimilation Among Chinese-Americans in Washington D.C.," *Sociological Quarterly* 18 (1977) 340-352.

[61] Clark Kerr, *Industrialism and Industrial Man* (New York: Oxford University Press, 1964) 18.

[62] Peter M. Blau and Otis Dudley Duncan, *The American Occupational Structure* (New York: John Wiley and Sons, Inc. Press, 1964) 431.

society can no longer afford the waste of human resources a rigid class structure entails.[63] Thus, industrialism suggests that:

> ...superior status cannot any more be directly inherited but must be legitimated by actual achievements that are socially acknowledged. Education assumes increasing significance for social status in general and for the transmission of social standing from fathers to sons in particular.[64]

What this implies for ethnic minorities is that occupational attainments should increasingly depend on educational qualifications and labour market experience and less on social origins and skin colour.[65] In other words, recruitment and promotion of workers should be based more and more upon what a person is capable of doing, rather than on who he is or what skin colour he has.

Given the assertions about industrialism, we expect the ethnic effect to be weaker for the native-born generation than immigrants, with regard to occupational differentials between ethnic minorities and majority whites. In other words, we expect the association between education and occupation to be stronger with succeeding generation. To do this, we need to test hypotheses concerning ethnic occupational attainments separately for immigrants and the native-born.

Human capital and status attainment of ethnic minorities

The human capital theory, as an integrated part of neo-classical economics, is concerned with the outcomes of the labour market, in particular wage differentials.[66] It assumes workers to be rational individuals, who intend to maximize their income by investment in those areas which will make

---

[63] Ibid., 431.

[64] Ibid., 430.

[65] Ibid., 430.

[66] According to neo-classic economics, "the theory of the determination of wages in a free market is simply a special case of the general theory of value. Wages are the price of labour; and thus in the absence of control, they are determined like all prices, by supply and demand...The demand for labour is only peculiar to this extent: that labour is a factor of production, and is thus demanded...not because the work to be done is desired for and by itself, but because it is to be used in the production of some other thing which is directly desired". See J.R. Hicks, *The Theory of Wages* (New York: St. Martin's, 1964) 1.

them more productive in the labour market.[67] The most important of these areas are education and on-the-job training.[68]

This theory, therefore, asserts the positive role of education and training in the advancement of ethnic minorities. It argues that success in schooling and formal education will increase the prospects of better paying, higher status and more satisfying employment.[69]

Critics have pointed out that the application of human capital theory to the attainment process largely ignores the complexity of earnings determination. Earnings are said to depend on the characteristics of jobs, personal characteristics, and a matching process which allows individuals with certain characteristics to be matched up with certain types of job.[70] Thus, the human capital approach is said to pay exclusive attention to individual characteristics and decisions, and to neglect job nature and matching processes. In other words, it "pays a little attention to the mechanisms by which investments generate a stream of income".[71] Status attainment research, is said to share the same weakness.

The empirical work on status attainment since Blau and Duncan's *American Occupational Structure*, has been heavily concentrated on models which assume that income is determined by background, personal characteristics and levels of educational and occupational achievements. The statistical model used is one of path analysis in which income difference is addressed by looking at path decomposition of the effect of various predicting variables. The basis of this model is "that socioeconomic background affects mental ability, that background, ability and education affect occupational attainment, and that all of the preceding variables affect earnings".[72]

Although status attainment research, like the human capital approach, has primarily given consideration to individual characteristics, it does provide a clear-cut picture of the extent to which personal characteristics affect the occupational outcome at different stages of transformation,

---

[67] G. Becker, *Human Capital* (New York: Columbia University Press, 1964).

[68] Apart from education and on-the-job training, investment also takes the form of migration and health. See T.W. Shultz. "Investment in Human Capital," *American Economic Review* 51 (1961) 1-17.

[69] T. Parsons, "The Social Class as a Social System: Some of its Functions in American Society," *Harvard Educational Review* (Reprint Series) 1 (1969) 69-90.

[70] Mark Granovetter, "Toward a Sociological Theory of Income Differences," in I. Berg ed. *Sociological Perspectives on Labour Market* (New York: Academic Press, 1981) 11-43.

[71] Ibid., p.18.

[72] W. Sewell and R. Hauser, *Education, Occupation and Earnings* (New York: Academic Press, 1975) 50.

through path analysis done for two ethnic groups. Duncan's study on the accumulative disadvantage of American blacks best illustrates the power of this approach:

> Disproportionate numbers of Negroes live in the South, where occupational opportunities are not so good as in the North. Within each region, moreover, Negroes are seriously disadvantaged. They have lower social origins than whites, and they receive less education. Even when Negroes and whites with the same amount of education are compared, Negroes enter the job market on lower levels. Furthermore, if all these statistical differences are controlled and we ask how Negroes would fare if they have the same origins, education and career beginnings as whites, the chances of occupational achievements of Negroes are still considerably inferior to those of whites. Within the same occupation finally, the income of Negroes is lower than that of whites.[73]

Thus, Duncan pointed out that "the multiple handicaps associated with being American Negro are cumulative in their deleterious consequences for a man's career".[74] And it is exactly on the basis of this finding that Duncan refutes the idea behind the "War on Poverty", which was intended to remedy gross discrepancies in occupational attainments between American blacks and whites. The more immediate problem does not lie so much in "inherited poverty" as in "inherited race", which is the cause of poverty.[75]

Status attainment research utilizes the method of multiple regression analysis where the socioeconomic returns to certain personal characteristics are explained by controlling all other context variables at the same time, such as age, gender, education, occupation, class, industry, labour market experience, etc. By including these other background variables in the same regression model, this method is an improvement on the path analysis because it helps bridge the gap between individual characteristics and the final occupational outcome, although critics of status attainment research

---

[73] Blau and Duncan, (1964) 405.

[74] Ibid.,405.

[75] Otis Dudley Duncan, "Inheritance of Poverty or Inheritance of Race" in D.P. Moynihan ed. *On Understanding of Poverty: Perspectives from the Social Sciences* (New York: Basic Books, Inc., Publishers, 1965) 85-110.

24

have not been entirely convinced of this.[76] The more detailed and complex processes of negotiation between personal characteristics and structural influences are not brought out effectively sometimes, because the survey data on which the analysis is based do not always provide all the necessary context variables.

The process of occupational attainment is a complicated one. A person has to clear several hurdles to achieve success. Previous studies have shown that members of non-white ethnic minorities may be penalized at every stage of transformation. But no study seems satisfactorily to have answered the question of how exactly the penalization happens, in particular the negotiation process between the worker's characteristics and the employer's requirement for the specified job position. Other more detailed studies in this direction may be useful in bringing out some hidden mechanisms.

The first hurdle is educational. Ethnic minorities, especially black people, share some of the educational deprivation of poor whites in terms of home and school influence. Many tend to work and reside in less prosperous regions of the country,[77] or in inner city neighbourhoods,[78] where inferior educational facilities make it likely that they acquire less knowledge and skill even given the same number of years of formal schooling. In the U.S, where a more or less uniform school system follows a pattern of incremental progress and is free to all, communities which provide educational facilities play an important role in determining the quality of output. In Britain, and at school level, this difference might be caused by the kind of school attended rather than the number of years of schooling. It has been found that Afro-Caribbean and Asian students are more likely to attend comprehensive secondary schools and given the varying culture of these schools, they are more likely to attend those that lack strong traditions of entry into higher education.[79]

The second hurdle, which is of major concern here, is to translate education into occupation. If an ethnic minority person possesses the same level of educational or technical qualification, or has the same number of years of formal schooling as a white person, then returns to human capital investment should be the same for them both, if the meritocratic principle applies. However, in many cases, they are not the same. This is because the same qualification may be evaluated by the employer differently for

[76] Mark Granovetter, 1981. pp.15-16.

[77] Blau and Duncan, 1964; p.405.

[78] Freeborne, 1980; p.289.

[79] John Brennan and P. McGeevor, *Ethnic Minorities and the Graduate Labour Market* (Council for National Academic Award, 1990) 29.

majority whites and ethnic minorities, and, among ethnic minorities, differently for those whose qualifications were obtained in the country of origin rather than the country of destination.

School type of the potential worker also affects the employer's decision. Despite the large scale growth and recognition of non-university higher education in Britain, attendance at polytechnic and colleges is still considered inferior to attendance at university, both by students and by employers. Some employers prefer to recruit their graduate personnel from universities. Evidence shows that ethnic minority students are less likely than white British students to attend universities.[80] Another source of study shows that they are more likely than white British students to attend polytechnics and colleges.[81]

The American higher education system makes a marked commitment to general education for all undergraduates. Still "America's colleges and universities are a mixture of public and private institutions with the privately supported institutions present at every level of excellence...".[82] If recruitment of graduates favours those students attending prestigious and mostly private institutions, the barriers for ethnic minorities, especially Asian Americans, lies in the unofficial "quotas" on the number of Asian American students imposed by several prestigious higher education institutions in the past few years.[83]

In addition, immigrants who were educated in their country of origin may find that their foreign qualifications are not seen to possess the same value as qualifications obtained in the country of destination. The kind of subject studied within higher education may be important too. Graduate employment prospects differ substantially according to the subjects studied. Concentration in certain subjects may cause concentration in certain occupations. Concentration of Asian students in engineering and science has long been a known fact both in Britain and the U.S, but the connection between these subjects and later concentration in related job positions, such

---

[80] Brennan and McGeevor, 1990. p.33.

[81] Tariq Madood, *Establishing the Numbers of Ethnic Minority Students in Degree or Equivalent Courses to Aid Graduate Recruiters* (CRE, 1991).

[82] Martin Trow, "American Higher Education: Exceptional or Just Different" in Byron Shafer ed. *Is America Different: A New Look at American Exceptionalism* (Oxford: Clarendon press, 1991) 142.

[83] Bob Suzuki. *Asian Americans in Higher Education: Impact of Changing Demographics and Other Social Forces*. A paper presented for a National Symposium on the Changing Demographics of Higher Education, New York City: The Ford Foundation, April 8, 1988. pp.46-48.

as scientific research and engineering, is not known to favour the Asian's occupational status particularly.[84]

When job hunting, in Britain, Afro-Caribbean and Asian students make more applications but obtain fewer jobs, which shows that members of ethnic minority groups experience greater difficulty in obtaining job offers than their white counterparts.[85] Perhaps because they anticipate such difficulties, ethnic minority graduates are more likely than their peers to continue in full time education. They are found to make more applications, but end up with fewer interviews.[86] Even among those who have reached the first, second and third stage of interview, they are less likely to be offered a job,[87] although the degree of difficulty is somewhat reduced for those studying favourable subjects.[88]

As a result, ethnic minorities are more likely to be found employed in the public and voluntary sectors than in the private sector, and South Asians are particularly more likely to take up self-employment.[89] Besides, they are more likely to be unemployed in the first few months following graduation.[90]

The third hurdle, though of little relevance to the present thesis, is the stage where occupation is transformed into income. Previously, we discussed the existing American literature on income disadvantages associated with being Chinese, in spite of occupational levels comparable to whites.[91] Similar studies are not available for Chinese in Britain, though evidence of ethnic penalties in income is available for other ethnic

---

[84] USCCR, *The Economic Status of Americans of Asian Decent: An Exploratory Investigation* (Washington, 1988).

[85] Brennan and McGeevor, 1990. p.55.

[86] R. Ballard and R. Holden, "The Employment of Coloured Graduates in Britain," *New Community* 4 (1975).

[87] K. Tanna, *The Experience of South Asian University Students in the British Educational System and in Their Search for Work* (Ph.D. Thesis, University of Aston, 1987).

[88] Brennan and McGeevor, p.56.

[89] Brennan and McGeevor, p.53.

[90] Ibid., p.55.

[91] As a matter of fact, more comparative results in this direction are also available. See: C. Hirschman and M.G. Wong, "Trends in Socio-economic Achievement Among Immigrant and Native-born Americans; 1960-1976," *Sociological Quarterly* 22 (1981) 485-514; C. Hirschman and M.G. Wong, "Socio-economic Gains of Asian Americans, Blacks and Hispanics," *American Journal of Sociology* 90 (1984) 584-607; R. Jiobu, *Ethnicity and Assimilation: Blacks, Chinese, Filipinos, Japanese, Koreans, Mexicans, Vietnamese and Whites* (Albany: State University of New York Press, 1988); H.R. Barringer, D.T. Takeuchi, P. Xenos, "Education, Occupational Prestige and Income of Asian Americans," *Sociology of Education* 63 (1990) 27-43.

minorities, provided that there is still differentiation within the ethnic minorities.[92]

An intervening variable to the level of socio-economic returns to education might lie in chances for promotion within the same occupation. Impediments to promotion for members from ethnic minority backgrounds look different in form for those who are well educated and those who receive little education, but they are all related to the employer's evaluation of the worker's performance. In the U.S, for instance, grievances are heard among immigrant professional Chinese working in corporations where their chances of advancement are blocked because their employers conceive of them as lacking efficient communicative skills in English. However, the situation for those who were educated in the U.S. and have no language problem is not so much better. This process is called "glass ceiling".[93]   Promotion within non-professional occupations, such as manufacturing, on the other hand, is often associated with on-the-job training. Access to development training often depends on favour from immediate bosses who write positive appraisals.[94]   Ethnic minority workers are said to have less chance to obtain this kind of training.[95]

It ought to be noted that in spite of slippage between educational achievements and possible occupational and income attainments among ethnic minorities as a whole, research does indicate generational differences, especially between foreign-born and native-born. Chiswick, for instance, concluded that American-born Chinese and Japanese earned about the same amount of income per year of education as did whites.[96] Fujii and Mak also discovered in the case of Hawaii that as of 1975, all minorities were disadvantaged compared to whites, although they found

---

[92] See McNabb and Psacharopoulos, 1980; Brennan and McGeevor, 1990, p.60-66.

[93] USCCR, 1991. For more on the "glass ceiling" process, see pp.66-69 and pp.72-90.

[94] Piore feels that secondary sector positions, in which many immigrants work, entail highly personalised relationships between supervisors and workers. See Piore, M.J. "Economic Fluctuation, Job Security, and Labour Market Duality in France, Italy and the United States" *Politics and Society* 9 (1980).

[95] There are basically two types of job training, induction training and development training. The former is given to new recruits on information such as company rules and regulations, fire precaution, operation of machinery and equipment, etc. This is said to be widely extended to majority of Black workers. The latter, however, which is given to existing employees who have been identified as people with specific future job or role, e.g. promotion to the level of supervisor or manager, reach only a small percentage of Black workers. See Commission for Civil Rights, *Ethnic Minorities and Employment*, No.4, March 4, 1977.

[96] Chiswick, 1983.

28

that non-white immigrants were more disadvantaged than the native-born.[97] This evidence seems to correspond to Lieberson's observation that the social and economic entry of a generation into American society precedes the high levels of education and occupational attainment of its children.[98] It also gives support to Blau and Duncan's explanation, i.e. minority handicap, though an obstacle to success, simultaneously provides a screening test which encourages a selected group of ethnic minority members to overcome initial handicaps and gain potential for continuing success.[99]

Ethnic enclave economy

The theory of ethnic enclave economy is important in discussions of ethnic occupational attainment because it provides an alternative mode of immigrant labour market incorporation. By doing this, it challenges the assimilationist and segmented labour market views on the entry point of immigrants into the host labour market. In this section, I shall introduce the ethnic enclave economy theory by way of discussing its differences from the existing theories.

The assimilationist view of ethnic occupational attainment admits that there is one labour market entry point for the immigrants. Historical studies show that turn-of-the-century immigrants to the U.S. ended up with menial, low-paid occupations in industry, canal and railway building, etc. They formed tightly-knit communities for self-protection and support and then gradually moved into the mainstreams of the society. This enables later writers to portray the immigrant adaptation as a uniform path in which newcomers took their place at the end of the labour market queue and proceeded to improve slowly but predictably their employment situations.[100]

The basic theme characterizing the segmented labour market theory emphasizes the importance of differences in economic organization for social structure and individual behaviour.[101] According to this view, the

---

[97] E.T.Fujii and J. Mak, "The Determinants of Income of Native and Foreign-born Men in a Multiracial Society," *Applied Economics* 15 (1983): 759-76.

[98] S. Lieberson, *A Piece of the Pie: Blacks and White Immigrants since 1880* (Berkeley: University of California Press, 1980).

[99] Blau and Duncan, 1964. p.407.

[100] Wilson and Portes.

[101]In discussing the importance of segmented labour market theory, Dale points out, "By use of a model of the labour market which incorporates the notion of barriers and of structure, it becomes possible to begin to explain the existing inequalities within the labour market and to explore ways of understanding how the labour market plays an active role

labour force in advanced capitalist society is segmented into two or more labour markets. The primary labour market is characterized by stable work conditions, high wages, scarce skill specifications, and internal labour markets which provide opportunities for upward job mobility within the firm. The secondary labour market is characterized by high turnover rates, low pay, low skill levels and lack of ladders for success.[102] With regard to upward mobility, jobs in this sector are said to be essentially dead-end. Not only do they offer little chance of advancement within the firm, but they offer little in the way of information, training or institutional connections which would facilitate advancement elsewhere in the labour market.[103]

Employment experiences of ethic minorities in advanced industrialized countries are seen as closely connected with the segmented labour market, especially the secondary labour market. The segmented labour market view supports one uniform labour market entry point for the ethnic minorities but seems to contradict the assimilationists on the possibility of eventual upward mobility. The minority workers, instead of queuing to improve their initial unfavourable employment condition, are likely to remain confined to the lower rungs of the job ladder and their chances for mobility are severely restricted by structural barriers in the segmented labour market. In the 1960s, this conceptualization emerged mainly as an attempt to explain the employment problems of the then predominantly Black labour force concentrated in low wage labour markets in the American inner cities,[104] though the same framework was also used for analyzing West Indian immigration to Britain at approximately the same time.[105] It has been observed by Castles and Kosack that,

> in the situation of full employment, the nationals of the countries concerned have taken advantage of opportunities for moving into better paying, more pleasant jobs, usually

---

in the stratification process". See Angela Dale, "The Role of Labour Market Segmentation in Understanding the Position of Women in the Occupational Structure", Occasional papers in Sociology and Social Policy, University of Surrey No. 4, 1986. pp.36-37.

[102] D.M. Gordon, *Theory of Poverty and Underdevelopment* (Lexington: Heath, 1972).

[103] M.J. Piore, "The Role of Immigration in Industrial Growth: A Case Study of the Origins and Character of Puerto Rican Migration to Boston," Working Paper 112, MIT: Department of Economics, 1973. p.11.

[104] R. Waldinger, "Immigrant Enterprise and the Structure of the Labour Market," Roberts, Finnegan and Gallie ed. *New Approaches to Economic Life* (Manchester: Manchester University Press, 1984) 214.

[105] C. Peach, *West Indian Migration to Britain: A Social Geography* (London: Oxford University Press, 1968) 64.

in the white-collar or skilled sectors. The immigrants have
been left with jobs deserted by others. Typically, such jobs
offer low pay, poor working conditions, little security and
inferior status.[106]

Recently, the notion of a uniform entry point advocated by both the
assimilationists and segmented labour market view has been challenged by
the ethnic enclave economy view. Portes et al suggest that like other
minorities, immigrant workers in the enclave economy meet with a hostile
reaction from the surrounding society to their cultural and racial
distinctiveness. They are barred from desirable occupations and forced to
make a living in marginal lines. However, they manage to escape the
lowest rungs of the economic ladder and through mobilization of ethnic
resources for economic advancement, sometimes acquire wealth and
achieve economic success despite societal hostility and initial
disadvantages.[107]

Other researchers discovered that immigrants increasingly enter the
labour market through immigrant owned firms. This is particularly true
among working class or lower middle class immigrants.[108]
Manufacturing firms managed by Cubans in Florida,[109] the garment
industry run by Chinese in New York City,[110] together with Chinese
restaurateurs[111] and South Asian shopkeepers in Britain,[112] are just a
few examples of ethnic entrepreneurship.

Researchers argue that the labour market within the ethnic enclave
economy operates differently from the secondary labour market. It is said
to be different, among other things, in maximum utilization of informal
resources by ethnic entrepreneurs to protect the immigrant economic niche
in a competitive and wider economic context.[113] The strategies employed
are found to be similar among ethnic minorities, despite differences in

---

[106] S. Castles and G. Kosack, *Immigrant Workers and Class Structure in Western
Europe* (London: Oxford University Press, 1973).

[107] Portes et al. 1980, 1985 & 1990.

[108] Waldinger, p.216.

[109] K.L.Wilson and A. Portes, "Immigrant Enclaves: An Analysis of the Labour
Market Experiences of Cubans in Miami," *American Journal of Sociology* 86 (1980).

[110] R. Waldinger, *Ethnic Enterprise and Industrial Change: A Case Study of the New
York Garment Industry* (University of Harvard: Ph.D. Thesis, 1983).

[111] Susan Baxter, 1981.

[112] Ivan Light and Edna Bonacich, *Immigrant Entrepreneurs* (Berkeley: University of
California Press, 1988).

[113] See Jeremy Boissevain et al., "Ethnic Entrepreneurs and Ethnic Strategies," *Ethnic
Entrepreneurs: Immigrant Business in Industrial Societies*. Waldinger et al ed. Sage Series
on Race and Ethnic Relations Volume 1 (1990) 131-156.

culture and economic backgrounds, and particular migration histories, etc.[114]

More recently, comparative studies on ethnic occupational success in the enclave as against the wider labour market indicate positive socio-economic returns to human capital in the enclave economy. Based on their study of the Cuban community in Miami, Portes et al. reported that, compared to immigrants employed in the secondary labour market, those in the enclave have occupations that correspond more closely with their educational attainments and income levels that correspond more closely with their occupational status. The level of socio-economic returns to human capital are said to be comparable to that of immigrants working in the primary industries.[115]

The important implication of these findings, according to Zhou and Logan, is

> that the enclave opens opportunities for its members that are not easily accessible in the larger society. The enclave...labour market...partially shelters ethnic group members from competition by other social groups, from discrimination and abuse on account of their ethnic origins, and from surveillance and regulations by the government. In many respects, the boundaries around the enclave provide tangible benefits to group members and seem to offer positive alternatives to assimilation.[116]

Following Portes el al., Zhou and Logan, using data on the New York City Chinese enclave, find considerable evidence for positive income returns for male enclave workers from education, labour market experience, etc. The rate of return for enclave workers is comparable to

---

[114] Ibid., p.156; Suzanne Model, "A Comparative Perspective on the Ethnic Enclave," *International Migration Review XIX* (1985) 64-81.

[115] See K.L.Wilson and A. Portes, "Immigrant Enclaves: An Analysis of the Labour Market Experiences of Cubans in Miami," *American Journal of Sociology*. 86 (1980) 295-319; A. Portes and A. Stepick, "Unwelcomed Immigrants: The Labour Market Experiences of 1980 (Mariel) Cuban and Haitian Refugees in South Florida," *American Sociological Review* 50 (1985) 493-514. The suppositions of Portes et al are disputed by Sanders and Nee who find that positive human capital returns are received only by the ethnic entrepreneurs and not by the employees in enclave. Thus they call for a reformulation of enclave economy hypothesis more sensitive to important differences between immigrants workers and immigrants bosses.

[116] M. Zhou and J. Logan, "Returns to Human Capital in Ethnic Enclaves: New York City's Chinatown," *American Sociological Review* 54 (1989) 809-820.

that of Chinese working outside the enclave. However, they find that none of these human capital variables are found to be positively related to the income of female enclave workers. Thus they suggest that attention be paid to more comparative research, where gender differences should be considered. This gives empirical support to gender segregation in the ethnic enclave economy, which other researchers had already speculated.[117]

In this thesis, I shall test the hypothesis that occupational returns to education and work experience are the same for Chinese working inside and outside the enclave economy.[118] The hypothesis will be tested for males and females separately. If, given the same education and age, working in the enclave makes no difference to the level of occupation, then we shall admit that the Chinese enclave economy serves as an alternative channel for job mobility which is as good as the wider labour market.

American exceptionalism

Towards the end of this thesis, I discuss American exceptionalism in relation to Chinese occupational attainment in Britain and the U.S.. The idea is used because of the comparative context it offers. Shafer, in defining American exceptionalism, suggested an "effort to highlight distinctively American clusters of characteristics, even distinctively American ways of organizing the major realms of social life".[119] The implication of American exceptionalism thus defined is simply that there is an American model, that is different from the models used by other nations. Thus this approach to American exceptionalism permits the essential counter-argument that the realm in question is not really exceptional. If one finds the "right" society, one can say that America is not different.[120]

---

[117] For more of this, see Annie Phizacklea's paper on "Entrepreneurship, Ethnicity and Gender", and Sue Baxter and Geoff Raw's paper on "Fast Food, Fettered Work: Chinese Women in the Ethnic Catering Industry" in Westwood and Bhachu ed. *Enterprising Women: Ethnicity, Economy and Gender Relations* (London: Routledge, 1988).

[118] In testing the hypothesis, I shall not divide the Chinese sample into those working in the primary and secondary labour markets. Too few Chinese work in the secondary sector to obtain a sample big enough for decent statistical analysis. Thus, the point of departure for this analysis is whether the Chinese enclave economy is equal in allowing chances for occupational success as the wider labour market as a whole.

[119] Shafer, Byron E. ed. *Is America Different: A New Look at American Exceptionalism* (Oxford: Clarendon Press, 1991) viii.

[120] Ibid., p.viii.

Comparative studies in support of the counter-argument have been done in the area of social stratification, even though much of it has only emphasized the movement between classes.[121]   In Erikson and Goldthorpe's study of social mobility for Sweden, Britain and America, for instance, the authors declared that they were unable to find evidence in favour of American exceptionalism. Thus, there is no basis for arguing, for the twentieth century at least, that American society is distinctively open, for it does not stand apart from all other nations in the amount of social mobility permitted to its members.[122] This thesis intends to throw light on another aspect of social stratification, i.e. whether America is exceptional in allowing ethnic minorities to achieve occupational success.

Temin, in celebrating American meritocracy, wrote,

> The United States nonetheless has remained somewhat open
> to the immigration of Asians and Latin Americans. These
> Americans are being absorbed into the economy and society
> of the United States in a free-wheeling fashion reminiscent
> of frontier settlements. Individuals are free to go their own
> way and the success of individual is celebrated. American
> education is very open and inclusive, providing an avenue
> for immigrants of all sorts to make their way into the higher
> levels of the economy in a very few generations.[123]

This seems to echo to earlier observations made by de Tocqueville on American equality of opportunity, when he noted that

> among a people whose ranks are nearly equal, no ostensible
> bond connects men together or keep them settled in their
> station. None of them have a permanent right to command,
> none are forced by their condition to obey; but every man
> finding himself possessed of some education and some
> resources, may choose his own path and proceed apart from
> all his fellow men. The same causes that make the members
> of the community independent of each other continually

---

[121] See Kerckhoff, A.C., R.T. Campbell and I. Wingfield-Laird, "Social Mobility in Great Britain and the Unites States" *American Journal of Sociology* 91 (1985) 281-301; Robert Erikson and John H. Goldthorpe, "Are American Rates of Mobility Exceptionally High? New Evidence on an Old Issue" *European Sociological Review*. 1 (1985).

[122] Erikson and Goldthorpe, 1985. p.19.

[123] Peter Temin, "Free Land and Federalism: American Economic Exceptionalism" in Shafer ed. *Is America Different? A New look at American Exceptionalism* (Oxford: Claredon Press, 1991) 92-93.

compel them to new and restless desires and constantly spur them onwards.[124]

Given the unique American frontier heritage, which celebrates equality of opportunity, we should expect the link of race to be unprecedentedly relaxed. Thus America might indeed be exceptional among all nations in applying the principle of meritocracy to its non-white minorities. If, apart from America, there is another country, which allows their ethnic minorities the same degree of occupational success, we can reject this assumption.

In the last chapter of the thesis, I shall compare America with Britain with regard to the relative level of occupational success of one ethnic minority, Chinese. Only three different results are possible. Either the Chinese American are more successful, or the British Chinese are more successful, or perhaps they are equally successful. Both first two results signify differential societal degrees of openness to the same ethnic minority. The last two results refute the notion of American exceptionalism with regard to one realm of social life, although, if the third case is proven to be true, notions about Chinese "exceptionalism" may arise. However, it is beyond the scope of the present thesis to investigate that issue.

---

[124] Alexis de Tocqueville, *Democracy in America* (New York: Vintage Books, 1945) 265.

2 Data and methodology

Data sources

The major data sets to be used in this thesis are extracted from the British national Labour Force Surveys (1983, 1984, 1985, 1986, 1987, 1988 and 1989) and the United States Census of Population and Housing Public Use Microdata Samples (1980). The author does not claim to have conducted surveys of her own. The research questions are thought to be best tackled by doing secondary analysis of existing large scale governmental sample surveys.

The British national Labour Force Survey (LFS) is part of a joint venture undertaken by countries of the European Community. The survey was first carried out by the six original members of the EC in 1960.[1] The main purpose of the survey is to provide statistics on the numbers of employed and unemployed persons and the kinds of job people do. Because different countries have different ways of recording these statistics for official purposes, it is difficult to make comparisons between countries in the EC. One of the major purposes of the LFS survey therefore is to provide this information on a strictly comparable basis for each country.[2]

The United Kingdom participated for the first time in 1973. Co-sponsored by the Department of Employment and the Commission of the European Community, the survey was carried out biennially from 1973 to

---

[1] ESRC, *ESRC Data Archive Catalogue: Study Descriptions* (Cambridge: Chadwyck-Healey, 1988).

[2] ESRC Data Archive, *SN:2029 Labour Force Survey: 1983 Interviewers Instructions* (Colchester: University of Essex, 1983). For more detailed description of the LFS surveys in different European Community countries, see Eurostat, *Labour Force Sample Survey: Methods and Survey* (Luxembourg: Office for Official Publications of the European Community, 1985).

1983. From 1983 onward, the survey was conducted annually.[3] The specific aim of the British survey is to "produce results about the population resident in private households and hotels, at regional as well at national level, and the overall sample size was dictated by this requirement". For instance, addresses selected for interview in 1983 numbered about 94,000 in England and Wales, 10,000 in Scotland, and 5,000 in Northern Ireland, i.e. about 1 address in 200 in Great Britain, about 1 in 100 in Norther Ireland.[4] The average response rate from 1983 onwards is 82-83%.[5]

Different sampling frames have been used in Great Britain and Northern Ireland. From 1983 onwards, the Postcode Address File (PAF) has been used in England, Wales and Scotland.[6] The Valuation Roll, a list of properties eligible for rating, has been used in Northern Ireland. The sample to be used in this study is obtained by pooling the annual LFS data sets from 1983 to 1989. The purpose of pooling is to obtain sufficient sample sizes for small ethnic minorities such as Chinese.[7] The sample covers the population normally resident in England, Wales and Scotland.[8] The total number of the pooled sample is 878,657.

The 1980 U.S. Census of Population and Housing Public Use Microdata Samples (PUMS) were collected by the U.S. Department of Commerce, Bureau of the Census and were made available by the Inter-university Consortium for Political and Social Research based at University

---

[3] For more details, see ESRC. *ESRC Data Archive Catalogue: Study Descriptions*, 1986. Section 2: 33132 (Cambridge: Chadwyck-Healey, 1988); Angela Dale and Judith Glover. "An Analysis of Women's Employment Patterns in the U.K., France and the U.S.A.: The Value of Survey Based Comparison," Department of Employment, Research Paper No. 75, 1990.

[4] *Labour Force Sample Survey* (Luxembourg: Office for Official Publications of the European Communities, 1985), 16.

[5] Personal communication with Michael Bradley from OPCS.

[6] Specifically, the "small-user" subfile of the Postcode Address File (PAF) has been used. The PAF, prepared by the Post Office and held on computer, is a list of all the addresses (delivery points) to which mail is delivered. Small users are delivery points, which receive fewer than 25 articles of mail per day; these are therefore likely to include all private households. See *Labour Force Sample Survey*, 17.

[7] Checks have been made to show that there are no systematic variations in the relationship between class and ethnicity from year to year.

[8] The British sample used in this thesis does not include Northern Ireland, because this study deals with ethnic minorities, and the question on "ethnic origin" was asked in England, Wales and Scotland but not in Northern Ireland. This information can be found in the document entitled *Questionnaires and Index to Respondent Variables*, which comes out once a year with other documents on the LFS by ESRC Data Archive. Thus, the subject of the following discussion may be more precisely defined as ethnic occupational attainments in Great Britain rather than in the U.K..

of Michigan, Ann Arbor.[9]   Three different PUMS series have been prepared.[10]   They are called PUMS A, B and C, each series having several nationally representative samples of different sizes, for instance PUMS A 5% Sample, PUMS A 0.1% Sample, etc.   The PUMS A 5% sample "identifies all states and various subdivisions within them, including most counties with 100,000 or more inhabitants".[11]   The PUMS A 0.1% Sample has been extracted from the PUMS A 5% Sample.   Both are nationally representative samples, containing information at both household and personal levels.[12]

The American data used for the secondary analysis in this thesis come from two sources.   The data on the Asian Americans, including Chinese, are from a tape prepared from the 1980 Census 5% PUMS A.[13]   Because all households containing at least one Asian were extracted from the sample, the procedure excludes houses without Asians.   It is thus necessary to draw a small nationally representative sample of non-Asians, such as whites, blacks and Hispanics.   A 0.1% Sample from the PUMS A was therefore ordered from the ICPSR.   This decision was made following the

---

[9] While every person and housing unit in the United States was enumerated on a questionnaire that requested certain basic demographic information (e.g. age, race, relationship), a sample of persons and housing units was enumerated on a questionnaire that requested additional information. The basic sampling unit for the 1980 census was the housing unit including all occupants. Two sampling rates were employed. One half of all housing units and persons in counties with fewer than 2,500 people, and one sixth of housing units and persons of all other places were enumerated. When both sampling rates were taken into account across the nation, approximately, 19% of the nation's housing units were included.   An iterative ratio estimation procedure, which resulted in the assignment of a weight to each sample person or housing record, was used. For details, see U.S. Department of Commerce, Bureau of the Census, *Census of Population and Housing, 1980 (United States): Public Use Microdata Samples* (Ann Arbor: ICPSR, 1983 & 1984), 35-36.

[10] A stratified systematic selection procedure with probability proportional to a measure of size was used to select each public-use microdata sample. The measure of size was the full sample weight that resulted from the 1980 census ratio estimation procedure described above. See U.S. Department of Commerce, Bureau of the Census, *Census of Population and Housing, 1980* (United States), 40.

[11] Ibid., page three from the beginning.

[12] Ibid., page three from the beginning. Descriptions of various PUMS samples are also available from the ICPSR. *Guide to Resources and Services 1989-1990* (Ann Arbor: ICPSR, 1990).

[13] The tape was originally prepared by the Pacific/Asian American Mental Health Research Centre headed by Dr. William Liu at University of Illinois at Chicago.   The tape was kept and supplied to me by the Social Science Data Archive at the University after the Research Centre was closed down.

procedure used by Barringer et al. in their study of Asian Americans.[14] In conducting the analysis, the two samples will be combined. Therefore, the combined sample represents an average of five out of every one hundred Asians and an average of one out of every one thousand whites, blacks and Hispanics in the 1980 Public Use Microdata Sample A. The total number of people in the sample is 375,083.

Basic statistical methods

As indicated in the introductory chapter, the central analysis of this thesis can be divided into three parts. In part one and part two, separate investigations on occupational success are carried out for Chinese in Great Britain and Chinese in the United States. Each of these two parts consists of three sections, i.e. demographic profile, educational attainments and occupational attainments. In part three, a comparative study of occupational attainments is conducted on Chinese in the two countries. Different statistical techniques are used in different parts of the analysis.

Chapters Three and Six, in which demographic profiles are drawn for Chinese in Britain and the U.S., serve as an introduction to later analyses. In these two chapters, I shall look at demographic characteristics such as ethnic origin, country of birth, age structure, sex ratio, and geographical distribution. These characteristics, or "demographic potentials", are considered important in contributing, positively or negatively, to socio-economic attainments of ethnic groups.[15] These results are preliminary. Therefore, the methodological tools include frequency tables and cross-tabular analysis.[16] Where necessary, graphic techniques are applied.[17]

Chapter Four and the earlier part of Chapter Seven look at the educational attainments of Chinese immigrants and their children in Britain and the U.S. Comparisons are made between majority whites and ethnic minorities and between Chinese and other ethnic minority groups. Education is assumed to be a strong predictor of subsequent level of ethnic

---

[14] Herbert R. Barringer, David Takeuchi and Peter Xenos, "Education, Occupational Prestige, and Income of Asian Americans," *Sociology of Education* 63 (January, 1990), 27-43.

[15] Robert M. Jiobu. *Ethnicity and Assimilation: Blacks, Chinese, Filipinos, Japanese, Koreans, Mexicans, Vietnamese and Whites* (Albany: State University of New York Press, 1988).

[16] The preliminary analysis is conducted by using SPSSX. See SPSS Inc. *SPSS-X User's Guide (3rd Edition)* (Chicago: SPSS Inc., 1988).

[17] All graphs in the thesis are created by using UNIGRAPH+2000. See UNIRAS. *UNIGRAPH+2000 User's Manual* (Soborg: UNIRAS, 1991).

occupational success, and it is the purpose of this thesis to bring out the hidden links between education and subsequent occupational attainments. Thus, the analysis of education in these two chapters is functionally preparatory for the analysis on occupational returns to education which follows.

Various statistical techniques are used in the study of educational attainments. In summarizing the educational levels for different ethnic groups, cross-tabulation tables are used. In determining the relationship between the educational level and selected demographic characteristics, such as age, sex and ethnicity, multinomial logit models are fitted.[18] In addition to quantitative analysis, secondary ethnographic material is also used. For instance, in accounting for the high educational attainments of Chinese, historical material is presented. It should be noted that historical material, especially that regarding the educational background of Chinese immigrants in their places of origin, applies to Chinese immigrants in both Britain and the U.S. Therefore, material presented in Chapter Three is not repeated in Chapter Seven.

Chapter Five and the latter part of Chapter Seven try to bring out the mechanisms through which education is translated into occupational attainments. In an attempt to account for group occupational disparity and disparity within the group, logistic regression analysis is applied. Guided by different theoretical hypotheses, different regression equations are obtained.

Chapter Eight deals with the comparison of the relative chances of Chinese to succeed occupationally in Britain and in the U.S. To estimate whether the effect on occupation of being Chinese varies from one country to another, holding structural differences constant, logistic regression analysis is again undertaken. An example of logistic regression analysis is given in the last section of this chapter for illustrative purposes.[19]

Brief description of dependent variables

One important goal of the statistical work in this thesis is to achieve as much comparability between countries as possible. Thus, variables to be included in the comparative models in Chapter Eight are usually made comparable first, if they were not so originally. I shall address the issue

---

[18] The multinomial logit models are fitted by using SPSS-X.

[19] The logistic regression analysis is conducted by using GLIM. See GLIM Party of the Royal Statistical Society. *The Generalised Linear Interactive Modelling System (Release 3.77)* (Oxford: Nag, 1985).

of comparability briefly as I introduce dependent and independent variables in this section and the next. More detailed discussion will be presented at the beginning of the analyses contained in separate chapters.

CLASS will be used as the indicator for occupational attainment. As a dependent variable in logistic regressions, class should be a dummy variable. In the analysis, two versions of class are used, with class first dichotomizing between the service class and the non-service class, and then between the employed and the unemployed. The former indicates the chances of reaching the most advantageous class level as against not reaching it. The latter concerns the chances of avoiding the most disadvantageous position as against being caught in it.

Class is a derived variable. In the British case, class is derived from two variables, i.e. socio-economic group and economic activity. To all those with a job, a socio-economic group is assigned in LFS. It can be used to distinguish the service class from the non-service class[20] as defined in Goldthorpe's Class Schema.[21] Then the variable of economic activity shows clearly who among the economically inactive are actually

---

[20] The variable on socio-economic status, itself being a derived variable of "occupation last week" and "current employment status" has 18 categories: (1) employers and managers in central and local government-large establishment (2) employers and managers in industry, commerce-small establishment (3) professional workers-self-employed (4) professional workers-employees (5) intermediate non-manual workers (6) junior non-manual workers (7) personal service workers (8) foremen and supervisors-manual (9) skilled manual workers (10) semi-skilled manual workers (11) unskilled manual workers (12) own account workers (13) farmers-employers and managers (14) farmers on own account (15) agricultural workers (16) members of armed forces (17) occupation inadequately described or no answer (18) not applicable. The service class consists of 1,2,3,4 excluding those whose SES is 2 and "current employment status" is "self-employed with/without employees". The excluded people are considered as petit-bourgeoisie and put into the non-service class. All the remaining categories, except for 13 to 18 are considered as the non-service class. Categories 13 through 18 are excluded, as these are of little relevance to Chinese occupational attainment in Britain.

[21] These class categories follow the earlier presentation of the class schema in holding together individuals with similar market situations, which are determined by their occupation and employment status. See John Goldthorpe. *Social Mobility and Class Structure in Britain* (Oxford: Clarendon Press, 1987), 41. Later, revisions are made in the presentation of the class schema. The purpose of the class schema is to "differentiate positions within labour markets and production units, or more specifically...to differentiate such positions in terms of the employment relations they entail". The revised class schema "seeks to bring out more clearly that the schema is intended ultimately to apply to positions, defined as social relationships, rather than to persons although for purposes of defining the classes distinguished, it is difficult to avoid referring to actual incumbents, e.g. managers, proprietors, workers, etc". See Robert Erikson, and John Goldthorpe, *Constant Flux: A Study of Class Mobility in Industrial Societies* (Oxford: Clarendon Press, 1992).

unemployed. Hence, there is an additional category of unemployed.[22] The first dummy variable of class dichotomizes between the service class and all the rest, which consists of the non-service class and the unemployed. The second dummy variable of class dichotomizes between the unemployed and the rest, which includes both the service class and the non-service class.

After deriving the variable of class within the British data set, the American data are translated into the class schema as closely as possible to allow comparisons between the two countries. This is done by combining variables of both occupation and employment status. More detailed descriptions of the recoding procedure are given at the beginning of Chapter 7.

Brief description of independent variables

AGE is a continuous variable, which is measured in years. It is considered an important determinant of the level of occupational attainment because, at least in the case of men, it is associated with length of time in the labour market, and seniority is normally positively related to higher occupational attainment.[23] People's chance to succeed occupationally also changes through the life cycle, with young people and old people having a relatively lower propensity to achieve higher socio-economic status than the middle aged. The variable on age is available in the same form in both the British and American data sets and remains completely comparable.

SEX is naturally a binary variable. It is believed that men and women's experiences in the labour market differ in terms of occupational distribution and career continuity, which affect their promotional prospects and eventual socio-economic status. In addition, gender difference might be complicated by the inclusion of ethnic minority women, whose

---

[22] The variable of "economic activity" has 25 categories, derived from 11 other basic variables. It includes the following: (1) full-time employee (2) part-time employee (3) employee time not stated (4) self-employed without employees (5) self-employed with employees (6) self-employed not stated employees (7) employment status not stated (8) YTS scheme (9) other scheme excluding TOPS (10) seeking work (11) temporary sick (12) holiday (13) waiting to start (14) awaiting results of application (15) TOPS course (16) full-time student (17) other student (18) sick or disabled (19) looking after house/home (20) retired (21) does not want/need employment (22) believes no jobs available (23) not yet started looking (24) other reason for not looking for work (25) no reason for looking for work. The "unemployed" includes categories 10,13, and 14.

[23] In the case of women, as shown in later analysis, class attainment is not necessarily related to seniority as child rearing interrupts employment.

occupational level is restricted by certain cultural values regarding the role of women. This variable is comparable across the two countries.

BIRTH refers to the place or country of birth. Although it is available in both data sets, with as many categories as there are countries in the world, the most useful distinction for this analysis is between those who are born in the host society, Britain or the U.S., and those born in foreign countries. The purpose of this distinction is to divide native-born ethnic minorities from foreign-born immigrants. Their patterns of occupational integration are found to differ considerably, according to existing empirical evidence, although the degree of differentiation may vary from group to group.

ETHNICITY refers to self-identified racial or ethnic group. It is a multinomial variable, which is available in both data sets, although it is called "ethnic origin"[24] in the British case and "race"[25] in the American case. In both cases, Chinese are listed separately from other ethnic groups. In the analysis, ethnicity is usually combined with country of birth. Thus a new variable of ETHBIR is created, in which categories refer to foreign-born Chinese, foreign-born Indians, native-born Chinese, native-born Indians, etc.

ENCLAVE is a binary variable derived from the base variable INDUSTRY, which is available in both data sets. It is used to distinguish between those Chinese who work in the traditional catering industries and those who work outside the ethnic enclave economy. For more details on how the variable is derived, see Chapter Five for the Chinese enclave economy in Britain and Chapter Seven for the Chinese enclave economy in the U.S..

---

[24] "Ethnic origin" includes the following categories: (1) White (2) West Indian or Guyanese (3) Indian (4) Pakistani (5) Bangladeshi (6) Chinese (7) African (8) Arab; Mixed Origin: (11) White (12) West Indian or Guyanese/White (13) Indian/White (14) Pakistani/White (15) Bangladeshi/White (16) Other Asian/White (17) African/White (18) Arab/White (19) Asian Mixture (20) African/West Indian or Guyanese (21) African/Asian (22) Miscellaneous 'Partly Coloured'(23) Miscellaneous 'coloured'; Other Origin: (24) White (25) West Indian or Guyanese (26) Indian (27) Pakistani (28) Bangladeshi (29) Chinese (30) African (31) Arab (32) other Asian (33) other origin mixture (34) mixed or not recodable (35) other origin and not recodable (36) no answer.

[25] The variable of "race" for American data is coded as follows: (1) White (2) Black (3) American Indian, Eskimo, Aleut Asian, and Pacific Islander (4) Japanese (5) Chinese (6) Filipino (7) Korean (8) Asian Indian (9) Vietnamese (10) Hawaiian (11) Other Asian and Pacific Islander, including Guamian and Samoan (12) Spanish write-in entry (13) other. The coding for a separate Spanish variable is as follows: (1) N/A (not of Spanish origin) (2) Mexican (3) Puerto Rican (3) Cuban (4) Other Spanish.

EDUCATION is the most crucial independent variable. In the British sample, information on the highest educational qualification[26] is available and it is a good measure of the level of formal schooling for Britain. Thus, in the analysis on the British alone, this measure is used. In the American data set, however, only information on the highest year of school attended is available.[27] Given a relatively uniform school system in the U.S., this measure is readily transferrable to the equivalent highest educational qualifications in the American system. The question of comparability arises only when the two countries are being directly compared. More detailed discussion of this issue comes at the beginning of Chapter Eight.

---

[26] The variable on the highest qualification is coded as follows: (1) higher degree (2) first degree (3) other degree-corporate or graduate member of professional institute (4) HNC/HND/BEC(higher)/TEC(higher) (5) teaching qualification-secondary (6) teaching qualification-primary (7) nursing qualification (8) ONC/OND/BEC(national/general)/TEC(national/general) (9) city and guild (10) A-level or equivalent (11) O-level or equivalent (including Grade 1 CSE) (12) CSE (other grades) (13) any other professional/vocational qualification (14) no qualification (15) don't know (16) no answer.

It should be noted that GCSE has replaced the previous dual system of GCE Ordinary-level and Certificate of Secondary Education (CSE) and like them, is a single subject examination. It was introduced in 1986 with a view to raising standards of performance. The first examinations were taken in 1988. The relation of GCSE grades to the former GCE O-level and CSE are as follows: GCSE grades A,B,C have standards as high as O-level grades A-C and CSE grade 1; GCSE grades D-G are equivalent to CSE 2-5. See The British Council, *International Guide to Qualifications in Education* (Third Edition), 1991. p.6.

The technical qualifications except the City and Guilds, may be grouped into BTEC (Business and Technician Education Council). There are three levels of BTEC qualifications: First Certificate/Diploma(FC/FD), National Certificate/Diploma(NC/ND) and Higher National Certificate/Diploma(HNC/HND). Each course is made up of a number of modules. These modules are marked with the following grades, pass, merit and distinction. City and Guilds qualifications are awarded at several levels from pre-vocational level upwards. There are three main occupational levels, level 1, level 2 and level 3. Certificates are awarded for successful performance demonstrated through a variety of assessment procedures. Some qualifications are awarded on the basis of grades: pass, merit, distinction or simply pass. Increasingly, however, certificates awarded are issued on the basis of acquisition of skills on knowledge for particular competences and may be accompanied by a Record of Achievement indicating specific competences demonstrated.

[27] The highest year of school attended is coded as follows: (0) never attending school or N/A (under 3 years of age) (1) nursery school (2) kindergarten; elementary (3) first grade (4) second grade (5) third grade (6) fourth grade (7) fifth grade (8) sixth grade (9) seventh grade (10) eighth grade; High School (11) ninth grade (12) tenth grade (13) eleventh grade (14) twelfth grade; college (15) first year (16) second year (17) third year (18) fourth year (19) fifth year (20) sixth year (21) seventh year (22) eighth year or more.

Why logistic regression

It ought to be pointed out that, in studying occupational attainments, I am going to use a fairly unconventional method of analysis, i.e. logit analysis. The most apparent difference of this method from the conventional method is, instead of using a continuous variable of occupational prestige, such as in multiple regression analysis, I use a multinomial variable with two sets of binary contrasts, i.e. service class versus the rest and unemployed versus the rest. The binary contrasts are adopted merely as expository devices to make explanations more straightforward. If necessary, a multinomial dependent variable can be used instead of two sets of binary contrasts.

This approach is adopted because I address theoretical questions, which can only be answered by doing logistic regression analysis. In studying occupational attainment, I posit a situation where members of different ethnic groups compete to reach a particular class position rather than not reaching it. Therefore, the measure of ethnic inequality in this competition is a log odds ratio, which is concerned with the relative chances of ethnic groups and therefore insensitive to absolute inter-group marginal differences.[28]

My decision to adopt such an approach is also based on the consideration that the traditional approach provides summary results, which tend to hide the complicated processes at work. For instance, education is found in general to be positively related to occupational level. This association may be represented by a single regression coefficient with a positive value between 0 and 1. It suggests a positive linear relationship whereby every additional year of education brings about a constant amount of increase in occupational prestige. A coefficient of this sort only summarises the relationship between education and occupation and tells little about how education may vary in its effects on access to different occupational levels. Summary results are obtained by theoretically assuming a uniform effect of education on occupation and by technically averaging out effects which can be revealed by a multinomial indicator. A lot of information is thus hidden from view and statistical parsimony itself entails obscuring central theoretical issues.

By using logistic regression with categorical dependent and independent variables, we end up with a greater number of regression coefficients,

---

[28] See Stephen E. Fienberg. *The Analysis of Cross-Classified Categorical Data (2nd Edition)* (Cambridge: MIT, 1980); David Knoke and Peter J. Burke. *Loglinear Models Series: Quantitative Applications in the Social Sciences* (Beverley Hill: Sage Publications, 1980); Anthony Heath, Colin Mills and Jane Roberts. "Towards Meritocracy? Recent Evidence on An Old Problem" (SCPR Working Paper No.3, 1991).

which provide a clearer picture of the process at work than continuous independent variables do. This is particularly valuable particularly when our theoretical concerns are occupational differentiation at the top and bottom reaches of the occupational structure. In other words, we do not want to assume that the same factors determine people's chances of reaching the service class to the same extent as they do for people's risks of unemployment. Summary coefficients, therefore, do not allow us to detect the finer yet significantly distinctive processes at work.

Logistic regression: an example

The logistic regression equation, known as the logit model, applies to analysis where the dependent variable is a binary variable, which cannot easily be scaled, such as house ownership, voting, etc. In short, such models are used in situations where the dependent variable is of the "yes" or "no" type, taking values of 1 or 0. In this study, a dummy variable of class may be "service class" or "the rest", taking values of 1 for "service class" and 0 for "the rest".[29]

We might want to study, for instance, class attainment as a function of age, ethnicity and education. Thus, the dependent variable class may take two values, 1 if the person is in "service class", 0 if belonging to "the rest". It should be noted that in social science research, it is often the case that the dichotomous dependent variable serves as an indicator for a probability, such as "probability of reaching the service class" and "probability of not reaching the service class". Thus, independent variables, such as age, ethnicity and education, are factors which we assume to affect the probability of class attainment. The logistic regression equation is written as:

$$\ln (P_i/1\text{-}P_i) = \theta_1 + \theta_2 X_i + \theta_3 X_j + \theta_4 X_k$$

where P_i is the probability of getting into the service class, X_i refers to age, X_j to ethnicity and X_k to education.

---

[29] Concerning the problems of logit models, Blalock wrote, "given that the dependent variable is a dichotomy, it may simply be recorded as 0 or 1 and used in a regression equation. This procedure creates two problems, however. First, if there are no restrictions placed on the values of the independent variables, the predicted value of the dependent variable may possibly exceed either of the limiting values of 0 or 1. Second, the assumption of homoscedasticity of the error term is also likely to be violated, especially if the proportions in the total sample are close to 0 or 1". See H.M.Blalock, Jr. *Social Statistics*. McGraw-Hill International Edition, 1979. p.541.

The values of δ_1, δ_2 and δ_3 are called parameter estimates of the independent variables, indicating the size and direction of the effects the independent variables have on the dependent variable. The estimates obtained from such regression equations are in the form of fitted log odds ratios, which need to be transformed first into odds and then into fitted probabilities for more straightforward interpretation.[30]

Here is one illustrative example of a logistic regression equation, in which it is assumed that chances of reaching the service class as against not reaching it depend on ethnicity and education. Note, ethnicity is binary, with 1 standing for Chinese and 0 for non-Chinese. Education is a multinomial variable, with 1 standing for degree and higher, 2 for A-level and equivalent, 3 for O-level and equivalent, and, 4 for no qualification. The logistic regression equation looks like this:

$$\ln\,(P/1\text{-}P) = \delta_1 + \delta_2(\text{ethnicity}) + \delta_3(\text{education}).$$

By fitting this model on the sample, which is assumed to be randomly selected, we look at the measures of goodness of fit of the model. The measures of goodness of fit include the G^2, which reflects the distance between the expected frequencies and the observed frequencies, and the degree of freedom, which refers to the minimum number of cells that have to be filled with frequencies in a particular contingency table for the frequencies of the other cells in the same table to be determined. In fact, the number of degree of freedom is equal to the number of cells in the cross-tabulation table minus the number of parameters.

In fitting the model, the null hypothesis says that an independent variable included in the regression equation does not have any effect on the dependent variable. With the loss of the same number of degrees of freedom, the bigger the change in G^2 (ΔG^2), the more likely it is that the null hypothesis will be rejected. Depending on the greatness of change in G^2, the null hypothesis can be rejected at .00 or .01, .05 level, etc. The decision is made by referring to a Chi-square distribution table. See, for instance, our example:

---

[30] The logistic regression analysis is done by using the newly released software, General Linear Interactive Models, developed by the Royal Statistical Society. The transformation of parameters estimates into odds and probabilities is also done by using macros within GLIM.

Model	G^2	d.f	ΔG^2	d.f.	rG^2(%)	P-value	ID
Class	12849	124					
+education	466	121	12383	3		0.000	
+ethnicity	400	120	66	1	97	0.000	3.7

This shows that both education and ethnicity have much effect on chances of reaching the service class as against not reaching it. Therefore, the null hypotheses as stated in both models are rejected.[31]

Measures of goodness of fit, though indicating important associations between variables, do not tell us the direction and size of the effects. Therefore, we turn to the parameter estimates. Written in the form of fitted log odds ratio as in logistic regressions, the coefficients are not usually straightforward for interpretation. See for instance,

Estimates	s.e.	Parameter
0.9399	0.02991	1
-2.115	0.03063	educ(2)
-3.113	0.06087	educ(3)
-4.118	0.08080	educ(4)
-0.2583	0.03193	ethn(2).

[31] It should be pointed out that this secondary analysis is conducted on a very large sample. Therefore, we are likely to obtain statistically significant results which are theoretically uninteresting to us. As a result, we are likely to encounter the situation where only the saturated model is a good fitting model, i.e. with P-value equal to or greater than 0.05. To cope with this, we have introduced two other summary measures, percentage of misclassified cases (ID) and percentage reduction in deviance (rG^2). If our model does not give a good fit by judging the P-value, and if we obtain an ID of around 2 or 3 percent, we can still say that the model is acceptable, because only 2-3% of the cases need to change their places to obtain the best fitting model.

Basically, the results show that compared with those with first degrees and higher, people with less education experience inferior fitted log odds of reaching the service class (versus not reaching it), and that the fitted log odds gradually decrease for people with increasingly lower education, even though the association between class and education is not perfectly linear. Likewise, being non-Chinese decreases the fitted log odds of reaching the service class (versus not reaching it), compared with being Chinese.

However, as the parameter estimates are in the form of fitted log odds ratio, it is not always easy to see exactly what is going on. Transformations are needed to simplify the fitted log odds ratios into fitted probabilities. To obtain fitted probabilities, we follow the procedure suggested by Davies.[32]

First, we fill in the model with parameter estimates obtained. We have,

---

$$0.9399\ (\beta_1) \quad \begin{array}{ll} +0.000\ [\beta_2(ed=1)] \\ -2.115\ [\beta_2(ed=2)] \quad +0.0000[\beta_3(eth=1)] \\ -3.113\ [\beta_2(ed=3)] \\ -4.118\ [\beta_2(ed=4)] \quad -0.2583[\beta_3(eth=2)]. \end{array}$$

To obtain the fitted probability of a person whose education and ethnicity are both 1, i.e. a Chinese with a degree, we first calculate the fitted log odds, in this case, 0.9399. We then exponentiate the value into the form of fitted odds, 2.5597. The fitted probability is obtained by dividing the fitted odds by the fitted odds plus one, 0.7191. Similarly, the fitted probability of a Chinese with an A-level reaching the service class is $P = \exp(0.9399-2.115)/[1+\exp(0.9399-2.115)] = .236$. It f&ollows that the fitted probability of a non-Chinese without qualification reaching the service class is $P = \exp(0.9399-4.118-0.2583)/[\exp(0.9399-4.118-0.2583)+1] = 0.0312$.

The same equations can be solved for all other parameter estimates to obtain fitted probabilities of Chinese or non-Chinese of various educational levels reaching the service class to obtain the following:

---

[32] Richard B. Davis. "Sample Enumeration Methods for Model Interpretation", Paper presented at the Sixth International Conference on Statistical Modelling held in Utrect, July 1991.

		Ethnicity	
		1 Chinese	2 non-Chinese
Education	1	.7191	.6641
	2	.2359	.1926
	3	.1022	.0808
	4	.0400	.0313.

Now, we can see more clearly that at all educational levels, Chinese have a greater fitted probability of reaching the service class. However, we also detect slightly greater advantage at the two highest educational levels. Likewise, for all ethnic groups, higher educational levels are associated with greater fitted probabilities of reaching the service class, even though the relationship between education and the better class position is not perfectly linear. For an even better illustration of this finding, we can draw a graph as in Figure 1.1, where the vertical axis stands for the fitted probability of reaching the service class and the horizontal axis stands for four categories of education. The two separate curves stand for Chinese and non-Chinese.

It should be noted that this example is a very simple one, with two independent variables and no interaction terms. In later analysis, regression equations will include a greater number of independent variables. Very often, the interaction terms between certain variables will be included. Thus, the interpretation of parameter estimates will be more difficult. To tackle this problem, I shall increasingly depend on transformation of fitted log odds ratios into fitted probabilities for a more straightforward way of summarizing the parameter estimates. Where there are huge tables, I shall not explain all the coefficients but only pick up a few for the sake of illustration. The procedures described above will I hope serve as a useful guide for later understanding of the analysis.

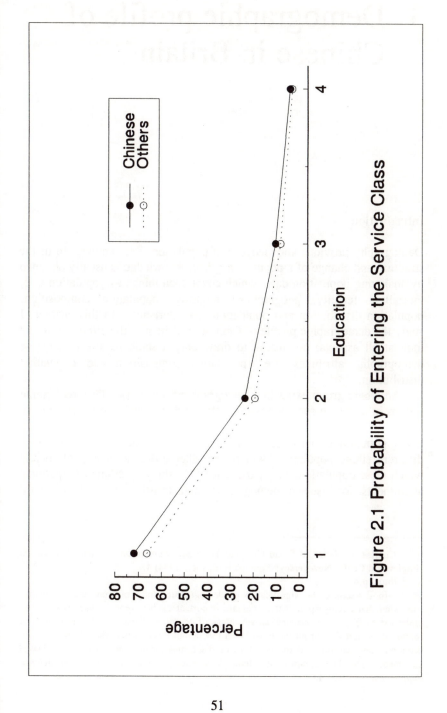

Figure 2.1 Probability of Entering the Service Class

3 Demographic profile of Chinese in Britain

Introduction

Demography provides knowledge of a population, i.e., knowledge of the structure and change of a population.[1] Such knowledge is usually obtained by analyzing population data, which cover such things as population size, mortality, fertility, geographical mobility, population composition, population distribution and population characteristics. In this chapter, I study the demographic profile of Chinese in Britain in the 1980s. I do not look at all aspects, but intend to draw only a static picture of Chinese demographic attributes, i.e., population composition and population distribution.

An ethnic group exists in a demographic framework. Different ethnic groups in the same society possess different demographic profiles. Given that demographic attributes are often useful in appraisal of how a particular ethnic population interrelates with other aspects of society,[2] knowledge of different ethnic populations will reveal other different aspects of society which these populations may experience.[3] In studying ethnic occupational attainments, for instance, demographic characteristics of an ethnic group,

---

[1] Charles B. Nam and Susan Gustavus Philliber, *Population: A Basic Orientation* (Englewood Cliffs, New Jersey: Prentice Hall, Inc., 1984) 4.

[2] Ibid., p.4.

[3] In discussing the significance of demographic study of minorities, Coleman suggested that demographic differences are important visible signs of what is going on under the surface. For instance, an advantage of one group versus another in respect of immigration, fertility, or mortality will be a function of its characteristic culture or socio-economic distribution, and the privilege or discrimination it experiences. See David Coleman. "The Demography of Ethnic Minorities" *Journal of Biological Science Supplement 8* (1983) 43.

which positively or negatively contribute to its socio-economic attainments are called demographic potentials.[4]

In this chapter, the demographic potentials of Chinese will be obtained primarily through comparisons of Chinese demographic attributes with those of the other major ethnic groups in Britain. First, I examine a few demographic attributes, such as group size, country of origin, year of arrival, sex composition, age distribution, and regional distribution. Then I discuss the possible impact of demographic attributes on Chinese occupational attainments, in relation to other ethnic groups. This chapter is functionally preparatory and the analysis descriptive. Questions such as causes of migration in particular historical period or causes of regional distribution are beyond the scope of this chapter.

The data set used in this chapter comes from the British national Labour Force Surveys (LFS) 1983-1989. It has been extracted to include majority whites and major ethnic minorities in Britain, by using the variable of ethnic origin. It consists of whites, Indians, West Indians, Pakistanis and Chinese.[5] The sample size is N=878,657.

Group size

Up until now, there have been no accurate official statistics on the actual population size of Chinese in Britain.[6] According to the Home Affairs Committee report released in 1985, there were approximately 100,000

---

[4] Robert M. Jiobu, *Ethnicity and Assimilation: Blacks, Chinese, Filipinos, Japanese, Koreans, Mexicans, Vietnamese and Whites* (Albany: State University of New York, 1988) 60.

[5] (1)People of African and Arab origins are not included. People who reported mixed origins are also excluded. (2) We should be aware that "the definition of race is probably the domain of the physical anthropologist. He recognizes that in the modern world most ethnic groups are of mixed racial origin and that fresh racial mixture is constantly occurring. In compiling demographic records, we have to be content with much grosser classifications than those of the anthropologist. These tend to be based on how members of groups identify themselves and how they are regarded by their compatriots. Racial or ethnic groups so defined, however, are usually more meaningful from the standpoints of social policy or demographic analysis than those defined by purely anthropometric criteria. The resulting classification is neither scientific nor objective, but it is reasonably consistent and reproducible in that most persons who know the person would place him in the same category or categories". See U.S. Bureau of the Census. "Racial and Ethnic Composition" *The Methods and Materials of Demography* (Washington, 1973) 252.

[6] The 1981 Census did not include any special ethnic question and only asked respondents about birth place. The 1991 Census included a question on ethnic origin, but data are not yet available.

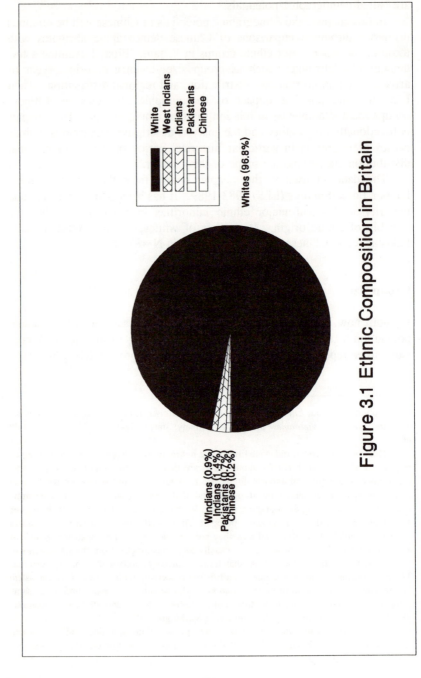

Figure 3.1 Ethnic Composition in Britain

Legend:
- White
- West Indians
- Indians
- Pakistanis
- Chinese

Whites (96.8%)

Windians (0.9%)
Indians (1.4%)
Pakistanis (0.7%)
Chinese (0.2%)

Chinese in Britain, based on estimates of local councils.[7] Chinese were said to form the third largest non-white ethnic group in Britain, following South Asians and Afro-Caribbeans.[8]

In the sample to be used in this thesis, which I will refer to as the LFS sample, there are 1,922 Chinese out of 874,986 people, a percentage of 0.2%. The percentages for Indians, Pakistanis, West Indians and whites are 1.4%, 0.7%, 0.9% and 96.7% respectively. The ethnic composition of the LFS sample is summarized in Figure 3.1.

Although Chinese rank third in size among the major British non-white ethnic groups, we can see that the size of the South Asian population, combining Indians and Pakistanis, is nearly eleven times that of the Chinese population. West Indians are four and a half times more numerous than Chinese. Therefore, Chinese in Britain are a relatively small non-white minority group in an ethnically homogeneous society, where over 95% of the population are of white origin.

Chinese: where they come from

The 1,922 people who claimed Chinese origin come from 36 different countries. About a quarter were born in Britain. Of the foreign-born Chinese, the single largest group comes from Hong Kong, forming nearly 35% of the Chinese sample. China[9] and Vietnam each contribute about 11%. The rest, amounting to 18% of Chinese, come primarily from South East Asian countries, such as Malaysia, Singapore, Philippines, etc. The country of birth of Chinese in Britain is summarized in Figure 3.2.

Based on the knowledge of country of birth, we can divide the Chinese sample into five main groups, Chinese born in Britain, Chinese born in Hong Kong, Chinese born in China, Chinese born in Vietnam and Chinese born elsewhere. Later analysis of demographic attributes will be conducted separately for these Chinese groups.

The reason for drawing distinctions among Chinese is that Chinese born in different countries, migrated to Britain with different purposes. Each group may have its own distinctive migratory history. Time of arrival, sex composition, age structure, regional distribution are all likely to be affected. This we shall discuss in detail later.

---

[7] The figure quoted by the OPCS based on the 1988-1990 LFS is 135,000.

[8] Home Affairs Committee, *The Chinese Community in Britain* (1985) 1.

[9] China includes mainland China and Taiwan.

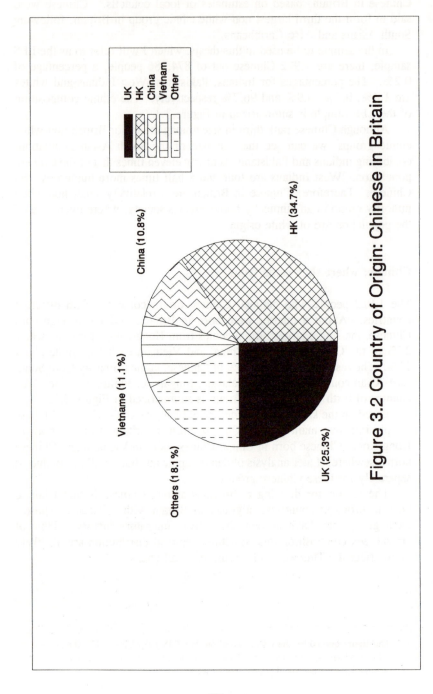

Figure 3.2 Country of Origin: Chinese in Britain

UK (25.3%)

Others (18.1%)

Vietname (11.1%)

China (10.8%)

HK (34.7%)

UK
HK
China
Vietnam
Other

Other ethnic minorities: where they come from

It has been shown in Figure 3.1 that apart from Chinese, other ethnic groups include British-born whites, Indians, Pakistanis, and West Indians. These categories are obtained by looking solely at ethnic origins and make no further distinction by country of birth. As a result, important ethnic minorities, such as Irish, may be buried within whites, while African Asians may be counted as Indians or Pakistanis.

The aim of this chapter is to bring out as many differences in the demographic profile of as many culturally distinctive groups as there are.[10] Only when finer ethnic categories are available, can we define more closely the uniqueness of the Chinese demographic profile. This will enable us to reduce the chances of wrongly attributing to Chinese alone what should be regarded as common to all or some ethnic minorities. Therefore, among whites, we shall distinguish those of Irish origin from those of British origin.[11] Among Indians and Pakistanis, we shall distinguish those born in India or Pakistan from those born in East Africa.[12] Among West Indians, we shall distinguish those who were born in Afro-Caribbean nations[13] from those who were born in Britain. In this way, we are able to identify 14 ethnic groups. The name and number of people in each group are listed in Table 3.1.[14]

---

[10] In a critique of studies of ethnic minority disadvantage in education, Plewis pointed out, "it is of course common practice, in statistical work to combine small and apparently similar groups to form a category of reasonable size in order to reduce the vagaries of random sampling. But sometimes, the labels we use for these categories take on unanticipated meanings and convey misleading messages. We should not always let the statistical arguments for combination outweigh substantive argument for separation. Indeed, there may sometimes be grounds for not presenting the data if the substantially meaningful groups are statistically too small and the statistically meaningful groups are substantially misleading". See I. Plewis, "Assessing and Understanding the Educational Progress of Children from Different Ethnic Groups" *Journal of the Royal Statistical Society*. Series A (Statistics in Society) 151 (1988) 316-326.

[11] No more distinctions are going to be made among whites of European origins.

[12] Indians or Pakistanis who claim to have been born in Kenya and Uganda are considered African Asians.

[13] Those West Indians born in Barbados, Jamaica, Trinidad and Tobago, West Indian Associate States, West Indies and other Caribbean Commonwealth countries are considered West Indians born in Afro-Caribbean nations.

[14] To understand the labels of ethnic group by country of birth in Table 3.1, UK/Chinese=Chinese born in UK; HK/Chinese=Chinese born in Hong Kong; CH/Chinese=Chinese born in China and Taiwan; VT/Chinese=Chinese born in Vietnam; EL/Chinese=Chinese born in other parts of the world; UK/Indians=Indians born in UK; IN/Indians=Indians born in India; UK/Pakistanis=Pakistanis born in UK; PK/Pakistanis=Pakistanis born in Pakistan; AF/Asians=Asians born in East Africa;

Table 3.1. Ethnic Groups by Country of Birth

Name of Ethnic Group	Number
UK/Chinese	487
HK/Chinese	667
CH/Chinese	207
VT/Chinese	213
OTHER/Chinese	348
UK/Indians	4,678
IN/Indians	4,651
UK/Pakistanis	3,017
PK/Pakistanis	3,064
AF/Asians	1,876
UK/West Indians	4,211
WI/West Indians	3,275
IR/Irish	8,767
UK/Whites	817,167
Total	852,628

Immigrants: when they come

Not all immigrant groups have the same migratory experience, nor do they come to Britain at the same time.[181] Brown pointed out that variations in year of arrival are "due to a combination of factors: different social and political forces prompted the migration from different areas; the migrants came from a variety of societies, which produced different patterns of migration; and above all, the number of black people moving into the U.K.

UK/West Indians=West Indians born in UK; AC/West Indians=West Indians born in Afro-Caribbean countries; IR/Irish=Irish born in Ireland; UK/Whites=Whites born in UK.

[181] This proposition has been proved to be statistically true. From a global Chi-square test, a likelihood ratio of 14,046 has been obtained with 40 degrees of freedom. It shows that statistically significant ethnic variations exist in year of arrival.

has been controlled by the government since 1962 by a series of legal and administrative measures".[16]

By the time Commonwealth immigrants came to Britain during the post-war economic boom, the Irish had already been in the country a few centuries. The latest group, Vietnamese refugees of Chinese origin, did not migrate to Britain until two decades ago. In this section, I examine the year of arrival for all immigrant groups as a way of briefly introducing the migratory experiences of various immigrant groups in Britain.

In Figure 3.3, cumulative percentages by year of arrival are drawn for all nine immigrant groups. Five time periods have been selected from 1950 to 1990, with ten years in each period. The percentage corresponding to a particular year represents the total number of people already in Britain by that year as a proportion of all people in the sample in Britain by 1990. Thus, a curve with a flatter shape, such as that for Irish (IRIR), indicates that Irish have the longest duration, compared to other groups, with over 30% of Irish already in Britain by 1950. At the other end of the spectrum, Vietnamese Chinese (VNCH) have the steepest curve, indicating that they are the latest comers to Britain, with no member of this group arriving before the 1970s.

Irish are the oldest minority group in Britain. The history of their immigration can be traced back to the seventeenth century. The population swelled in the nineteenth century when famine prompted a mass exodus from Ireland. The 1851 census estimated that there were at least half a million Irish-born people living in the ports and industrial areas of England, Scotland, and Wales. Although the pace of Irish migration slackened somewhat after this period, it continued at a steady level and even accelerated in the twentieth century. Irish migration reached its peak this century during the immediate post-war period.[17] Attracted by a short-lived economic miracle at home, a net flow back to Ireland occurred in the 1970s. The 1980s, however, saw a new wave of Irish immigration to Britain.[18]

Vietnamese Chinese came as political refugees. After the fall of Saigon in 1975, Chinese in Vietnam were persecuted and many had to flee the country. Britain received about 20,000 Vietnamese refugees as part of

---

[16] Colin Brown, *Black and White Britain: The Third PSI Survey* (Policy Studies Institute, 1984) 18.

[17] M. Haralambos, Sociology: New Directories (1985) 21-22.

[18] Ceri Peach et al., "Immigration and Ethnicity" in A.H. Halsey ed. *British Social Trends since 1900* (London: MacMillan, 1988) 571.

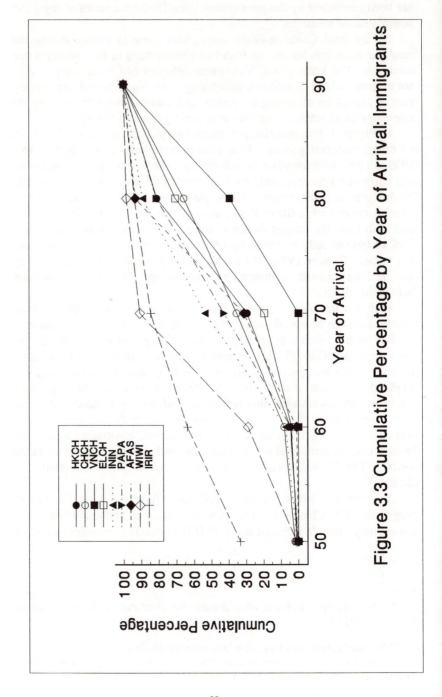

Figure 3.3 Cumulative Percentage by Year of Arrival: Immigrants

an international resettlement effort.[19]   The presence of this group in Britain was unknown up until the mid-1970s, as already shown.

As shown in Figure 3.3, between the two extremes of Irish and Vietnamese Chinese, there is a whole spectrum of ethnic groups. Distributed from left to right are West Indians (WIWI), Indians (ININ), Pakistanis (PAPA), African Asians (AFAS), and Chinese (HKCH, CHCH, ELCH). It is obvious that, of these ethnic groups, the earliest migration was of West Indians, who came at an increasing rate in the 1950s and 1960s to fill labour shortages in expanding British industry.[20]   Asians came at a time when West Indian migration was in decline. They came primarily after the 1962 Commonwealth Immigration Act, although the pattern of arrival varies within the Asian groups. Pakistanis seem to have arrived a bit later than Indians.[21]

Note, however, that the great majority of African Asians did not come until the 1970s and presented a case different from that of both Indians and Pakistanis. It is said that their ancestors migrated to East Africa as early as the 13th century and through time established and strengthened their middle class status through education and penetration into white-collar jobs. From the mid-1960s till the early 1970s, persecution of Asians in Kenya and Uganda took the form first of removal of non-citizens from public employment and then of expulsion from the country. As a result, lots of Asians were forced to migrate to Britain. In the beginning, only young males from wealthy backgrounds were sent on behalf of their families to assess economic opportunities in Britain. In 1972, when Amin ordered all Asians out of Uganda, people from all kinds of socio-economic backgrounds came, many being extended families with little resources.[22]

The Chinese migration into Britain, as discussed in Chapter One, followed the classic pattern of economic migration.   Up until WWII, Chinese immigration, which consisted mainly of single male immigrant labours, remained a trickle. The second wave of migration brought into Britain the majority of today's Chinese population. The post- war British demand for ethnic cuisine coupled with deteriorating economic conditions in rural Hong Kong formed the major pull-push factors. Although the resurgence of Chinese immigration started as early as the 1950s, the large influx of Chinese did not follow until the 1960s. Thus, the figure shows

---

[19] P. Jones, *Vietnamese Refugees: A Study of Their Reception and Resettlement in the U.K.* (Home Office, 1982) 1.

[20] A.H. Halsey. p.578.

[21] This result is different from that of Brown, who observed that the bulk of Pakistanis migration was a little earlier than the Indians.

[22] Vaughan Robinson, *Transients, Settlers and Refugees: Asians in Britain* (Oxford: Clarendon Press, 1986) 41-43.

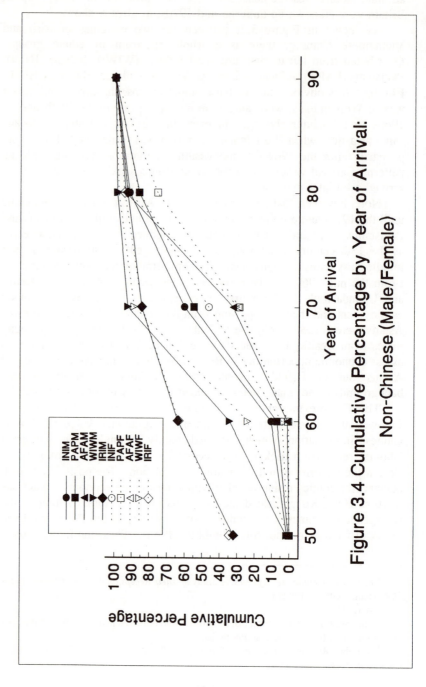

Figure 3.4 Cumulative Percentage by Year of Arrival:
Non-Chinese (Male/Female)

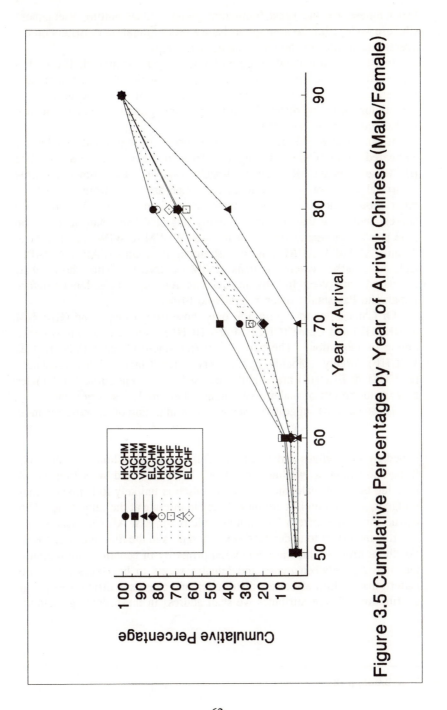

Figure 3.5 Cumulative Percentage by Year of Arrival: Chinese (Male/Female)

that Chinese are the latest immigrant group. Even putting Vietnamese Chinese aside, Chinese immigrants have a shorter duration in Britain on the average than most of the other immigrant groups.

In addition to general group variations in year of arrival, Brown has suggested that the timing of migration also varied between men and women.[23] He found that Asian women migrated later than Asian men, even though time lag differs for different ethnic groups. Similar evidence is also found in the present sample.

It can be seen in Figure 3.4, where curves for males and females are compared for non-Chinese immigrants, Irish are the only group whose male (IRIM) and female (IRIF) curves largely coincide. This shows that time of arrival does not differ between Irish men and Irish women. All the other groups, however, have female curves lying to the right of male curves, indicating that females generally migrated later than males. The time lags are closest among West Indians (WIWM & WIWF) and African Asians (AFAM & AFAF), but widest among Pakistanis (PAPM & PAPF) and, to a lesser extent, Indians (INIM & INIF). This shows that, compared with West Indians and African Asians, it took longer before Indian and Pakistani women migrated to Britain.

Of Chinese, as in Figure 3.5, only those from Hong Kong (HKCHM & HKCHF) and China (CHCHM & CHCHF) show sex variations in the timing of migration. The curves for Vietnamese Chinese (VNCHM & VNCHF) largely coincide. The curves for Chinese born elsewhere (ELCHM & ELCHF) are slightly reversed in that the curve for females appears to the left of males, even though the time lag is very small.

These patterns suggest that sex variation in timing of migration is most likely to happen among economic immigrants. Male sojourners form the majority of the early immigrants. Only when they decide to settle are they joined by their wives and families. This is true for Chinese from Hong Kong and China, as well as for Indians, Pakistanis, and West Indians. A time lag between male and female migration is unlikely to happen among refugees, whose families are more likely to migrate at the same time. This is true for Chinese from Vietnam as well as for East African Asians.

It is important to understand sex differences in the timing of migration. For those groups which are composed primarily of economic immigrants, the time lag between males and females seems to be consistent. This pattern may in turn affect sex distribution and cause sex differences in age distribution. These attributes we shall address in the following sections.

---

[23] Brown, p.18.

Sex distribution

First, to see if group differences in sex distribution are statistically significant, I have done a global Chi-square test. The Chi-square test yields a likelihood ratio of 135 with 14 degrees of freedom. The overall differences between cell values and expected frequencies are thus found to be statistically significant. This leads us to believe that sex distributions differ among ethnic groups.

Secondly, to find out the specific sex distribution of each group defined above, I have calculated the sex ratio. The sex ratio is usually defined as the number of males per 100 females, or

$$(P_m / P_f) \times 100$$

where P_m represents the number of males, and P_f the number of females.[24] The calculated sex ratios for all the groups are listed in Table 3.2.

Table 3.2. Sex Ratio by Ethnic Groups

Ethnic Group	Sex Ratio
UK/Chinese	113
HK/Chinese	114
CH/Chinese	90
VT/Chinese	99
OTHER/Chinese	79
UK/Indians	105
IN/Indians	98
UK/Pakistanis	105
PA/Pakistanis	116
AF/Asians	115
UK/WestIndian	89
WI/WestIndian	89
IR/Irish	88
UK/Whites	94

[24] U.S. Bureau of the Census. *The Methods and Materials of Demography (Volume 1)*. p. 191. Note, demographic measures such as sex ratio are usually taken from the total population. Since we do not have data on the total population but on a sample of the population, it has to be to be taken on the sample data instead.

To interpret the sex ratio, 100 is the point of balance between the sexes according to this measure. A sex ratio above 100 denotes an excess of males. Accordingly, the greater the excess of males, the higher the sex ratio; the greater the excess of females, the lower the sex ratio.

British-born whites have a sex ratio of 94, which means that for every 100 females within our British-born white sample, there are 94 males. The lowest sex ratio of 79 is found among Chinese born elsewhere and the highest of 116 among Pakistanis born in Pakistan. Some group differences in sex ratio are clearly affected by historical circumstances, others may be caused by the selection bias of the sample.

Of the Chinese groups, only those born in China and Vietnam have fairly balanced sex compositions. The high sex ratio for Chinese from Hong Kong and Chinese born in Britain is noticeable, with 114 and 113 males for every 100 females respectively. The excess of males among the Hong Kong Chinese may reflect an earlier migration, which consisted mainly of single men or married men leaving their families behind.[25] Although they were normally joined by their wives and children several years later, males seemed to form a higher proportion of the immigrant population from Hong Kong to Britain at all times.

The excess of British-born Chinese males, however, is intriguing.[26] The only likely explanation lies in reverse migration. Among immigrants from Hong Kong, particularly those in the traditional catering business, the practice of sending British-born Chinese children back to Hong Kong to receive traditional education is said to be common.[27] Parents might prefer to send their daughters back to be brought up in Chinese culture, which they compare favourably to western culture, while preferring to keep their sons working in the family business in the hope that the male children would inherit the family fortune in the future.[28]

Among Chinese from elsewhere, the sex ratio is very low. Chinese in this group are most likely to be second time migrants, born in countries

---

[25] As a matter of fact, male dominance among economic immigrants is not true only for Chinese. Castles and Kosack suggest that in all migratory movements, males tend to go abroad by themselves in search of employment. They are unmarried, or if married, they leave their wives and children behind. If they decide to settle permanently, they are usually joined by their families later. See Steven Castles and Godula Kosack, *Immigrant Workers and Class Structure in Western Europe* (London: Oxford University Press, 1985) 50.

[26] I have conducted a Chi-square test on the sex ratio of majority whites and British-born Chinese. The Chi-square value is 361 with 1 degree of freedom. It shows that there is a statistically significant difference in sex ratio between majority whites and Chinese born in Britain.

[27] Kwee Choo Ng, *The Chinese in London* (London: Oxford University Press, 1968).

[28] Ibid.

other than China and Hong Kong. Among the immigrants, many were young professionals, who were established in their country of birth, but came to Britain for better chances of occupational success.[29] Many of them might be well educated young women, whose socio-economic aspirations were blocked by limited job opportunities for women at home. In addition, British men who married Chinese women during service abroad are likely to bring their wives with them to settle in Britain when their service terminates.[30] These two factors might contribute to an excess of females.

Compared to Chinese, relatively high sex ratios are generally found among other Asian immigrant groups, except for Indians born in India. Pakistanis, in particular, have a very high sex ratio of 116. Studies have shown that among early Commonwealth immigrants, the sex balance for coloured Commonwealth migrants was 1,384 males per 1,000 female. Among them, the proportions of women among Indian and Pakistani migrants were much lower than that among West Indians. Pakistanis were the extreme case, with more than four men for each woman. This imbalanced sex distribution, which was formed many years ago, may still have some bearing on the present day Pakistani immigrant population, where a male surplus has not vanished.

An interesting thing to notice about Pakistanis is that the sex distribution of the second generation is much closer to that of British-born whites than the first generation. This forms a contrast with second generation Chinese, who have a higher male dominance than all the other Chinese immigrant groups. This appears to support the postulated reverse migration of primarily British-born female Chinese.

Lastly, West Indian and Irish immigrants both have lower sex ratios than most of Asian immigrants. The dominance of women among these immigrants may be caused by selective migration, which favoured women rather than men.

It has been suggested by Peach that early West Indian migration was sensitive to the employment situation in Britain because of its highly significant reverse relationship with unemployment rates in Britain.[31]

---

[29] Susan Baxter, *The Chinese and Vietnamese in Birmingham* (Birmingham City Council, 1986) 28.

[30] Of the present Chinese population in Britain, it is about twice as likely for a Chinese woman to marry a white spouse than for a Chinese man to do so. This may indicate that more Chinese women settle in Britain due to marriage. See David Coleman. "The Demography of Ethnic Minorities" in *Journal of Biosocial Science Supplement* 8 (1983) 77.

[31] Ceri Peach. "The Caribbeans in Europe: Contrasting Patterns of Migration and Settlement in Britain, France and Netherlands," ESRC Research Paper, 1991.

This is particularly true of West Indian men, whose settlement was more dependent on the demand for labour than that of women. Therefore, Peach suspected that a section of the male immigrants became "floating migrants", whose proportion among the total West Indian immigrants was influenced by British economic conditions.[32] Because of this, the major West Indian immigrants were women and children, who might be less likely to travel and more likely to settle in Britain.

The reason for female dominance among Irish is similar to that among Chinese born elsewhere. Among recent Irish immigrants, many are well educated young professional women, who came to Britain for jobs more commensurate with their qualifications. Lots of these jobs were simply not available to them at home.[33]

In this section, I have looked at sex distribution and differences in sex distribution between groups. The most important finding is that sex ratios are still higher for the Asian immigrants in general. The sex ratios of Chinese, however, are generally lower than Pakistanis and African Asians. Male dominance, which was pronounced among earlier immigrants, has weakened but is still evident among the present immigrant population.

The puzzling finding is that while the sex ratio becomes normal among the second generation of other Asian groups, the sex imbalance is sustained among British-born Chinese. Whether this bears any relation to the practice of sending British-born Chinese young women to Hong Kong remains speculative. But the very high sex ratio is only a sign of what is going on under the surface, and it may be indicative of the consequences of such practices on related aspects of social life. For instance, when the young people, young women in particular, come back to Britain after several years of traditional Chinese education, how do they adjust to British society again, schools, and employment?

Age distribution

Age has an important effect upon an ethnic group's level of socio-economic success. This is because "a group with a low mean age, one composed of many youths and children, has a different demographic trajectory than a group with high mean age. Both groups require resources from society but of vastly different kinds. Socialization-family structure, peer group

---

[32] Ceri Peach, "Factors Affecting the Distribution of West Indians in Great Britain" *Journal of Biosocial Science Supplement* 8 (1983) 153.

[33] D. McMohan, "The Integration of the Irish in Britain" *International Migration Review* (Forthcoming).

pressure, formal education, job training-is the most basic requirement for a young group. Its future lies ahead of it and its contribution to society will be made later. The opposite applies to an old group".[34]

In this section, I shall look at group mean age first to obtain a general age profile for various ethnic groups. It can be seen in Table 3.3 that British-born whites have an average age of 37. Among the other groups, the biggest difference lies between foreign-born and native-born. All foreign-born immigrants have entered their thirties on average, except for Vietnamese Chinese. Native-born Chinese, Indians, and Pakistanis have an average age below ten. British-born West Indians have entered their teenage on average, probably due to the longer duration of their parents in Britain. This guess is partially confirmed by the mean age of West Indian immigrants, which is generally higher than those of Asian immigrant groups.

The mean age is only a summary measure, which indicates an overall age level. In the next section, I shall use a more detailed measure with age categories to show similarities and differences in the age distribution of all ethnic groups. Population pyramids and percent distributions will be used as graphical representations of the measure.

Table 3.3. Mean Age by Ethnic Groups

Ethnic Group	Mean Age
UK/Whites	37
UK/Chinese	10
HK/Chinese	32
CH/Chinese	43
VN/Chinese	26
OTHER/Chinese	31
UK/Indians	10
IN/Indians	40
UK/Pakistanis	9
PA/Pakistanis	32
AF/Asians	31
UK/West Indians	16
WI/West Indians	44
IR/Irish	49

---

[34] Jiobu, *Ethnicity and Assimilation*, 70.

Age categories are divided into five year age cohorts. Placing all people over the age of 85 in one cohort, we have obtained 18 age cohorts. From the Chi-square test, we obtain a likelihood ratio of 40,522 at 238 degrees of freedom. It shows that there are statistically significant differences in age distribution among the ethnic groups.

In Figures 3.6-3.11 and Figures 3.14-3.21, population pyramids are constructed for all ethnic groups. They represent age-sex composition of a population.[35] The basic pyramid form consists of bars, representing age groups in ascending order from the lowest to the highest. The bars for males are given to the left of a central vertical axis and the bars for females to the right of the axis. The number of males or females in a particular age group is indicated by the length of the bar measured from the central axis.

The population pyramid for the host population, British-born whites, is presented in Figure 3.6. It has a gentle slope, with a narrow base gradually expanding in the middle portion and tapering at the top. It illustrates a case where there are fewer children and even fewer older people, although the age cohorts do not differ very much in the number of people they contain.

Although profiles of the age structure of all five groups of Chinese differ in one way or another from that of British whites, it is Chinese born in Britain who present the most striking contrast. As seen in Figure 3.7, British-born Chinese are concentrated in the four lowest age categories, from 0 to 19. This shows that the great majority are still under the age of 20 and are likely to be engaged in full time studies or just at the beginning of a career.

It is known that these people were born in Britain and that they are likely to be second generation Chinese. As mass immigration into Britain, which included most of the parents of this group did not start until the 1960s, and the survey was taken in 1980s, the time gap of about twenty years in between may well explain the concentration of this group in age categories of under 20.

Differences in age distribution from majority whites exist among the other four Chinese groups, too. Among Chinese born in Hong Kong, as shown in Figure 3.8, concentration is obvious in age categories between 20 and 40 for both males and females. This might be explained by the fact that migrants of the 1950s onwards, who were likely to be young people then, were entering their middle age when the survey was undertaken. On the other hand, the small number of children and older people in this

---

[35] Again, the data on which the population pyramids are drawn do not represent the population but the sample of the population.

Figure 3.6 Age by Sex: British-born Whites

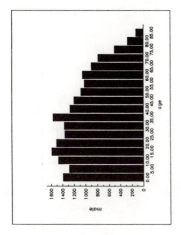
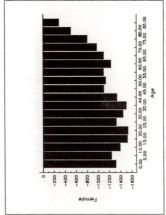

Figure 3.7 Age by Sex: British-born Chinese

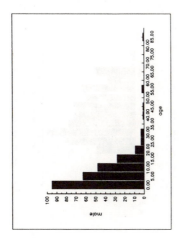
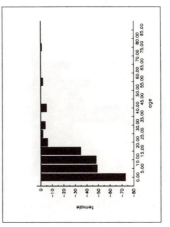

Figure 3.8 Age by Sex: Chinese Born in Hong Kong

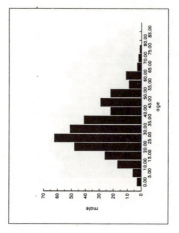

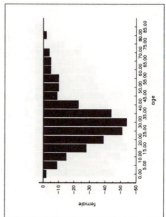

Figure 3.9 Age by Sex: Chinese Born in China

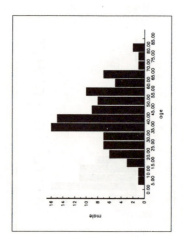

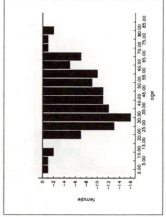

Figure 3.10 Age by Sex: Chinese Born in Vietnam

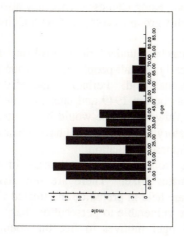
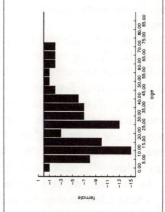

Figure 3.11 Age by Sex: Chinese Born Elsewhere

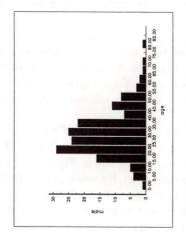
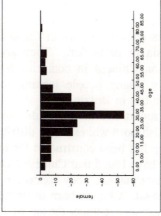

group, as well as in other immigrant groups, may be determined by the characteristics of immigrants, who are more likely to be able bodied workers than dependents.

Similar patterns also apply to Chinese born in China. In Figure 3.9, the highest frequencies occur in the middle age categories, especially at 35-44 for males and 25-34 for females. However, senior citizens are not as under-represented as in the case of Hong Kong Chinese. This may also be confirmed by the higher mean age of this group as compared with Chinese from Hong Kong.

Emigration from mainland China has been under strict control since the Communists took power in 1949. Clearly, not all people in this group are likely to be direct migrants from the mainland. Perhaps some of them migrated first to Hong Kong or Taiwan before 1949 and later migrated again to Britain. These mainland or Taiwan Chinese would have entered at least middle age in the 1980s. Migratory history may still have a bearing on the present age structure of this Chinese population.

Figure 3.10 shows that Chinese from Vietnam concentrate in age categories below 40, males and females alike. There are few senior citizens. In Vietnam, where Chinese are held in prejudice and treated with hostility, young Chinese may be more vulnerable to persecution than elderly people. They may have stronger motives to flee the country. Besides, compared with their seniors, they are more able to bear the physical hardships of life in exile. Therefore, senior citizens are less likely to join the exodus.

The last group consists of Chinese born elsewhere. As seen in Figure 3.11, higher frequencies are likely to occur in certain younger and middle age categories for both males and females. These categories range from 20 to 39. Due to their Chinese descent, people in this group should have ancestors who were born in China and later migrated overseas, to South East Asia in particular. They are likely to be second or subsequent generation Chinese in countries from which they migrated. They are primarily young people looking for better occupational and economic opportunities in Britain.

To summarize the major differences between the five Chinese groups and British-born whites in age distribution, a percentage distribution of age by group has been constructed for males and females in Figures 3.12 and 3.13. I have found that Chinese males are generally younger than British-born white males. They concentrate in young and middle age categories of under 40. Chinese born in Britain present an extreme case, where the great majority are under the age of 20. Similar patterns are also applicable to female Chinese, compared with British-born white women.

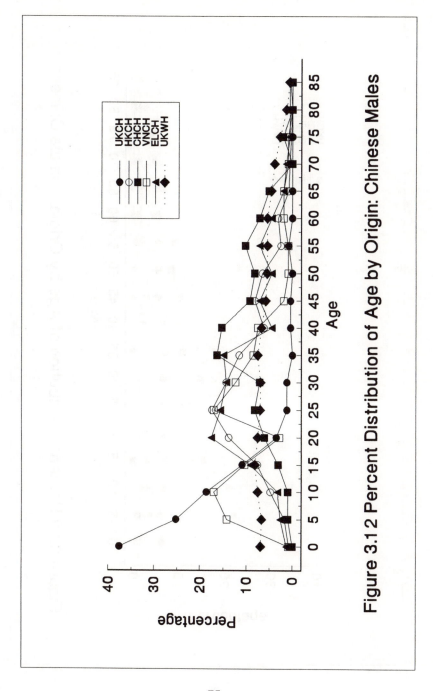

Figure 3.12 Percent Distribution of Age by Origin: Chinese Males

75

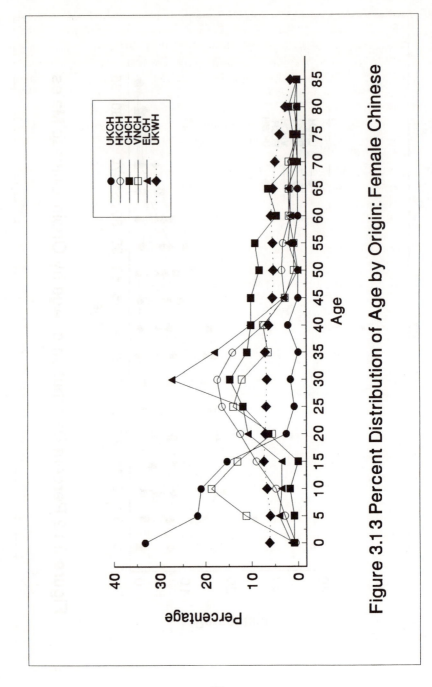

Figure 3.13 Percent Distribution of Age by Origin: Female Chinese

Among other minority groups, which have been selected as control groups, similar patterns emerge among the second generation. In Figures 3.14, 3.15, and 3,16, the great majority of Indians and Pakistanis born in Britain are under the age of 20, whereas most British-born West Indians are under the age of 30. The earlier arrival of West Indian immigrants may cause the average age of their second generation to be slightly higher than the offspring of Asian immigrants.

Among Asian immigrants, those from East Africa have been singled out as a separate group on account of their unique migratory experiences. An immediate impact of this migration on the present age structure of East African Asians may be the absence of children under the age of 15, as shown in Figure 3.17. The bulk of the population, both males and females, is found to be between 15 and 39. Children and young people who migrated in the 1970s had entered their youth and middle age by the time of the survey.

Profiles of the age structure of Indian, Pakistani, West Indian, and Irish immigrants, as presented in Figures 3.18, 3.19, 3.20, and 3.21, reflect interesting age distributions that correspond to the approximate length of duration of each group in Britain. The bulk of population distribution shifts upwards gradually from Pakistanis to Indians, West Indians, and Irish.

As discussed earlier, Irish are the longest-established minority group in Britain. Massive migration of West Indians to Britain also preceded that of Asians, because the first influx of Indians and Pakistanis did not occur until the early 1960s. Timing of migration may have much bearing on the age structure of a minority group. For instance, as young West Indians who came during the 1950s reached late middle age at the time of the survey, young Indians and Pakistanis who followed nearly a decade later may have just entered the middle age.

To summarize the findings on ethnic minorities other than Chinese, especially immigrants among these groups, percentage distributions of age by group have also been constructed for males and females separately in Figures 3.22 and 3.23. It can be seen that, compared with British-born whites, the proportions of young people under 30 are higher for Asian immigrants, and the proportions of middle-aged people are higher for West Indians and Irish. It follows that there are much lower percentages of children and older people among all immigrant groups than among the indigenous white population.

In this section, I have examined the age structure and age distribution of fourteen ethnic groups. The ethnic minorities are over-represented in the young and middle age categories, when compared with British-born whites. Concentration of foreign-born immigrants is obvious in the middle

Figure 3.1 4 Age by Sex: British-born Indians

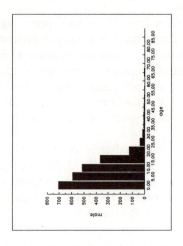
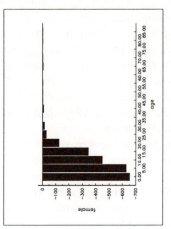

Figure 3.1 5 Age by Sex: British-born Pakistanis

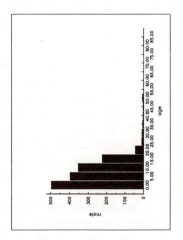
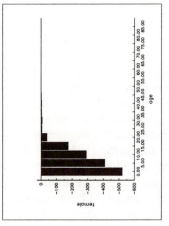

Figure 3.1 6 Age by Sex: British-born West Indians

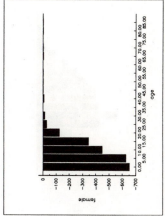

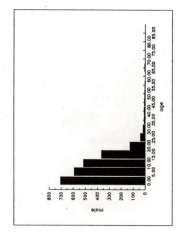

Figure 3.1 7 Age by Sex: East African Asians

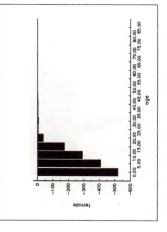

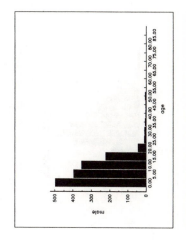

Figure 3.1 8 Age by Sex: Indians Born in India

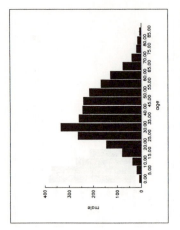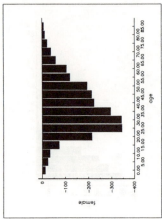

Figure 3.1 9 Age by Sex: Pakistanis Born in Pakistan

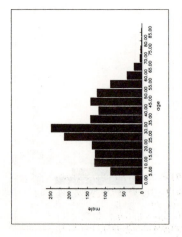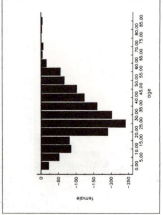

Figure 3.20 Age by Sex: West Indians Born in West Indies

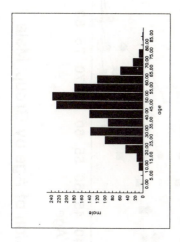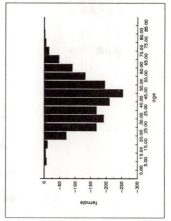

Figure 3.21 Age by Sex: Irish Born in Ireland

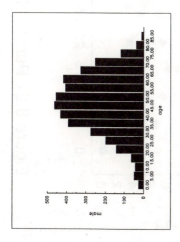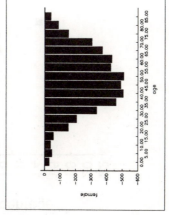

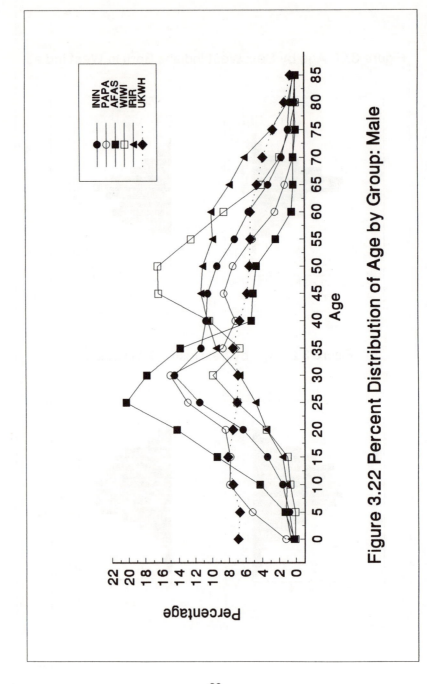

Figure 3.22 Percent Distribution of Age by Group: Male

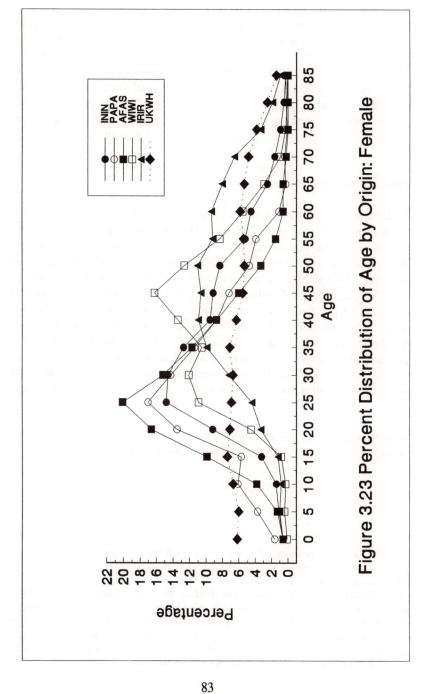

Figure 3.23 Percent Distribution of Age by Origin: Female

age categories, as is concentration of native-born in the young age categories.

As discussed earlier, different ages entail different stages of life cycle. The age distribution patterns obtained so far suggest that the economically active as a proportion of the immigrant population may be higher than that of the host population and the majority of British-born ethnic minority members may still be in full-time study or at an early stage of their career. Chinese, who migrated to Britain later than most immigrant groups, may be even less advanced in the life cycle although the age distributions of various Chinese groups hardly present a uniform pattern.

Regional distribution

To look at regional distribution, I cross-tabulated the variable of region of usual residence[36] with ethnic groups. The Chi-square test was then conducted to examine the fit of the observed frequencies to the expected. A huge likelihood ratio of 27287.58 has been obtained with 126 degrees of freedom. This shows that ethnic group distribution differs by region.

The geographical distribution of British-born whites is first compared with that of the five groups of Chinese. As shown in Figure 3.24, the biggest concentration of majority whites (UKWH) is found in the Southeast, with nearly 28% of the sample. The Northwest and Scotland are two other regions where over 10% of this population reside.

Compared with British-born whites, the most noticeable pattern of regional distribution for Chinese is higher concentration in the Southeast. Percentages of Chinese in the Southeast, in descending order, are 68% for Chinese born elsewhere (ELCH), 58% for Chinese from Vietnam (CHVN), 49% for Chinese from China (CHCH), 47% for Chinese from Hong Kong (HKCH), and 44% for Chinese born in Britain (UKCH).

---

[36] The variable on regional distribution is derived from the original variable "region of usual residence showing metropolitan counties" (URESCOM). URESCOM has 17 categories as follows: 1 Tyne and Wear; 2 Rest of North Region; 3 South Yorkshire; 4 West Yorkshire; 5 Rest of Yorkshire and Humberside; 6 East Midland; 7 East Anglia; 8 GLC; 9 Rest of Southeast; 10 Southwest; 11 West midland; 12 Rest of West Midland; 13 Greater Manchester; 14 Merseyside; 15 Rest of North West; 16 Wales 17 Scotland. These areas are recoded into ten major regions following this scheme: North=1,2; Yorkshire=3,4,5; East Midland=6; East Anglia=7; Southeast=8,9; Southwest=10; West Midland=11,12; Northwest=13,14,15; Wales=16; Scotland=17.

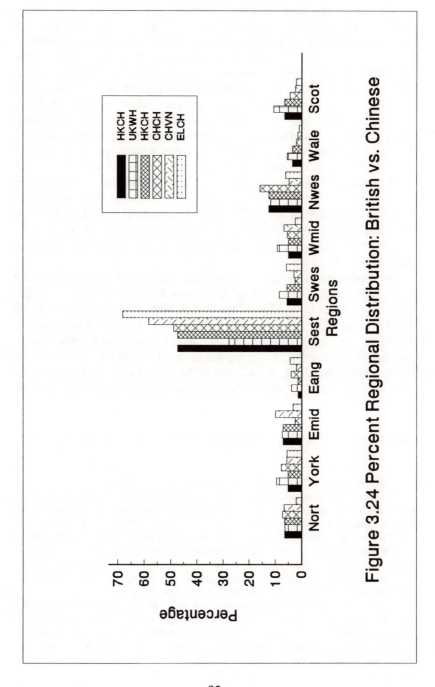

Figure 3.24 Percent Regional Distribution: British vs. Chinese

Researchers have suggested that population clustering in the Southeast is a general pattern applicable to almost all ethnic minorities in Britain.[37] This is again confirmed by the findings presented in Figure 3.25. All immigrant groups, except Pakistanis, are over-represented in the Southeast. The number of people residing in this region as a proportion of the whole population are 47% for Indians born in India, 61% for African Asians, 63% for West Indians born in Afro-Caribbean nations, 48% for Irish born in Ireland. As in Figure 3.26, British-born Asians and West Indians, except Pakistanis, also have a greater propensity to be in the Southeast. Note, the proportion of the Pakistani immigrants residing in the Southeast, is about 2% lower than that of the British-born whites, and the proportion of the British-born Pakistanis is 3% lower than that of British.[38]

Researchers have also suggested that regions with large concentrations of ethnic minorities are normally areas with large urban centres. In their studies of migration in the 1960s, Castles and Kosack already discovered a marked concentration of immigrants in urban areas.[39] The degree of concentration is found to be even higher among Indians, Pakistanis and West Indians.[40]

According to the present sample data, over half of all immigrant and native-born ethnic minorities in the South East are found in Greater London, whereas only 32% of the British-born white population in the Southeast reside in Greater London. Within the Chinese population, the degree of concentration in Greater London, measured as a percentage of people in the Southeast, is the highest among Chinese from Vietnam and Chinese born elsewhere, at 74% and 72%. The degrees of concentration are lower for Chinese born in Britain, China, and Hong Kong, at 64%, 58% and 57%.

To explain ethnic over-representation in the Southeast and a few other regions, social geographers suggested that the regional distribution of a

---

[37] Brown, 1984. p.20-21. Halsey, p.561-610.

[38] The Pakistanis concentrate in Yorkshire, West Midlands and Northwest, where traditional textile industries are found. This partly reflects the fact that Pakistani labour migration was correlated with the availability of economic opportunities in Britain.

[39] According to the 1961 Census, Castles and Kosack pointed out, " altogether 56 per cent of immigrants are in the six major conurbations, compared with the 36 per cent of the total population. More than a third of all immigrants are to be found in Greater London, compared with only one sixth of the population. Immigrants make up 12 per cent of the population of London". See Castles and Kosack, 1985, p.49.

[40] New Commonwealth immigrants were even more concentrated than other immigrants; nearly two thirds of them are actually in London. Nearly five percent of London inhabitants came from the New Commonwealth, and the concentration is particularly high in certain boroughs-Brent, Hackney, Lambeth, Haringley, Islington and Hammersmith. See Castles and Kosack, 1985, p.49.

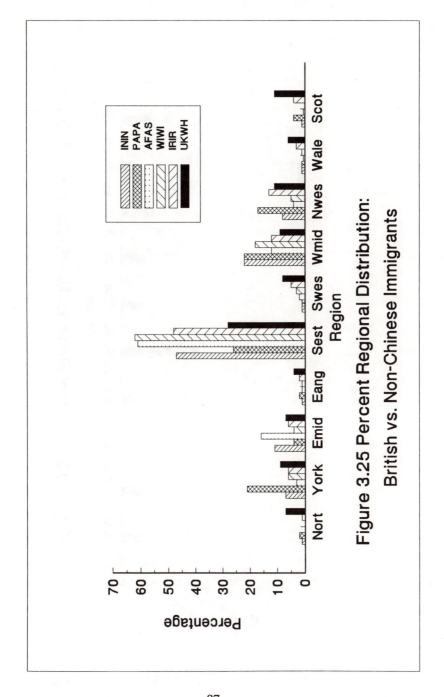

Figure 3.25 Percent Regional Distribution:
British vs. Non-Chinese Immigrants

87

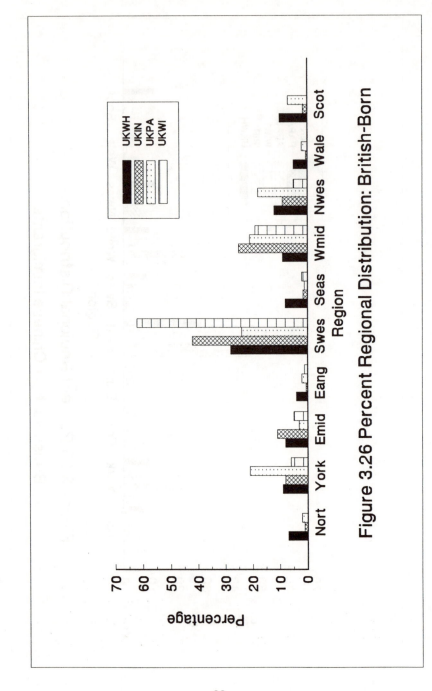

Figure 3.26 Percent Regional Distribution: British-Born

population, particularly an immigrant population, is primarily affected by the local demand for labour.[41] Peach proposed that the demand for labour is the primary control over settlement, separating regions into positive and negative ones. The positive regions are those with growing industries and high demand for labour. These are usually where the indigenous population are likely to migrate. The negative regions are just the opposite, with declining industries and a net outward flow of population. In between the two categories, there are regions with moderate demand for labour, where the outflow of the local population is balanced by an inflow of ethnic minorities desperate for jobs.[42]

During the early days of immigration, positive regions included London and the South East, the combined Southern and Eastern region, and the South West. The North Midlands, the Midlands, and the East and West of Ridings of Yorkshire were regions of moderate demand. The North West, Wales, the North, and Scotland were negative regions. With the exception of the South East, all the regions with the strongest demand for labour have lower proportions of coloured immigrants than regions of moderate demand.[43] Much must have happened to change the job oriented region distribution since the 1960s. But the early patterns must still have a bearing on the present day ethnic regional distribution, especially in explaining concentrations of ethnic minorities in areas traditionally known for moderate job opportunities.

The Irish settlement pattern, too, seems to be affected by the demand for labour. Early settlement started in Scotland and the North West. In the 1950s and 1960s, the Midlands proved to be an attractive place with growth industries and labour deficits. So Irish moved from the North to the Midlands. In the 1970s, economic recession in the Midlands prompted another movement to the Southeast. Today, about 48% of the Irish live in the South East, the single largest concentration in one region. In addition, Irish are also over-represented in the North West and West Midlands, compared to the indigenous population. Concentration in these two regions might just be a reminder of the Irish southward movement.

---

[41]With regard to South Asians, researchers also suggested that settlement concentration is a product of local job availability and chain migration. See Muhammad Anwar, "The Participation of Asians in the British Political System" and Vaughan Robinson, "Boom and Gloom: the Success and Failure of South Asians in Britain" in Colin Clarke, Ceri Peach and Steven Vertovec ed., *South Asians Overseas: Migration and Ethnicity* (Cambridge: Cambridge University Press, 1990).

[42] Ceri Peach, "Factors Affecting the Distribution of West Indians in Great Britain" in *Journal of Biosocial Science Supplement* 8 (1983) 155-156.

[43] Ibid., p.156-157.

It should be noted, however, that this demand for labour explanation may not be as appropriate for Chinese as it is for Asians, Afro-Caribbeans, and Irish. Unlike other immigrant groups who came to participate in the British labour market, Chinese developed over the years an economic niche of catering, mostly outside the dominant economy. Thus, patterns of regional distribution, at least for catering Chinese, follow the need for expansion of the catering industry itself. Demand for Chinese food by local people rather than demand for labour in the local labour market affects the regional distribution of catering Chinese.

It has been suggested that Chinese are more dispersed geographically than most ethnic minorities, as a result of the development of the catering business.[44] The growth of Chinese take-aways and restaurants started in the 1960s, when British demand for ethnic food encouraged the diffusion of Chinese into progressively smaller towns and even villages across the country.[45] Thus, higher percentages of Chinese are found in several regions with lower proportions of Asian or Afro-Caribbean immigrants, to name a few, the North, East Anglia, the North East, the South West, Wales, and Scotland.[46]

To test whether Chinese are more dispersed geographically at a national level in the 1980s, I have constructed cumulative percentage distributions for the major non-white minorities, Chinese, Indians, Pakistanis, and West Indians. Separate comparisons are made between immigrants and native-born.

In Figure 3.27, Chinese born in Hong Kong and China are compared with Indian, Pakistani, African Asian, and West Indian immigrants. It can be seen that both groups of Chinese are less concentrated geographically as their curves fall consistently below those of other groups except

---

[44] Craig Livesey, *The Residential Dispersal and Social Isolation of Chinese in Greater Manchester* (Unpublished B.A. Thesis, Oxford: Oriel College, 1988).

[45] Peach et al. p.595.

[46] The majority of Vietnamese Chinese came to Britain as political refugees. Thus, their geographical distribution is likely to be affected by resettlement policies. Resettlement after the first influx of the Vietnamese Chinese in 1978 involved deliberate dispersal of the group with 4 to 10 families per town throughout the country, but this was not a success. Then these people were located wherever housing was available, usually areas which the local population was abandoning because of a lack of job opportunities. With few transferable skills and no English, Vietnamese Chinese were unlikely to succeed where the British had failed. Unemployment rates in these areas ran as high as 80% and have remained so ever since. Many Vietnamese reacted to dislocation and a devastating economic situation by moving from their dispersed location into the major cities. Thus, the population of Vietnamese Chinese in London increased twofold. Today nearly 60% of them reside in the South East region. The resettlement dispersal scheme has thus given way to a spontaneous secondary migration. See A.H.Halsey, p.608.

90

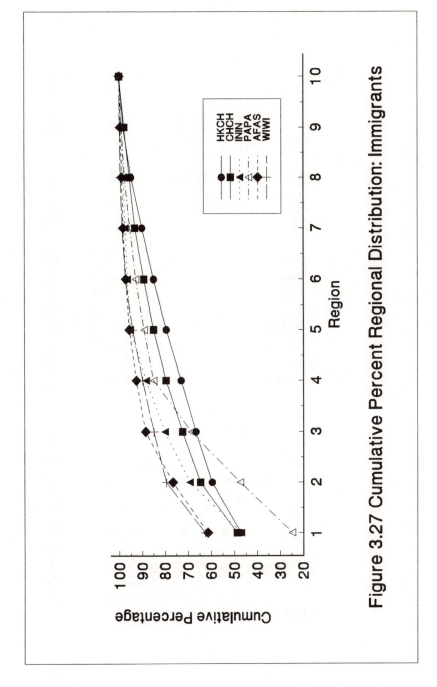

Figure 3.27 Cumulative Percent Regional Distribution: Immigrants

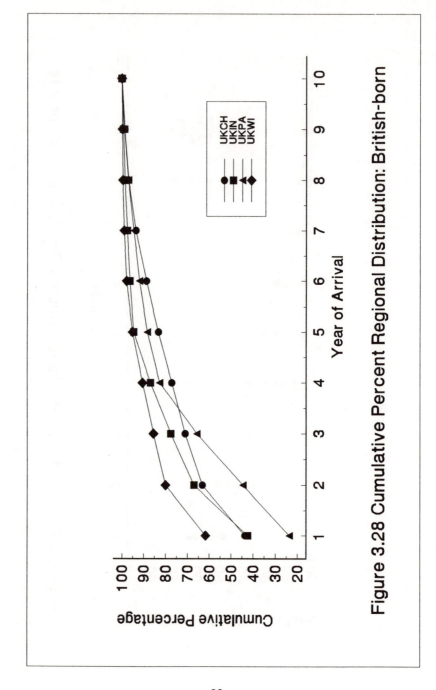

Figure 3.28 Cumulative Percent Regional Distribution: British-born

Pakistanis. In Figure 3.28, where British-born Chinese are compared with Indians, Pakistanis and West Indians born in Britain, Chinese are found again to be more geographically dispersed than all other groups except Pakistanis.

To summarize, compared to the indigenous population, the ethnic minorities, foreign or native-born, exhibit greater degrees of concentration in the South East and in areas traditionally known for moderate job opportunities. Although they share with other ethnic minorities the tendency to concentrate in the South East, and London in particular, Chinese are still more geographically dispersed than other Asians and Afro-Caribbeans, with the exception of Pakistanis.

Conclusions

In this chapter, I have examined the demographic attributes of Chinese in Britain in a comparative context. As the data show, Chinese arrived on the British scene later than most immigrant groups. They are smaller in size, younger in age, more dispersed geographically, and have sex ratios which are closer to the host population than most immigrant groups, except West Indians and Irish. Thus, compared with South Asian and Afro-Caribbean immigrants, Chinese appear less prominent and they may therefore be considered to pose less of threat to the indigenous population than other immigrant groups.

The Chinese group itself may be divided into several subgroups possessing different demographic profiles. Among immigrant Chinese, those from Hong Kong, China, and elsewhere have demographic profiles closer to the indigenous population than Chinese from Vietnam. As the refugees from Vietnam only form a tiny proportion of the total Chinese population, the demographic potentials of Chinese as a combined group may still contribute favourably to Chinese occupational outcomes.

Compared with other ethnic minorities, the native-born form a smaller proportion of the Chinese population. They are younger in age and have a more imbalanced sex ratio in favour of males. Most second generation Chinese may still be engaged in full time studies. Thus speculation on their occupational attainment may be premature. However, the practice of sending female children back to Hong Kong for primary education casts doubt on the continuous process of Chinese educational and occupational integration into British society.

4 Educational attainments of Chinese in Britain

Introduction

In modern industrial societies, education is assumed to be increasingly important in determining occupational attainment. As Heath puts it, "one theme common to post-war sociological writing has been the functionalist view that a stable industrial society requires a greater emphasis to be placed on a man's achievements and a lesser one on his ascribed characteristics. It is not who a man is but what he does that matters. Furthermore what he does is to be judged by 'universalistic' criteria, such as educational attainment, which can be applied to all and be empirically verified. Nepotism and the 'old school tie' must give way to publicly demonstrable merit. On this view, we would expect to find that the importance of ascription has declined whereas that of achievement has increased overtime".[1]

The increased emphasis on occupational success being achieved through personal merit does not imply that ascriptive attributes no longer have an effect. What it does imply is that superior status cannot any more be directly inherited but must be legitimated by actual achievements that are socially acknowledged. For this reason, education assumes increasing importance for social status in general and for the transmission of social standing from parents to children in particular. Superior family origin increases the chances of superior occupational status because it helps in attaining a better education.[2]

---

[1] Anthony F. Heath, *Social Mobility* (Fontana Paperbacks, 1981) 43-44.

[2] Peter M. Blau and Otis D. Duncan, *The American Occupational Structure* (New York: John Wiley & Sons, Inc., 1967) 430; Hans-Peter and Yossi Shavit, "Persisting Barriers: Changes in Educational Opportunities in Thirteen Countries," in *Persistent Inequality: Changing Educational Stratification in Thirteen Countries*, ed. Shavit and

The rise of universalism is seen as a response to the needs of industrial society. According to Blau and Duncan, in today's highly industrialized societies, "technological progress has created a need for advanced knowledge and skills on the part of a large proportion of the labour force, not merely a small professional elite. Under these conditions society cannot any longer afford the waste of human resources a rigid class system entails. Universalistic principles have penetrated deep into the fabric of modern society and given rise to high rates of occupational mobility in response to this need".[3] This indicates that the connection between education and occupational attainment has been strengthened unprecedentedly.

Marsh argues that, if industrial societies institutionalize universalistic achievement values in the area of social mobility to a greater extent than pre-industrial societies did, when inter-societal differences in occupational demands are held constant, industrial societies should still exhibit more mobility than traditional societies. This hypothesis, however, was only weakly supported by his comparative study of social mobility at elite levels between modern American society and traditional Imperial China. Therefore he suggested that the greater openness of industrial societies may be due almost wholly to sheer quantitative occupational demand,[4] rather than to values and norms of a universalistic achievement type.[5]

According to Marsh, Imperial China perhaps presented an exceptional case of a traditional society, in which link between education and occupation was not necessarily weaker than in an industrial society. The idea of achieving higher occupational status through education may not be less familiar to people in a traditional society like Imperial China. Studies conducted by Marsh and others on elite circulation in imperial China have not rejected such speculation.

In this chapter and at the beginning of Chapter Seven, I shall study the relative educational attainments of Chinese immigrants and their subsequent

---

Blossfeld (Boulder, CO: West View Press, 1992); Jan O. Jonsson, "School Reforms, Educational Expansion, and Changes in Inequality of Educational Attainments in Sweden," *Persistent Inequality*, ed. Shavit and Blossfeld, 1992.

[3] Ibid., 431.

[4] In their studies of social mobility in industrial societies, Erikson and Goldthorpe found the net association between origin and destination to be constant across cohorts. Thus, upward social mobility is likely to be caused by structural changes in the economy. No evidence has been found to indicate that these societies have otherwise become more open. For more details, see Robert Erikson and John Goldthorpe. *The Constant Flux-A Study of Class Mobility in Industrial Societies* (Oxford: Clarendon Press, 1992).

[5] Robert M. Marsh, "Values, Demands and Social Mobility," *American Sociological Review* 28 (1963): 565.

generations in contemporary Britain and America. It is therefore valuable to first understand Chinese attitudes towards education, and the role of education in determining occupational success, in those societies from which the Chinese migrants came. The cultural values and social outlook brought by the immigrants from their society of origin are considered to exert a continuous influence on their aspiration for socio-economic success in the host society.

This chapter is divided into two main parts. In the first part, I shall use secondary material to look at the link between education and occupation in the traditional sending societies of Chinese immigrants,[6] i.e. Imperial China, Taiwan, Hong Kong, and South East Asia. In the second part, I shall use crosstabular and logit analysis to study the educational success of Chinese, relative to that of other ethnic groups in Britain.

Imperial China

In Imperial China, public officials, especially those of high rankings, were appointed primarily on the basis of their performance in competitive civil-service examinations. Thus education, with a view to success in the examinations, was pursued by all ambitious males as the regular channel to that official status, which was for thirteen centuries the ultimate goal of upward social mobility.[7]

Traditional Chinese society was necessarily hierarchical, because its component classes had unique rights and obligations. There was an essentially feudal concept demarcating rights and obligations between rulers and ruled. Its guiding principles were postulated by Mencius nearly two thousand years ago:" some labour with their minds and some labour with their physical strength. Those who labour with their minds rule others. Those who labour with their physical strength sustain others and those who rule are sustained by others. This is a principle universally recognized".[8]

A social hierarchy based on such a division of labour needed an effective ideological argument to sustain itself. The answer was a principle

---

[6] China, Taiwan, Hong Kong and South East Asia are considered as traditional sending places of the Chinese immigrants in both Britain and America. Thus, discussions on historical materials in this chapter are also applicable to the Chinese in America.

[7] See Robert M. Marsh, *The Mandarins: The Circulation of Elites in China, 1600-1900* (New York: The Free Press of Glencoe, 1961); Ping-ti Ho, *The Ladder of Success in Imperial China: Aspects of Social Mobility*, 1368-1911 (New York: Columbia University Press, 1962); Yung-Teh Chow. *Social Mobility in China: Status Careers Among a Chinese Gentry Community* (New York: Athernon Press, 1968).

[8] Ho, *The Ladder of Success in Imperial China*, 17.

of elite circulation, whereby membership of the ruling class was made available to all those demonstrating superior moral qualities and academic capabilities. The concrete solution for this principle was provided by the Confucian school, i.e. the equal educational opportunities for all.

As early as the latter half of the third century, "the Imperial Academy was established and an ad hoc system of recommending men of talents for state services was introduced. This marked the first step towards the implementation of the Confucian social ideology. By the seventh century, a further stride was made in this direction, as the Tang empire made the competitive civil-service examination a permanent system by which men of talents were selected as officials. From the eleventh century onward, more schools and private academies were established. Until after the founding of the Ming empire, China began to have a rudimentary but nationwide state school and scholarship system. The repeated early Ming imperial exhortations for setting up community schools further tackled the problem of elementary education".[9]

One may wonder why so much effort was invested in developing a public examination system. It was partly because the Imperial Chinese rulers believed that no unchanging elite could stay in power forever. The accumulation of superior elements among the commoners would eventually threaten the power and order of the elite. By recruiting such elements into the elite class, the civil-service examination served as a functional prerequisite for maintaining social stability and securing the power of the ruling class. Commoners who became upwardly mobile through this channel tended to conform to the values and norms of the elite class.

In traditional China, the elite formed only a small minority, while the great majority of people belonged to the commoner's class. However, among the commoners, occupations and roles were also divided into different levels, which were called the "four people" - scholars, farmers, artisans and merchants. Commoners occupied an intermediate position within the class structure as a whole. They were inferior to the emperors, royal families and officials, but generally superior to the military. Of the commoners, scholars possessed the greatest potential for developing elite careers in the bureaucracy and local leadership, as many aspired to scholarship in Imperial China.

---

[9] Ho, 255-256. Though it is doubtful whether the Confucian ideal was fully realized in any historical period, Ho suggested that the institutionalization of a competitive examination system as the main avenue of social-bureaucratic mobility and the existence of a large number of state and private schools are probably without parallel in major societies prior to the Industrial Revolution and national compulsory education.

With regard to the attractiveness of officialdom, Marsh wrote, "the supreme status of officials was based upon several factors: they were closely associated with the emperor, 'the son of Heaven', as administrators of his realm; their prestige and authority were second only to his and to that of a small group of nobility; official appointment and advancement presupposed, at least for many of them, the most extensive preparatory education of any career in the society, an education consisting wholly of the highly revered classics and humanistic orientation; they maintained and transmitted the core values of the culture; they held the highest earning power in wealth in the society, aside from the imperial court itself".[10]

A significant aspect of this elite career in China is that, legally, recruitment into officialdom was open to virtually all males in the society on an achievement basis. This created a Chinese version of the "log-cabin to White House" myth, whereby poor but talented boys from humble backgrounds could succeed, by hard work and outstanding academic results, to the highest reaches of officialdom. As China did not have a caste system, it was not entirely irrational for a commoner, even a peasant commoner to seek to become an official. Many elements of the Chinese culture encouraged the view that this goal was the definite objective for all "men of talent". Ideally speaking, office and its rewards were to devolve upon the wise, the virtuous, and the talented.[11]

However, the effects of such a system were double-edged. In evaluating it, Ho said, "At its best, the examination system, with its curricular centring on classics, literature, history and administrative problems, produced men of sound common sense and judgement, even statesmen. At its worst, it produced parrot-like scholar-officials without imagination and originality and fostered ideological conformity".[12]

In fact, the latter effect is just what the Imperial rulers wanted to see. There is a story that the great Tang emperor, Tai-tsung (reigned 627-649 A.D.), after seeing the august procession of newly elected Chin-shi (scholars who passed the highest level of public examination) remarked with gratification, "the world's men of unusual ambitions have thus been trapped in my bag". The rulers well understood that a certain amount of continuous elite circulation was vital to the stability of the dynasty. By adopting an open system of recruitment, the Imperial government intended to ease the tension between rulers and ruled, thus reducing the amount of social discontent and undermining the potential for social conflict. "In fact, the examination system's long history of thirteen centuries is a most

---

[10] Marsh, *The Mandarins*, p.1.

[11] Marsh, p.3.

[12] Ho, p.259.

eloquent testimonial to its usefulness as a main channel of mobility and a politically and socially stabilizing factor".[13]

The imperial examination system was abolished in 1911, at the time when the first emigration of Chinese started. Stanley observed a strong achievement element among the early Chinese immigrants in America. He wrote, "differing...from the coolie of Hindustan, the Chinese is ignorant of the blight effects of caste, and is as strongly bent on raising himself to a higher position as he is on acquiring wealth".[14] Stanley's observation implies that Chinese, coming from a society with a unique examination channel to upward mobility, perceived a stronger connection between hard work and socio-economic success, than did immigrants from countries where upward mobility was more restricted.

My contention throughout this chapter is that Chinese immigrants, long educated in a culture which emphasizes the role of education in achieving occupational success, should be more ready to take advantage of widely available educational opportunities, when they settle in a more advanced industrial society. In saying this, I agree with Lieberson's remark on Jewish occupational success in America.[15] It is hardly a distinctive subcultural pursuit of education, which is incidental to occupational success. It is rather the recognition on the part of the individual of the potential rewards of education, which propels painstaking pursuit of high educational success.

Hong Kong

Hong Kong was part of imperial China until 1842, when it came under British rule. It was ceded to Britain by the Treaty of Nanking at the end of the Opium War. Due to its strategic and commercial significance, lying right on the path of the chief trade route to China and with a deep and sheltered harbour, it served as a commercial, diplomatic, and military post for Britain in the East.

After WWII, the colony entered a new era, with a booming economy, unprecedented population growth, and urban development.[16] One important component of this population growth was an influx of immigrants

---

[13] Ho, p.258.

[14] Lone-Poole Stanley, *The Life of Sir Harry Parke*, quoted in Marsh, *The Mandarins*, p.4.

[15] Stanley Lieberson and Mary Walters, *From Many Strands: Ethnic and Racial Groups in Contemporary America* (New York: Russel Sage Foundation, 1984) 145.

[16] Ainslie T. Embree, ed. *Encyclopedia of Asian History* (New York: Charles Scribner's Sons, 1988), 76.

from China. In 1947, the local population of Hong Kong amounted to 1.8 million. The war and disturbances in China caused a mass influx of refugees. Although entry to Hong Kong was restricted by quota from 1950 onward, both legal and illegal immigrants continued to flow in. This immigration, together with a high rate of natural increase, brought the population to about 3 million in 1960. The rate of natural increase began to drop in the 1960s, but immigration was on the increase, particularly in the early 1960s and late 1970s.[17] During this time, farmers from the mainland brought more advanced farming methods and prospered in the rural area of Hong Kong, i.e. the New Territories. Their success edged out less competitive local farmers. It was against this background (plus a call for foreigners to fill up the labour shortage in Britain) that the exodus of Chinese from Hong Kong started in the 1950s.

The population of Hong Kong may be grouped into two types of communities, the urban community in Hong Kong and Kowloon, and the farming and fishing communities in the New Territories. It is said that the great bulk of Chinese immigrants in Britain came from the New Territories with a minority coming from Hong Kong and Kowloon.[18]

In the New Territories, further distinctions were made according to people's dialect. The indigenous population of the New Territories consisted of four principal dialect groups: Cantonese, Hakka, Hoklo, and Tanka. The first two groups were traditionally land dwellers and the latter two boat dwellers. The largest two dialect groups were Cantonese and Hakka, between whom intermarriage was rare as there was once animosity. They became more amicable in time, but the Cantonese were still better off than the Hakkas.[19] These two dialect groups form the majority of the Chinese population in Britain.[20]

Because of the nature of local economies developed in the urban and rural communities, Chinese in the New Territories were largely engaged in agricultural activities before migrating overseas, while Chinese from urban Hong Kong were integrated to different degrees into the post war industrialized economy. As a matter of fact, distinctions of a geographical nature affect the educational level of these immigrants and their subsequent occupational destinations. People in rural Hong Kong were less exposed to western culture and received less western education than people in urban Hong Kong. While people from the New Territories were channelled into

---

[17] Ibid., 76.

[18] Anthony Shang, *The Chinese in Britain* (London: Batsford Academic and Educational, 1984).

[19] Ng, *Chinese in London*, p.8.

[20] Home Affairs Committee, *The Chinese Community in Britain*, p.1.

the family oriented catering trade via a kinship network already established in the niche of catering, many people from urban Hong Kong, normally professionals with a good western education, were directly recruited into the booming post-war British service industry.[21] Occupational difference will in turn affect the educational level of children of immigrants from different parts of the colony.

Urban Hong Kong

Free primary schooling in Hong Kong was introduced in 1971 and extended to nine years in 1978.[22] Before this, Hong Kong's educational system was marked by its diversity. According to Mitchell, in the mid-1960s, only 5% of urban secondary schools were controlled and financed by the government while 81% of them were privately run profit-making institutions. Other small schools were run by the many religious groups. On the whole, the schools were extremely academically oriented. Students were trained to pass examinations that would qualify them for entrance into university. Even the curriculum of the few vocational schools (only 2% of the total) also had a fairly strong academic emphasis.

About 30% of all schools were Chinese schools, which means they taught in Chinese, although English was a typically required foreign language. The other schools were in the Anglo-Chinese stream. They used Chinese only in their courses on Chinese literature, history, and language itself. English was used for most other subjects. Cantonese was the Chinese dialect spoken in these schools, although some schools taught Mandarin as part of the Chinese language instruction programme.[23]

In addition to structural differences, schools differed widely in the quality of education they provided and the quality of the students they attracted. Top quality schools tended to be government schools and government assisted schools. More emphasis was given by these to extra-curricular activities that helped develop their pupils' academic and non-academic interests. There were also more facilities to provide the pupils with wider educational experiences.[24]

For secondary school graduates, entrance to university was extremely competitive. In a study of family life in urban Hong Kong, Mitchell

---

[21] Watson, *Emigration and the Chinese Lineage*, pp.194-195.

[22] Embree, 76. It is also suggested by Lee that governmental policies towards educational expansion have been geared at industrial and economic growth of the colony. See O.N.Lee, *Education and Social Changes in Japan, Singapore and Hong Kong* (London: MacMillan, 1991).

[23] Robert Edward Mitchell, *Pupil, Parent and School: A Hong Kong Study*, 1969.

[24] Ibid.

explained that Hong Kong's two official universities had only about five thousand students. Perhaps as many as seven thousand other children attended overseas universities. But this figure of 12,000 represents less than 5% of all young people between the ages of 19 and 23 in Hong Kong.[25]

Despite severe competitiveness in securing places in universities, aspirations for higher education were commonly held by both pupils and their parents. For instance, in 1967, 52% of parents wanted their children to attend a university and 59% of Form Five pupils wanted to do so, although only 25% were either quite or very certain that they would attend. Fifty-seven per cent of the pupils felt that their parents wanted them to go to university.[26]

Research has also been done on actual educational attainments and their determinants. It is commonly believed that Chinese place a very great emphasis on education. In the Hong Kong urban community this emphasis was translated into an examination and certificate orientation in the labour market. Higher levels of careers and jobs were particularly oriented towards the successful completion of certain educational programs. Success is obtained by passing recognized examinations, for example, the first credential for students completing Form Five was the School Leaving Certificate, which was obtained by passing an examination applicable to all secondary school students. In 1967, 59% of Form Five students passed it.[27]

Despite the importance of schooling in job placement, aspirations and attainments were found to be class stratified. It was found that children from lower class families had less opportunity than children from upper class families to attend secondary school, and once in school, they were less likely to do well, especially in high quality schools. The reason for this gap was summarized as differing value emphasis, whereby lower class parents were less likely to set high goals for their children and encourage them by rewarding them for educational achievements. Thus lower class children were less likely to be inclined towards a university course of studies than their middle class counterparts.[28]

Last but not least, pessimism was found to be prevalent among both upper and lower class children. They felt dismayed by the restricted

---

[25] Robert Edward Mitchell, *Family Life in Urban Hong Kong*, p.312.

[26] Ibid.

[27] Mitchell, *Pupil, Parent and School*, p.15.

[28] A. Sweeting, "Hong Kong," *Schooling in East Asia* ed. R.M. Thomas and T.N. Postlethwaite (Oxford: Pergamon Press, 1983); S. Pong and D. Post, "Trend in Gender and Family Background Effects on School Attainments: the Case of Hong Kong," *British Journal of Sociology* 42 (June 1991) 249-271.

educational and occupational opportunities in Hong Kong. Many wished to pursue higher education and work overseas and not come back to Hong Kong.

Rural Hong Kong

Although Chinese are traditionally known for emphasizing education, and parents would deprive themselves in many ways to send their children to school, this ideal was far from being translated into reality in rural areas of Hong Kong. It was suggested by Osgood that "We cannot help being impressed by the Chinese attitudes towards education and things of the mind. Almost every writer has noted the high regard for knowledge in Chinese culture...Some Europeans were so excited by this pleasing state of affairs that they attributed literacy and schooling to almost everyone in the empire".[29]

In the rural communities of New Territories, education and schooling were largely based on the village and made possible by the self-reliance of villagers. According to Jarvie and Agassi, in 19th century China the burden of providing education for village children lay with the elders of the village in conjunction with the parents of the children of school age. Thus the education of children depended to a large extent on the amount of effort made by the grown-ups. The smaller villages usually could not afford regular schools. Teachers from outside the community were sometimes invited to set up a small school in the ancestral hall and stay as long as they could make a living. In consequence, parents who wished to educate their children had to send them to school elsewhere. It was said that there was a good deal of movement among children of the smaller villages at the time. Education thus became a means for bringing people together.[30]

An evaluation of rural education has been given by Hayes, who compiled data on duration of school (in years) and place of school (ancestral hall, monastery, private school, village school, etc) by interviewing villagers in the New Territories. He wrote, "it will be seen that few of my village informants claimed that they had no education. On the one hand, given the small numbers of boys in the classes, changes in the teachers, as well as periods in which there was perhaps no teachers available, it seems likely that some boys did not even receive a rudimentary schooling in what, at that time, was a wholly private system of education.

---

[29] Cornellus Osgood. *The Chinese: A Study of a Hong Kong Community* (Tucson: University of Arizona Press, 1975), 1153.

[30] I.C. Jarvie and J. Agassi, *Hong Kong: A Society in Transition: Contributions to the Hong Kong Society* (London: Routledge and Kegan Paul, 1969) 44-45.

Even so there seems to have enough evidence to hint that a good proportion of them must have attended classes".[31]

Apart from very remote and isolated villages, where the traditional style of education was maintained, the New Territories experienced major economic changes in the 1960s. After WWII, industrial and commercial development in the urban areas of Hong Kong created new jobs and economic opportunities for the villagers. As a result, they moved rapidly into every sector of the expanding economy from service jobs to work in textile factories. During the first half of the century, there had already been a gradual trend of rural men and women moving into non-agricultural occupations, and this process was greatly accelerated by economic growth in the colony. Participation in occupations outside the villages led to a higher standard of living among the rural people, who now could afford a better education for their children. Better education enabled many rural youths to move into higher status and better paid jobs in government and business.[32]

Based on his observation of the Hakka community, Ng wrote, "the aspirations of today's educated young men is not to stay on the farm or even to become a village leader. It is a rare thing to find a young man behind a plough in the valley today. Dissatisfaction with the life of the village and the inability to make use of the education obtained there are compelling reasons for these youths to leave the rural home to seek better life in the city".[33]

Nevertheless, contrary to the trend of rural youths seeking better occupational opportunities through good education, a somewhat different trend was discovered by Watson in his studies of an emigrant community,[34] San Tin, in rural Hong Kong settings. Unlike other rural youths who were eager to take advantage of local economic prosperity, people from the emigrant community looked overseas for economic opportunities.

---

[31] James Hayes, *The Hong Kong Region 1850-1911: Institutions and Leadership in Town and Countryside* (Folkstone: Wm Dawson and Sons Ltd, 1977) 217. Based on Hayes's sample of 50 people, mean year of schooling has been calculated to be four years. Of course, as information on temporary interruptions due to unavailability of teachers, etc. is not given, the actual average duration of schooling must be shorter than four years.

[32] Jarvie and Agassi, *Hong Kong: A Society in Transition*, p.18.

[33] Ronald Ng, quoted in Jarvie and Agassi, p.59.

[34] An emigrant community refers to a community from which a considerable number of people have for sometimes emigrated and continue to emigrate. Emigrants from this type of community usually retain close ties with their kinsmen behind, even after many years of settlement abroad.

In the past, emigrants from San Tin became very successful in building profitable catering businesses abroad. Many semi-literate restaurant workers later came back home building sterling houses and driving automobiles. This made youngsters extremely sceptical of the idea that education was necessary for material success. They began to think that the only qualification needed for employment in high paying restaurants abroad was membership of the Man[35] lineage. As a result, many adolescents dropped out before finishing middle school and waited idly, sometimes for years, until they were old enough to obtain vouchers or work permit to go abroad. As one youth put it, "What good are history and geography to me? How will it help me to work in a restaurant? I know how to read and how to use an abacus. That's enough for anyone".[36]

Unfortunately, similar attitudes were sometimes shared by parents, who felt reluctant to send their children to the better primary schools in the New Territories or to encourage them to attend middle schools. Their expectation of their children seldom went beyond prospective restaurant workers, even though, as later research revealed, their attitudes might change once they were in Britain.[37]

To summarise, previous research on education in Hong Kong suggests that urban areas were on the whole far more advanced than rural areas in educational arrangements, such as school facilities, teaching qualities, and course provisions. Within urban communities, social class based differentiations existed at the level of entry to particular types of school, degree of preparedness for higher education, and education related occupational aspirations. Though education was commonly believed to serve as a channel for upward mobility, expectations for career success tended to be lower among lower class students.

Meanwhile, education was gradually accepted by rural communities as an effective means of entering high paying jobs in the cities and enjoying material comforts away from the village. Both parents and the younger generation were eager to take advantage of the local economic miracle and better their living standards. Unfortunately, such motivation was not evident in certain emigrant communities, where people observed no direct correlation between a good education and high economic rewards in the catering trade.

---

[35] Name of the lineage in San Tin village.

[36] Watson, p.195.

[37] Alfred Chan, *Employment Prospects of Chinese Youths in Britain* (London: CRE, 1986).

105

China and Taiwan

After the Communists came into power in 1949, great efforts were made to equalize opportunities for education. Little research has been done on the association between social origin and educational success. A few existing empirical studies suggest that education is a strong determinant of higher occupational status, and, possibly upward occupational mobility.

In their study of occupational attainment in urban China, Blau and Ruan observed that career success was not entirely independent of family class background, but found that the influence that existed was transmitted by human capital. Therefore, they concluded that occupational success in urban China is greatly dependent on education. Women especially improved their occupational status through education more so than men.[38] A similar gender pattern is also found by Lin and Bian.[39] Nee studied the process of economic attainment in rural China and found evidence in support of positive educational returns on earnings in the countryside too.[40]

Recently, Cheng et al studied social mobility in contemporary China, using the 1986 national sample. It has been found that despite apparent self-recruitment among professionals and administrative elites, there are significant inflows of people with agricultural backgrounds into these jobs. This is true for both male and female respondents in urban China. Association between father's occupation and son's occupation has not weakened over time, but there is evidence from female respondents that the impact of parental occupation on a daughter's class has reduced significantly.[41] More recent analysis of the same data set confirms that education has an important effect on the occupational attainments of urban residents.[42]

The modern system of education in Taiwan is said to have evolved through a series of modifications to the School law promulgated by the Manchu court in 1902.[43] Since Taiwan became the seat of the Nationalist

---

[38] Peter M. Blau and Danching Ruan, "Inequality of Opportunity in Urban China and America," *Research in Social Stratification and Mobility*, 9 (1990) 3-32.

[39] Nan Lin and Bian Yanjie, "Getting Ahead in Urban China," *American Journal of Sociology*, 97, no. 3 (November 1991) 657-688.

[40] Victor Nee, "A Theory of Market Transition: From Redistribution to Markets in State Socialism," *American Sociological Review* 54 (October 1989) 267-282.

[41] Yuan Cheng, Jianzhong Dai and John Goldthorpe, "Social Mobility in Urban and Rural China". Paper presented at the ISA RC28 Social Stratification Conference, Trento, May 14-16, 1992.

[42] See incoming results by Yin, Dai and Goldthorpe.

[43] Ministry of Education, *Educational Statistics of the Republic of China* 1989, p.xii.

central government, it has experienced rapid growth.[44]   Notably, percentage representation of women among the student population has increased rapidly.[45]

In spite of educational expansion, researchers found that the effect of social origin on educational attainment remains constant over time. While it has become easier for children with poorly educated parents to receive primary and secondary education, children with well educated parents generally have the advantage in competition for entrance into universities.[46]

It should be noted that over the four decades, the number of students pursuing higher education abroad has generally been on the increase (except during the early 1970s). The most popular subjects for foreign study are engineering and natural science.[47] The amount of studying abroad may be partially explained by the fact that higher education in Taiwan is far from universal. The rate of admission, defined as the number of students admitted over the number of applicants, hovered around 20%.[48] Another factor may well be aspirations for greater occupational and economic success abroad, especially among the well educated. Although the number of returners has been on the increase with the rapid growth of the Taiwanese economy, the proportion of people staying abroad after the completion of their studies rather than returning to Taiwan has also increased. This is especially true of those studying in the United States.

South East Asia: overseas Chinese communities

Although the bulk of the Chinese immigrants in Britain are from Hong Kong, China, Taiwan, and to a lesser extent, Vietnam, still one out of five come from elsewhere -principally Malaysia and Singapore. For many decades, Chinese communities in South East Asia were familiar only with the traditional way of life they brought with them from China. Then in the 1950s, the introduction of western technology and ideology began to

---

[44] Ibid., xiv.

[45] Shu-ling Tsai, Hill Gates and Hei-Yuan Chiu, "Schooling Taiwan's Women: Educational Attainment in the Mid-Twentieth Century". Paper presented at ISA RC Social Stratification, Trento, Italy. May 1992.

[46] Hou-sheng Chan and Ying Chan, "Origin and Destination: The Case of Taiwan," *Taiwan: A Newly Industrialised State* ed. H.H. Hsiao (Taipei: National Taipei University, 1989).

[47] Ibid., 55-56.

[48] Ibid., 36-37.

modernize both material and social life among Chinese communities there.[49]

In traditional Chinese emigrant society, occupational placement was largely hereditary and determined by the socio-economic status of the family, so little value was placed on education. In the western-influenced modern societies, however, education played a vital role in occupational placement, especially in the more highly rewarded white collar and professional jobs. In East Malaysia, education at English schools was highly valued because it was regarded as the key factor in obtaining favoured positions in the occupational structure. For some people with humble family origins, education especially at high levels, had become the main instrument of vertical social mobility.

Formal schooling was not the only factor bringing about changes in these Chinese communities. The Western press, pictorial magazines and movies, and above all, the example of British colonial officials' life styles, helped change the life styles of local residents, directly and indirectly affecting their employment tendencies and educational levels.

For instance, one important aspect of westernization was an increasing demand for durable consumer goods. This demand gave rise directly to new commercial enterprises such as electrical appliance shops and car dealers. It also indirectly stimulated related economic activities such as car repairs and petrol stations. The expansion of service industry required people with basic education and good training, who were knowledgeable and skilful enough to tackle all sorts of technical problems.

Due to much exposure to western technology, cultural values, and life styles, Chinese immigrants from western-influenced modern societies, should be easily assimilated into the educational system and occupational structure of British society than immigrants from more traditional societies with little western influence.

Hong Kong Chinese in Britain

Factors affecting the educational attainments of immigrants in the host society are different from factors affecting educational attainment in the country of origin. In addition to socio-economic status, which usually affects entry and performance in the educational system, difficulties arise from language barriers and cultural differences, a few things rarely found

---

[49] Sin Fong Han, *The Chinese in Sabah East Asia* (The Chinese Association for Folklore, 1975) 143.

in one's country of origin. The problems faced by Hong Kong Chinese immigrants in Britain have been discussed by Freeborne.[50]

The first difficulty faced by Chinese, especially those from rural backgrounds is an inability to communicate well in English. Most of the parent generation did not come from the sophisticated modern environment of urban Hong Kong, which means few had much education in English or contact with foreigners. After they arrived in Britain, many had to work long unsocial hours in restaurants, which kept contact with the British to a minimum. Handicapped by poor or non-existent English and trapped in catering, most of the parents hoped that their children would benefit from better educational opportunities in Britain and take career jobs.[51]

However, the language problem also threatened the younger generation of Chinese who were brought over to Britain in their school years. Freeborne found that many Chinese children arrived at primary school speaking little or no English. Teachers without training in working with multi-racial classes were unable to provide help. In some cases, teachers were even unwilling to help due to lack of interest and sympathy with the particular difficulties of immigrant children. Under such circumstances, a high school drop out rate was likely among immigrant youths and the language barrier may further handicap their job opportunities in the wider society. Worse, some disaffected school leavers group together and become involved in illegal activities since they could get no satisfaction from school.[52]

Cultural differences, especially adjustment to the style of teaching and learning in British schools, posed another big challenge to Chinese children. In this case, Freeborne made a comparison between Chinese and other Asian children: "The children who enter school direct from Hong Kong may need a longer time to adjust to their new school than those from the Asian sub-continent. They will find difficulties in reading, in so far as they may not be aware of that each letter or group of letters represents a sound; they will need extra help in comprehension; they will find the pronunciation of some sounds difficult. They have been accustomed to way of formal methods of teaching and may find the friendly and bustling activities of a primary schoolroom bewildering".[53]

He also noticed that older Chinese students such as school leavers who came back for further education, lacked flexibility and 'gamesmanship' in

---

[50] John Derek Michael Freeborne, *The Chinese Community in Britain: With Special Reference to Housing and Education.* (Ph.D. thesis, University of London, 1980).

[51] Freeborne, *The Chinese Community in Britain* 295.

[52] Ibid., 301.

[53] Ibid., 304.

learning. They might be highly motivated, but they sometimes found it difficult to adjust to the more open-ended western system of education. Therefore he called for efforts to be made to understand the particular needs of Chinese students and to deal with their problems.

Thirdly, as far as the pre-school, primary, and secondary education of Chinese children is concerned, it is suggested that they must often experience educational deprivation. "This is partly due to the residential and working distribution of a majority of the Chinese community and a centrifugal force dragging some of them towards the inner city rather than out into suburbia". Chinese children, like children of other ethnic minorities and white working class children, may suffer inadequate school buildings, overcrowding, a high staff turn-over, inadequately trained staff, inappropriate organization and curriculum, lack of resources, vandalism and truancy, and an environment of poor housing, poverty and social neglect.[54]

Educational attainments of Chinese: a descriptive analysis

In the above sections, social attitudes towards education and the role of education in determining occupational success have been examined for the major places of origin of Chinese immigrants in Britain (as well as in America). It is generally agreed by researchers that traditional Chinese society values education because of its function as a major channel for upward mobility. A strong association between occupational attainment and education was also evident in urban and rural Hong Kong (except the emigrant communities), China, Taiwan, and Southeast Asia. Thus Chinese, compared to immigrants from societies where social demarcation is more rigid and fixed, may be better positioned to take advantage of the educational system in the host society to improve their occupational status. Because of this, the level of Chinese educational attainment is assumed to be higher than those of other ethnic minorities, and similar to that of British-born whites. This hypothesis, I shall test for both foreign-born and native-born Chinese in Britain.

The level of educational attainment, however, may vary between Chinese immigrants from different places. Migrants with urban backgrounds and those previously exposed to western influence might have better school facilities, better teaching, a more stimulating academic environment, and wider academic interests. Therefore, they may be more adaptive and competitive in the educational system of the host society.

---

[54] Ibid., 289.

These include Hong Kong urbanites and Chinese from Southeast Asia and other parts of the world. Chinese from Vietnam form the other extreme. They speak little English, possess few transferrable skills, and have little chance to improve their educational level in a very short time. Thus, their level of education may be significantly lower than that of other Chinese immigrants in Britain. We should be aware of these differences in later analysis.

The indicator for educational attainment is the "highest qualification". It is coded as (1) higher degree; (2) first degree; (3) other degree - corporate or graduate member of professional institute; (4) HNC/HND/BEC(higher)/TEC (higher); (5) teaching qualification - secondary; (6) teaching qualification-primary; (7) nursing qualification (8) ONC/OND/BEC (national/general)/TEC (national/general); (9) city and guild; (10) A-level or equivalent; (11) O-level or equivalent (including Grade 1 CSE); (12) CSE (other grades); (13) any other professional/vocational qualification; (14) no qualification; (15) don't know; (16) no answer.

The first step of the analysis is to look at the distribution of the highest qualification by ethnic origin. This is done by crosstabulating education by ethnicity for immigrant and native-born males and females separately.

In Tables 4.1, 4.2, 4.4 and 4.5, percentage distributions of the highest qualification by ethnic group are displayed for foreign-born and native-born males and females. British-born white males and females have been included as contrast groups. In the following, I shall compare Chinese with majority whites and other ethnic minorities in terms of the highest qualification obtained.

From Table 4.1[55], it can be seen that 31% of British-born whites claim to possess no qualifications, leaving 69% qualified. About 7% have university degrees and above. O-level and City and Guild are the most common qualifications, possessed by 16% and 15% of people.

---

[55] In Tables 4.1 and 4.2, the row stands for qualifications and the column different ethnic groups. To understand the labels in the column, HD=higher degree, FD=first-degree, MP=member of professional institute, HN=HNC/HND, TS=teaching qualification: secondary, TP=teaching qualification: primary, NU=nursing qualification, ON=ONC/OND, CG=city and guild, AL=A-level, OL=O-level, CS=CSE, OP=other qualifications, and NQ=no qualification. To understand the labels in the column, HKCH=Chinese born in Hong Kong, CHCH=Chinese born in China, VTCH=Chinese born in Vietnam, ELCH=Chinese born elsewhere, ININ=Indians born in India, PAPA=Pakistanis born in Pakistan, AFAS=African Asians, WIWI=West Indians born in West India, IRIR=Irish born in Ireland, UKWH=British born whites.

Table 4.1 Percent Distribution of Qualification by Ethnicity: Foreign-Born Males

	HKCH	CHCH	VTCH	ELCH	ININ	PAPA	AFAS	WIWI	IRIR	UKWH
HD	4.1	0.0	0.0	6.6	5.7	2.0	3.9	0.6	1.5	1.8
FD	9.7	11.9	2.6	13.1	10.6	5.3	10.2	2.5	3.8	5.1
MP	0.0	1.7	0.0	4.1	1.7	0.4	1.5	1.1	2.0	2.7
HN	2.8	3.4	0.0	2.5	2.5	1.3	2.6	1.2	1.1	3.2
TS	0.0	0.0	0.0	1.6	0.4	0.1	0.4	0.2	0.4	0.6
TP	0.0	0.0	0.0	0.0	0.1	0.2	0.7	0.0	0.3	0.1
NU	1.8	1.7	0.0	4.9	0.3	0.1	0.0	1.6	1.3	0.5
ON	1.8	1.7	0.0	2.5	1.3	1.9	4.3	1.7	0.8	3.3
CG	1.6	0.0	2.6	3.3	4.7	3.8	7.4	13.6	8.3	15.2
AL	14.3	8.5	15.8	21.3	7.9	7.1	14.1	3.0	6.2	7.0
OL	19.4	6.8	13.2	16.4	11.9	11.8	22.4	8.7	9.2	16.0
CS	3.7	0.0	2.6	2.5	4.4	5.4	5.9	4.4	2.1	5.2
OP	5.1	8.5	23.7	17.2	14.3	8.8	8.2	10.4	12.4	8.0
NQ	35.5	55.9	39.5	4.1	34.2	51.7	18.4	51.0	50.5	31.2
	100.0	100.0	100.0	100.0	100.0	100.0	100.0	100.0	100.0	100.0
N	217.0	59.0	38.0	122.0	1569.0	891.0	744.0	994.0	2339.0	10368.0

Chi-square=1725 d.f=117

Compared with the indigenous population, Chinese from Hong Kong and China seem to have a polarized distribution of qualification. Both groups have larger proportions of people with university degrees, 14% for Hong Kong Chinese and 12% for Chinese from China. Yet, both groups have greater percentages of people without qualifications, 36% for Hong Kong Chinese and 56% for Chinese from China.

Vietnamese are much worse educated than majority whites, with a lower percentage of people reaching university level and a higher percentage of people without qualification. The most common qualification of this group is "other professional qualifications", or rather "foreign qualification".[56] Few Vietnamese refugees have had time to acquire British qualifications. Chinese born elsewhere are by far the most highly educated. Nearly 20% have degrees, and only 4% claim to have no qualifications. The most common qualification is A-level, which is held by 21% of this group.

Among other immigrant groups, African Asians and Indians from India are relatively well educated. Indians fare particularly well at the top, with 16% reaching degree level. African Asians have a very low percentage of 18% without qualifications. In comparison, Pakistanis, West Indians, and Irish have lower percentages of highly qualified and much greater proportions of unqualified. On the whole, Indians look similar to Hong Kong Chinese and African Asians close to Chinese born elsewhere. Pakistanis, West Indians, and Irish are more like Vietnamese Chinese.

In Table 4.2, percentage distributions are listed for female immigrants as well as for British-born white women. Patterns emerging from similar inter-group comparisons as above show the effect of gender on the highest qualification, in addition to ethnic differences. The most obvious finding is that, unlike males, the most common qualification is nursing for West Indians, Irish, and Chinese from elsewhere. This pattern, reflecting distinctive migratory experiences, may have direct effect on the occupational attainments of women in these groups.

The second finding is that Pakistani women, unlike their male counterparts, have a greater proportion of highly qualified people, their percentage with degrees somewhat higher than that of British-born white women.[57]

---

[56] In LFS, all foreign qualifications are listed under "other professional qualifications".

[57] The economically active women from Pakistani origin tend to come from upper class background and receive western style education. This may explain the relatively greater proportion of qualified Pakistani women in the Labour Force Survey. See M. Anwar, The *Myth of Return-Pakistanis in Britain* (london: Heinemann, 1979).

Table 4.2 Percent Distribution of Qualification by Ethnicity: Foreign-Born Females

	HKCH	CHCH	VTCH	ELCH	ININ	PAPA	AFAS	WIWI	IRIR	UKWH
HD	1.1	0.0	0.0	3.5	2.8	1.1	1.1	0.1	0.6	0.5
FD	4.9	12.9	0.0	14.6	7.9	3.7	5.2	1.2	1.9	4.0
MP	0.0	0.0	0.0	2.1	0.2	0.4	0.5	0.4	0.5	0.6
HN	0.0	0.0	0.0	1.4	0.6	0.0	0.8	0.5	0.2	0.5
TS	0.0	0.0	0.0	2.1	1.1	0.1	0.3	0.3	0.8	1.5
TP	0.5	0.0	0.0	0.7	1.6	0.4	0.8	0.3	1.3	1.9
NU	7.1	6.5	0.0	31.3	2.0	0.9	3.8	20.1	14.0	4.5
ON	1.6	1.6	0.0	1.4	0.6	0.1	2.9	0.6	0.4	1.4
CG	2.2	0.0	0.0	1.4	0.7	0.4	2.4	2.4	1.5	3.3
AL	11.0	6.5	6.1	11.8	5.8	4.0	8.5	4.0	6.7	6.6
OL	18.7	4.8	21.2	13.9	13.9	10.5	34.9	13.8	14.3	24.5
CS	5.5	0.0	6.1	1.4	5.5	4.0	8.4	8.7	2.1	6.9
OP	3.8	9.7	15.2	5.6	9.7	8.3	7.8	8.8	10.4	6.9
NQ	43.4	58.1	51.5	9.0	47.7	65.9	22.8	38.6	45.3	36.9
	100.0	100.0	100.0	100.0	100.0	100.0	100.0	100.0	100.0	100.0
N	182.0	62.0	33.0	144.0	1414.0	698.0	657.0	1237.0	2477.0	9997.0

Chi-square=2035 d.f=117

114

Lastly, while over half claim to be unqualified, none of the Chinese women from Vietnam have qualifications higher than A-level. They are by far the least educated group among both women and men. It is expected that their level of occupation may be severely jeopardized by a very low level of education.

The above crosstabular analysis informs us that the highest qualification varies not only with ethnic group, but also between males and females. In addition, the highest qualification may vary for people of different ages. In the next section, I shall explore the relationship between the highest qualification and ethnic origin, gender, and age. I shall not do complicated data analysis, but will simply use logit analysis to describe the relationship between these variables.

In multinomial logit analysis, I assume having any specified qualification (as against having no qualification) to be a function of age, sex, and ethnicity. The purpose is to see how Chinese fare in achieving a certain educational level, as against being unqualified, compared to other ethnic groups, after age and sex are held constant. The logit model looks like this:

$$\text{Ln } (P_i/1-P_i) = \beta_1 + \beta_2 X_i + \beta_3 X_j + \beta_4 X_k$$

where X_i represents age, X_j represents sex and X_k represents ethnic origin. Education categories are numbered from 1 to 5, with 1 corresponding to higher educational levels.

In conducting the analysis, we first need to collapse certain categories of the response and explanatory variables in order to avoid a big number of zero cells in a four-way contingency table. The variable on "the highest qualification" is collapsed approximately into five categories of degree and above, A-level, O-level, CSE, and no qualification.[58] Age is collapsed into four ten year cohorts, 25-34, 35-44, 45-54 and 55-64. Sex is a binary variable. Ethnicity is collapsed from ten to seven categories, as the four Chinese groups are combined into one category. Thus, no distinctions are made among Chinese because of the small N problem.

In Table 4.3, parameter estimates and standard errors are listed only for ethnicity, as they are of primary interest. Note, no-qualification is the base category for education, and Chinese the base category for ethnicity.

---

[58] To show the relationship between revised and original educational level, (1) degree and above=higher degree, first degree, member of professional institute and teaching qualification; (2) A-level and equivalent=A-level, HNC/HND and nursing; (3) O-level and equivalent=O-level, ONC/OND; (4) CSE and equivalent=CSE, C & G and other qualifications (including foreign qualification); (5) no qualification.

The parameter estimates are in the form of log odds ratios (in the simple case with no interaction), the numerical expression of which is written as follows:

$$\text{Ln} \left[\ (F_{ij}/F_{0j}) \ / \ (F_{i0}/F_{00}) \ \right]$$

i.e. we compare the fitted odds in the jth ethnic group with those among Chinese, where i is qualification, j is ethnic group, $i=0$ represents no qualification, and $j=0$ represents Chinese.

Thus, when age and sex are held constant, Indians, African Asians, and British whites have similar fitted log odds as Chinese of having a degree as against having no qualification. All ethnic groups have lower log odds than Chinese of having A-level as against having no qualification, although the coefficients are not significant at 0.05 level for African Asians, West Indians, and Irish. Except for Pakistanis, whose log odds of having both O-level and CSE are lower than those of Chinese, all the other groups seem to have greater log odds than Chinese of having O-level and CSE as against having no-qualification.

Table 4.3 Parameter Estimates: Qualification by Ethnicity
Foreign-Born (N=25,569)

	Degree	A-level	O-level	CSE	None
CHIN	0.	0.	0.	0.	0.
ININ	.0609	-.8740	.1029	**.3740**	0.
	(.1348)	(.1330)	(.1494)	(.1447)	
PAPA	**-1.2117**	**-1.669**	**-.6779**	**-.4880**	0.
	(.1623)	(.1602)	(.1661)	(.1592)	
AFAS	.2101	-.1280	**1.2537**	.6973	0.
	(.1623)	(.1551)	(.1609)	(.1668)	
WIWI	-1.6967	-.1756	.1460	**.5829**	0.
	(.1833)	(.1275)	(.1529)	(.1458)	
IRIR	-.9758	-.1866	**.2904**	**.3422**	0.
	(.1412)	(.1200)	(.1439)	(.1409)	
UKWH	-.1709	**-.3063**	**.9605**	**.7198**	0.
	(.1255)	(.1141)	(.1368)	(.1355)	

$G^2=745$ d.f$=180$

116

The above findings imply that when age and sex are controlled for, Chinese enjoy some ethnic advantage in achieving degree level and even greater advantage in getting A-level. But they suffer an ethnic penalty in obtaining O-level and CSE.[59] Thus, compared to other ethnic groups, Chinese immigrants seem to be polarized in educational attainments. In other words, there are some Chinese who have greater odds of being better qualified as against being unqualified than most other ethnic groups, but there are other Chinese whose odds of gaining intermediate or minimum qualifications as being completely unqualified are even lower than most other ethnic groups.

Next, we shall look at the educational attainments of British-born Chinese in comparison with British-born Indians, Pakistanis, West Indians and whites. As in the case of immigrants, we shall first examine the distribution of the highest qualification among ethnic groups. Then, we shall conduct logit analysis, where we assume qualifications to be a function of age, sex and ethnicity. As we already know from Chapter Three that British-born ethnic minorities are much younger than immigrants, we include those of age 24 and below. In conducting logit analysis for immigrants, we excluded this age group, because many below the age of 24 would still be in full time education.

In Table 4.4[60], the most obvious pattern is that ethnic minority males are under-represented in higher qualifications, such as degree and above, when compared to British white males. As a matter of fact, no Chinese male falls into this category. At the other end of the spectrum, again, all ethnic minorities are under-represented among those without qualifications. The percentage without qualifications is lowest for British-born Chinese, at 9%. It follows that compared with the indigenous population, ethnic minorities are concentrated in intermediate qualification brackets, A-level, O-level and CSE. As a matter of fact, three quarters of British-born

---

[59] I have used another variable, "age terminating continuous full-time education" to check the relative advantage of the Chinese immigrants in the highest qualification. As it normally takes longer to get higher qualifications, I assume that the better educated a group is, the later it is to terminate continuous full-time education on the average. I calculated the mean score of terminal age and found that the Chinese have a mean score of 17.76. This score is higher than those of all other ethnic groups, except African Asians. Among the Chinese immigrants, the mean scores are 17.27 for Hong Kong Chinese, 17.23 for Chinese from China, 16.54 for the Vietnamese Chinese and 19.41 for Chinese from elsewhere.

[60] To understand labels in the row in Tables 4.4 and 4.5, UKCH=Chinese born in U.K., UKIN=Indians born in U.K., UKPA=Pakistanis born in U.K., UKWI=West Indians born in U.K., and UKWH=Whites born in U.K..

Table 4.4 Percent Distribution of Qualification by Ethnicity: British-Born Males

	UKCH	UKIN	UKPA	UKWI	UKWH
HD	0.0	1.0	0.7	0.5	1.8
FD	0.0	2.5	1.4	0.9	5.1
MP	3.0	0.3	0.7	0.4	2.7
HN	3.0	3.0	0.7	1.0	3.2
TS	0.0	0.0	0.0	0.1	0.6
TP	0.0	0.3	0.0	0.0	0.1
NU	0.0	0.0	0.0	0.2	0.5
ON	3.0	3.8	2.0	3.4	3.3
CG	6.1	8.9	3.4	14.0	15.2
AL	33.3	15.7	11.6	7.0	7.0
OL	33.3	36.7	48.3	24.9	16.0
CS	9.1	13.9	11.6	22.8	5.2
OP	0.0	1.8	2.0	1.7	8.0
NQ	9.1	12.2	17.7	23.1	31.2
	100.0	100.0	100.0	100.0	100.0
N	33.0	395.0	147.0	802.0	10368.0

Chi-square=914 d.f=52

Table 4.5 Percent Distribution of Qualification by Ethnicity: British-Born Females

	UKCH	UKIN	UKPA	UKWI	UKWH
HD	3.3	0.5	0.0	0.4	0.5
FD	0.0	1.1	0.0	0.8	4.0
MP	0.0	0.0	0.0	0.2	0.6
HN	0.0	1.1	0.8	0.4	0.5
TS	0.0	0.0	0.0	0.4	1.5
TP	0.0	0.3	0.0	0.1	1.9
NU	6.7	1.9	1.7	3.4	4.5
ON	0.0	4.9	5.1	3.3	1.4
CG	3.3	3.0	1.7	6.5	3.3
AL	16.7	12.7	7.6	8.7	6.6
OL	53.3	44.7	40.7	37.2	24.5
CS	3.3	13.8	20.3	22.5	6.9
OP	0.0	1.9	0.0	2.1	6.9
NQ	13.3	14.1	22.0	14.1	36.9
	100.0	100.0	100.0	100.0	100.0
N	30.0	369.0	118.0	1017.0	9997.0

Chi-square=882 d.f=52

119

Chinese claim to have one of these qualifications, the highest percentage across all groups.

Similar patterns are also discernable from Table 4.5, where distribution of the highest qualification is presented for females. It is noticeable, however, that unlike their male counterparts, 3.3% of Chinese females have degrees. Moreover, 6.7% have nursing qualifications. In spite of these differences, the degree of concentration in A-level, O-level, and CSE combined is still highest among female Chinese across all groups.

The obvious concentration of Chinese in intermediate qualifications might reflect the age structure of British-born Chinese. We know from previous analysis that the average age of British-born Chinese is only slightly higher than 7, the youngest of all British-born minority groups included in the study. It appears necessary, therefore, to control for age and sex in summarizing the effect of ethnicity on qualification. The logit model is as follows:

$$Ln(P_i/1-P_i) = \theta_1 + \theta_2 X_i + \theta_3 X_j + \theta_4 X_k$$

where X_i represents age, X_j represents sex and X_k represents ethnic origin. Education categories are numbered from 1 to 5 with category 1 corresponding to the highest educational level.

Table 4.6 Parameter Estimates: Qualification by Race
British-Born (N=21,606)

	Degree	A-level	O-level	CSE	No-qual
UKCH	0.	0.	0.	0.	0.
UKIN	.6182	-.6726	-.4702	.5234	0.
	(1.097)	(1.226)	(1.090)	(1.073)	
UKPA	-.8318	**-1.7205**	**-1.5941**	**-1.3902**	0.
	(.4678)	(.5034)	(.4576)	(.4500)	
UKWI	-.4055	-.8010	-.8263	-.8711	0.
	(.4455)	(.4612)	(.4357)	(.4313)	
UKWH	.5984	.0151	.7710	.3512	0.
	(.6042)	(.6242)	(.5942)	(.5908)	

$G^2 = 281$ d.f = 88

In Table 4.6, parameter estimates and standard errors are presented for qualification by British-born ethnic groups. As in the previous case, a five category variable of education is used, the base category being no-qualification. There are five ethnic groups, among which the British-born Chinese serve as the base category.

It can be seen that no group difference is found in obtaining a degree or higher as against having no qualification. In addition, we can see that, except for Pakistanis, who show consistent disadvantage (defined as fitted log odds of obtaining certain qualification as against being unqualified), no group difference is observed for access to A-level, O-level, and CSE as against being unqualified. Thus, holding age and sex constant, we find little difference in educational level between British-born Chinese, other British-born ethnic minorities, and the indigenous population.[273]

Conclusions

In this chapter, I have examined secondary materials with regard to the role of education in occupational success in Imperial China, Hong Kong, China, Taiwan, and Southeast Asia. I argued that rather than as a distinctive cultural value, education was pursued more because of its function as a channel of upward mobility. Likewise, realization of the important role of education in socio-economic success might motivate Chinese migrants overseas to pursue higher educational attainments.

This contention is supported by findings on the relative level of educational success of Chinese in Britain. I have found that when age and sex are held constant, Chinese immigrants have relatively better chances of being highly qualified than most other ethnic groups, although there are a portion of Chinese who find it more difficult than other ethnic groups to obtain intermediate and low qualification. This polarized pattern is not found among British-born Chinese, who appear to have similar chances as other British-born ethnic minorities of obtaining all qualifications.

In studying the highest qualification of Chinese, I did not make distinctions within each educational level between foreign qualifications and British qualifications. Such distinctions become meaningful only where employers attach different values to the same educational level attained in

---

[273] As in the case of immigrants, I also calculated the mean age terminating continuous full-time education for the native-born groups. The mean scores are 17.34 for Chinese, 17.27 for Indians, 16.52 for Pakistanis, 16.77 for West Indians and 16.25 for British. Although Chinese still have the highest mean score, the difference in duration of schooling between the Chinese and other groups seems much smaller, compared to the case of immigrants. Again, our findings are supported.

different countries and employees with foreign qualifications receive lower occupational returns to the same educational level than employees possessing British qualifications. I shall address this issue in the next Chapter.

5 Occupational attainments of Chinese in Britain

Introduction

In western liberal societies, the dominant notion of social justice is perhaps the one that advocates equality of opportunity: equal effort and talent should be equally rewarded regardless of class, sex, age, race, or religion. Economic efficiency likewise requires that workers should be paid according to their actual productivity rather than to ascribed (and economically irrelevant) characteristics such as race or sex.[1] This liberal argument, when applied to the occupational attainments of ethnic groups in industrialised society, implies that universal achievement values discourage discrimination against ethnic minorities. Ascriptive characteristics, such as ethnic minority backgrounds, should become less relevant than formal schooling to occupational success.

In the previous chapter, Chinese, long cultured in a tradition emphasizing the role of education in upward mobility, were actually found to be disproportionately over-represented among the well-qualified, despite a substantial proportion of unqualified people. Now, given the increasing connection between education and occupation in industrialised society, as posited by the liberals, we would expect Chinese to have relatively better chances for occupational success too.

This chapter is divided into four parts. First, I shall do simple cross-tabular analysis of ethnic distribution in occupation related variables, such as employment status, industry, and socio-economic status. The purpose is to present preliminary results on Chinese occupational attainments, in comparison with other ethnic groups. Secondly, I shall test three

---

[1] Anthony Heath and John Ridge, "Social Mobility of Ethnic Minorities," *Journal of Biosocial Science, Suppl*, 8 (1983), 169.

hypotheses with regard to ethnic differences in occupational attainments, drawing elements from theories of industrialism, human capital, and the occupational attainment process of ethnic minorities. Thirdly, I shall examine the recent theory of occupational returns to education in the ethnic enclave economy by comparing Chinese occupational attainments inside and outside the Chinese catering trade. The findings are summarized in the conclusion.

Occupation of Chinese: preliminary analysis

Employment status

Employment status has two main categories, employee and self-employed.[2] In Table 5.1 and 5.2, percentage distributions of employment status are listed for foreign-born and native-born ethnic minorities and British whites. It can be seen from Table 5.1 that 31% of Chinese are self-employed, the highest proportion of all ethnic groups. This probability is 2.5 times that of British-born whites and Irish-born in Ireland, and approximately 1.5 times that of other Asians. West Indians have the lowest percentage of self-employed, at 5%.

Table 5.1 Percent Distribution of Employment Status by Ethnic
         Origin: Foreign-born

	Self-employed	Employee	Total	N
Chinese	31.3	68.8	100.0	432
Indian	20.9	79.1	100.0	1543
Pakistanis	23.9	76.1	100.0	494
African Asian	22.3	77.7	100.0	740
West Indian	5.4	94.6	100.0	1427
Irish	13.6	86.4	100.0	2827
British Whites	12.5	87.5	100.0	10226

Chi-square=47 d.f=4

---

[2] The variable of "employment status" is coded in more detail in 1983 LFS. Since 1984, it is coded in two categories only, i.e. employee and self-employed. To allow for coding differences between 1983 and the years after it, we adopt the two category form by collapsing the more refined variable on "employment status" in 1983 LFS.

Interestingly, the percentage of self-employed is the lowest for British-born Chinese, compared with all other British-born ethnic minorities and whites. Only 3% claim to be self-employed. British born Indians, Pakistanis, and British whites are over 3 times more likely to become self-employed. Only British born West Indians have a similar, but still slightly higher, proportion of self-employed.

Table 5.2 Percent Distribution of Employment Status by Ethnic
Origin: Native-born

	Self-employed	Employee	Total	N
Chinese	3.0	97.0	100.0	33
Indian	9.9	90.1	100.0	304
Pakistanis	11.3	88.7	100.0	62
West Indian	3.7	96.3	100.0	945
British Whites	10.4	89.6	100.0	13265[3]

Chi-square=355 d.f=6

Rapid inter-generational reduction in the proportion of self-employed among Chinese may be due to two alternative factors. One factor is that the second generation managed to escape the traditional catering business, where most of the Chinese self-employment takes place. Alternatively, the second generation, like their parents, may still be caught in catering - working as employees, since still too young to take up self-employment. This will become clear when we examine the distribution of foreign-born and native-born Chinese in industry.

Industry

The variable of "industry", or Standard Industrial Classification, has 312 detailed industry codes. For the sake of presentation, we have collapsed

---

[3]Since no age restriction is imposed on the native-born, we have obtained a bigger sample size for British-born whites in Table 5.2 compared to Table 5.1, where people under the age of 25 were excluded.

Table 5.3 Percent Distribution of Industrial Group by Ethnic Origin: Foreign-born

	Chinese	Indian	Pakistani	African Asian	West Indian	Irish	Brit. Whites
Agricu.forest.fish	0.5	0.0	0.0	0.1	0.1	0.5	2.1
Energy.water.supply	0.7	0.9	0.4	0.9	1.2	2.0	3.3
Mineral extraction	0.9	2.9	5.7	1.8	2.9	2.3	3.5
Metal goods	3.5	16.4	14.0	15.9	13.6	9.4	11.0
Other manufacturing	2.8	18.3	22.7	10.0	8.8	6.4	9.3
Construction	0.9	2.5	1.4	2.0	5.1	16.3	7.7
Catering related	56.7	25.0	28.7	32.7	9.7	15.2	17.0
Transport	3.2	9.7	13.4	8.4	11.6	6.4	6.5
Banking	7.9	6.8	4.5	12.0	5.3	7.1	8.9
Other service	22.9	17.6	9.3	16.1	41.7	34.3	30.6
Total	100.0	100.0	100.0	100.0	100.0	100.0	100.0
N	432.0	1543.0	494.0	740.0	1427.0	2827.0	10226.0

Chi-square=2046 d.f=90

126

Table 5.4 Percent Distribution of Industrial Group by Ethnic Origin: Native-born

	Chinese	Indian	Pakistani	West Indian	British Whites
Agricu.forest.fish	0.0	0.0	0.0	0.1	2.1
Energy.water.supply	0.0	2.0	0.0	1.0	3.1
Mineral extraction	0.0	0.7	1.6	1.4	3.3
Metal goods	0.0	10.2	3.2	9.2	11.0
Other manufacturing	9.1	14.1	17.7	9.8	9.7
Construction	3.0	1.0	1.6	7.3	7.7
Catering related	51.5	34.5	48.4	23.1	19.2
Transport	3.0	3.3	1.6	7.6	6.1
Banking	18.2	13.2	14.5	11.6	9.8
Other service	15.2	21.1	11.3	28.9	28.1
Total	100.0	100.0	100.0	100.0	100.0
N	33.0	304.0	62.0	945.0	13265.0

Chi-square=251 d.f=36

127

them into 10 industrial groups.[4]   When necessary, we shall discuss
detailed industries, otherwise, we shall follow the shortened scheme.

From Table 5.3, we find that Chinese immigrants have the highest
proportion engaged in catering. Over half of Chinese, or 57%, work in
"distribution, catering, hotel and repairs". This percentage is about twice
that of Indians, Pakistanis and African Asians, about three times that of
Irish and British whites, and five times that of West Indian immigrants.

The next biggest concentration of Chinese immigrants (23%), is found
in "other service", which consists of public administration, education,
medical health, recreational and personal services. The proportion of
Chinese in this group is higher than that of other Asian immigrant groups,
but still falls below that of West Indians, Irish, and British-born whites.
In addition, Chinese seem to be over-represented in banking, compared
with other immigrant groups, except African Asians. On the other hand,
Chinese are under-represented in energy and water supply, extraction of
minerals, metal goods, other manufacturing, construction, and transport.

In Table 5.4, industry distribution is listed for the native-born. On the
whole, there are very few native-born Chinese working in any of the
industrial groups. Of these Chinese, the single largest concentration of
51% is still found in the catering related group. Their percentage in
banking is also higher than that of all other ethnic groups. Previously, we
found the percentage of self-employment to be extremely low for British-
born Chinese. We wondered whether it was a reflection of the second
generation Chinese escaping the traditional catering trade, or simply a life
cycle factor. Now it seems clear that the majority of British-born Chinese
are still engaged in catering, where they might be too young to take up
self-employment yet.

Socio-economic group

This variable, from which our dependent variable "class" will be primarily
derived in the following section, has 16 categories, as shown in Tables 5.5
and 5.6. Compared with other ethnic groups included in Table 5.5,
Chinese are much over-represented in the category of "employers and
managers in small establishments". But they are three times less likely
than British-born whites and twice less likely than Irish to become
"employers and managers in large establishments". The distinction
between big and small establishments is the number of people working in

---

[4] See ESRC Data Archive, *SN: 2029 Labour Force Survey: 1983 Index of SOEC
Mnemonics OPCS Classification of Occupation and Derived Variables* (Colchester: ESRC
Data Archive, 1983) Appendix C.

Table 5.5 Percent Distribution of Socio-economic Group by Ethnic Origin: Foreign-born

	Chinese	Indian	Pakistanis	Af. Asian	West Indian	Irish	British Whites
employer/manager/large	3.5	3.8	1.8	2.4	3.7	7.2	9.3
employer/manager/small	23.8	9.7	11.7	12.7	1.6	6.8	8.3
s-employed professional	1.6	2.7	0.4	4.2	0.4	1.4	1.0
employee professional	8.3	6.4	3.4	7.6	1.0	2.3	4.1
intermed. non-manual	17.4	9.4	6.7	9.6	24.8	17.1	15.5
junior non-manual	12.0	6.9	22.3	10.4	12.2	17.8	11.8
personal service	14.1	2.1	1.6	1.2	6.6	7.9	4.6
manual supervisor	0.2	2.7	3.0	2.7	4.5	5.3	4.6
skilled manual	2.5	13.7	21.5	10.8	17.1	12.3	13.4
semi-skilled manual	2.1	23.3	23.3	15.8	18.1	10.5	8.1
unskilled manual	3.5	4.3	4.9	1.5	7.4	8.3	4.4
own account	11.1	9.9	14.6	8.8	4.0	7.8	6.2
farm employer/manager	0.0	0.0	0.0	0.0	0.0	0.1	0.5
farmer own account	0.0	0.0	0.0	0.0	0.0	0.0	0.4
agricultural worker	0.0	0.0	0.0	0.1	0.1	0.3	0.9
armed forces	0.0	0.1	0.2	0.3	0.4	0.5	0.7
Total	100.0	100.0	100.0	100.0	100.0	100.0	100.0
N	432.0	1543	494	740.0	1427.0	2827.0	10226.0

Chi-square=2,014 d.f=90

Table 5.6 Percent Distribution of Socio-economic Group by Ethnic Origin: Native-born

	Chinese	Indian	Pakistanis	West Indian	British Whites
employer/manager/large	3.0	4.3	0.0	3.5	7.7
employer/manager/small	6.1	6.3	4.8	1.5	7.1
s-employed professional	0.0	0.7	0.0	0.6	0.8
employee professional	0.0	3.6	3.2	0.7	3.6
intermed. non-manual	18.2	14.5	8.1	15.3	14.5
junior non-manual	36.4	32.9	43.5	36.9	21.6
personal service	18.2	4.6	8.1	7.5	5.1
manual supervisor	0.0	1.6	4.8	1.4	3.9
skilled manual	9.1	10.9	8.1	14.6	14.5
semi-skilled manual	6.1	13.2	9.7	11.2	8.9
unskilled manual	3.0	3.3	1.6	4.1	4.5
own account	0.0	4.3	8.1	2.3	5.3
farm employer/manager	0.0	0.0	0.0	0.0	0.5
farmer own account	0.0	0.0	0.0	0.0	0.3
agricultural worker	0.0	0.0	0.0	0.2	1.0
armed forces	0.0	0.0	0.0	0.0	0.7
Total	100.0	100.0	100.0	100.0	100.0
N	33.0	304.0	62.0	945.0	13265.0

Chi-square=325 d.f=60

the same establishment. Those with 25 or more people are considered large establishments and those with less than 25 people small establishments.

In professional jobs, Chinese immigrants have a lower percentage of self-employed professionals than Indians and African Asians. Their percentage of professional employees, however, is higher than all other groups. The other two categories where Chinese concentration is obvious are "personal service" and "own account", with 14% and 11%, which are both higher than those of all other ethnic groups. It follows that Chinese are generally under-represented in manual work, skilled and unskilled alike. Few Chinese work in farming or the armed forces, the same being more or less true of other immigrant groups.

As shown in Table 5.6, native-born Chinese are less likely than all other ethnic groups, except Pakistanis, to be employers or managers of large establishments, but they are more likely to become employers and managers of small establishments than all other groups. They are also highly represented in personal service. These findings are similar to those for Chinese immigrants. Surprisingly, no native-born Chinese is found in a professional job. Instead, they are almost as well represented in intermediate and junior non-manual work as all other native-born groups. Access into professional jobs, unlike access into managerial or routine non-manual jobs, normally requires higher education. Our previous analysis of educational attainments informs us that, because of a very young mean age, few British-born Chinese have yet taken a university degree. Therefore, a better way of examining Chinese occupational success would be to control for the effects of age and education. This we shall discuss in the next section.

Hypothesis testing

In this section, I shall test a series of hypotheses with regard to ethnic differences in occupational attainment. The major focus of the analysis is the relative level of occupational attainment of Chinese in comparison with majority whites and major non-white ethnic minorities in Britain. Hypothesis testing is done through logit analysis.

The dependent variable is class, which takes the form of two binary contrasts, the service class versus the non-service class, the unemployed versus those in work. The purpose of studying these two extreme splits is to contrast the chances of reaching the most advantageous position with the risks of being in the least desirable position for people of different ethnic origins, Chinese in particular. The service class is derived from the

131

variable "socio-economic group".[5] It consists of the first four categories of SEG, employer and manager of large establishment, employer and manager of small establishment, self-employed professionals, and employee professionals. To exclude the petit-bourgeoisie from the service class, we assign those who claimed themselves to be employer and manager of small establishment and, at the same time, self-employed to the non-service class, with the help of another variable "economic activity".[6] The unemployed are obtained by simply extracting those who claimed themselves to be unemployed in the variable of "economic activity".

The independent variables include age, education and ethnicity, all of which are multinomial:

Age:
    1=25-29
    2=30-34
    3=35-39
    4=40-44
    5=45-49
    6=50-54
    7=55-59
    8=60-64

Education:
    1=first degree and higher
    2=A-level and equivalent
    3=O-level and equivalent
    4=CSE and equivalent
    5=no-qualification

Ethnic origin:
    1=Chinese
    2=Indians
    3=Pakistanis

---

[5] The variable of "socio-economic group" has 16 categories as follows: 1=employer and manager of large establishments of and above 25 people; 2=employer and manager of small establishments below 25 people; 3=self-employed professionals; 4=professionals working as employees; 5=intermediate non-manual; 6=junior non-manual; 7=personal service; 8=supervisor of manual workers; 9=skilled manual; 10=semi-skilled manual; 11=unskilled manual; 12=own account; 13=farmer as employer or manager; 14=farmer on own account; 15=agricultural worker; 16=armed forces.

[6] The variable "economic activity" is coded: (1) unemployed (2) self-employed in employment (3) employee in employment (4) not stated in employment.

4 = African Asians
5 = West Indians
6 = Irish
7 = British-born whites.

The first hypothesis, drawing elements from the theory of human capital, posits that class is a function of age and education only. Age is considered a proxy of labour market experience and education stands for the highest formal qualification. This model suggests that at the same age, people with the same qualifications will achieve similar levels of occupational success, regardless of ethnic background.[7] This model, which we call the "baseline model", is written as follows:

$$\text{Ln } (P/1\text{-}P) = \theta_0 + \theta_1(AGE) + \theta_2(EDUC).$$

Our experience tells us that the baseline model rarely fits. Thus, the second hypothesis we shall test assumes that given the same age and education, class varies with ethnicity. This model, which we call the "ethnicity model", looks like this:

$$\text{Ln } (P/1\text{-}P) = \theta_0 + \theta_1(AGE) + \theta_2(EDUC) + \theta_3(ETHN).$$

The third hypothesis assumes that the effect of ethnicity on class varies for people with different educational levels. It suggests that people with different qualifications tend to compete in different labour markets. Those with higher qualifications, though of various ethnic backgrounds, tend to look for jobs in more bureaucratic enterprises where educational credentials are given more credit in recruitment and promotion of workers. Therefore, testing this hypothesis implies examining the interaction effects of education and ethnicity, other things being equal. To conduct a conservative test, in which we want to exclude from the effect of "ethnicity by education" on class, which could be accounted for by the effects of other two-way interactions, we also control for "age by education" and "age by ethnicity", should any of them be statistically significant at the 0.05 level. Therefore, we compare the fit of the following two models, which we call the "control" model and the "ethnicity by education" model:

---

[7] It ought to be noted that the same educational level may not necessarily entail the same value in determining occupational success. In the case of immigrants, for instance, education received in Britain may be considered of better quality than that received overseas. Thus, even at the same level, people holding British qualifications may have better chances for occupational success than those holding foreign qualifications. This I shall test for all immigrant groups. The results will be given in the footnotes.

$$\text{Ln } (P/1\text{-}P) = \theta_0 + \theta_1(AGE) + \theta_2(EDUC) + \theta_3(ETHN)$$
$$+ \theta_4(AGE.EDUC) + \theta_5(AGE.ETHN);$$
$$\text{Ln } (P/1\text{-}P) = \theta_0 + \theta_1(AGE) + \theta_2(EDUC) + \theta_3(ETHN)$$
$$+ \theta_4(AGE.EDUC) + \theta_5(AGE.ETHN) + \theta_6(EDUC.ETHN).$$

Male immigrants

The first part of the analysis in this section involves hypothesis testing, which is done by fitting logit models. As shown in Table 5.7, I have fitted four nested models, which contain the baseline model, the ethnicity model, the control model and the ethnicity by education model for access to the service class. Hypothesis testing for risks of unemployment will be discussed in the second part of this section.

It can be seen that the baseline model does not fit well, with deviance of $G^2 = 743$ and d.f $= 257$ and an Index of Dissimilarity of 12.42. When ethnicity is added to the baseline model, the change in G^2 is 376 for 6 degrees of freedom. By fitting the ethnicity model, we reduce deviance by 51% and the Index of Dissimilarity by 5.06. This implies that when age and education are equal, class varies with ethnicity. Therefore, the null hypothesis of the ethnicity model is rejected.

It is also shown in Table 5.7 that when the interaction term of ethnicity by education is introduced into the model, the change of G^2 is 85 for 24 degrees of freedom, compared to the control model. By fitting the ethnicity by education model, we reduce deviance by 72% and the Index of Dissimilarity by 7.46, compared to the baseline model. It implies that other things being equal,[8] the effect of ethnicity on class is different at different educational levels. As a result, the null hypothesis of the ethnicity by education model is also rejected.

Table 5.7 Modelling Male Immigrants Access to the Service Class
(N=11,466)

Models	G^2	d.f	ΔG^2	Δd.f	p-value	rG^2(%)	ID
Baseline	743.4	257			0.0000		12.42
Ethnicity	367.2	251	376	6	0.0000	51	7.36
Control	291.6	209	76	42	0.0001	61	6.12
Ethn.Educ	206.7	185	85	24	0.1341	72	4.96

[8]The interaction effect of age by education is not statistically significant at 0.05 level and has been excluded from the control model.

The parameter estimates for the ethnicity by education model are presented in Appendix 5.1. They are in the form of fitted log odds ratios and are not straight forward for explanation. Besides, not all the coefficients are of theoretical interests to us. For the sake of clarity of presentation, I translate the parameter estimates into fitted probabilities following the method described in Chapter Two. Then I do a simple graphic representation of the association between education and class for all ethnic groups, reflecting our concern about the ethnic differences in translating education into occupational attainments. Any age cohort may be selected, as the interaction effect of education by ethnicity has not been found to vary with age group.[9] The reason for selecting people between 35 and 39 is simply that occupation is likely to mature within this age span.

Figure 5.1 shows the fitted probabilities[10] of reaching the service class for each male immigrant group and British-born white males between the ages of 35 and 39 at five given educational levels. The vertical axis stands for the predicted probabilities of reaching the service class in percentage form with values ranging between 0 and 100, and the horizontal axis stands for five educational levels in descending order, where 1 = degree and above, 2 = A-level, 3 = O-level, 4 = CSE, and 5 = no-qualification.

It can be seen that the curve representing Chinese lies somewhere below the curves representing British-born whites and Irish, but in most cases, above the curves representing other Asians and Afro-Caribbeans. The vertical distance between the curve of Chinese and those of other groups indicates the difference in likelihood between Chinese and any other groups reaching the service class, given a particular educational level.

On the whole, it can be seen that the spectrum of curves in Figure 5.1 approximately indicates a negative linear relationship between access to the service class and decreasing educational levels for all ethnic groups. However, the curves are more spread out at degree and A-level than at CSE and no-qualification. Hence, there are bigger variations in the likelihood of different ethnic groups entering the service class at higher rather than lower educational levels.

Compared to Pakistanis, Indians, West Indians, and African Asians, Chinese are better placed to reach the service class at all educational levels, except at O-level. But Chinese with degrees and A-levels clearly enjoy even greater ethnic advantage (defined as fitted probability) than Chinese

---

[9] In testing if the interaction effect of ethnicity by education varies with age cohorts, we have fitted the three way interaction term of age by ethnicity by education. The change in G^2 is 171 with 155 degrees of freedom. It is not statistically significant at 0.05 level.

[10] The probabilities are calculated from the log odds ratios in ethnicity by education model, using the method described in Chapter Two.

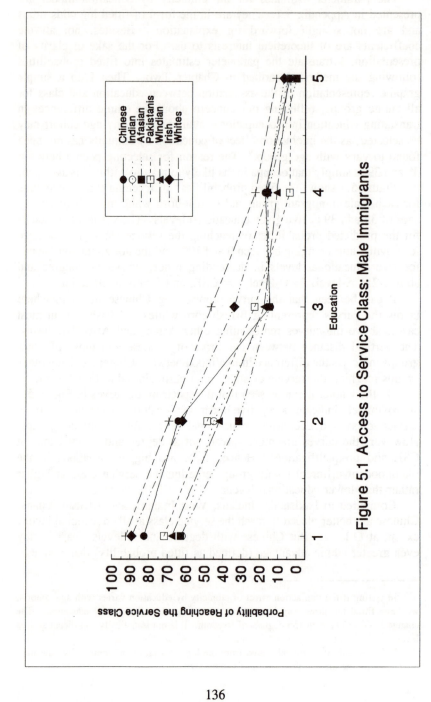

Figure 5.1 Access to Service Class: Male Immigrants

with CSE and no-qualification. On the other hand, Chinese have nearly parallel curves to Whites and Irish at all educational levels, except O-level.[11] Thus, compared to the indigenous population and Irish, the ethnic effect appears to be independent of education (except for O-level) for Chinese.[12]

It should be pointed out that in order to obtain a more parsimonious model, I tried different ways of fitting the final interaction effect of ethnicity by education. The method was to collapse the original categories of ethnicity or/and education variables and fit the interaction term with the recoded variables. Unfortunately, I was unable to obtain a unique superior model better than the existing full model in terms of goodness of fit.[13]

---

[11]The findings with regard to occupational returns to education did not make distinctions, within the same level of education, between those qualifications obtained in Britain and those obtained outside Britain. To test whether British qualifications and foreign qualifications of a similar level do carry different weights in recruitment and promotion of workers, we divide immigrant workers into those with British qualifications and those with foreign qualifications, at all educational levels. From Appendix 5.4.a, where parameter estimates are listed for the immigrant groups further divided into those with British and foreign qualifications, we can see that for most male immigrant groups, relative chances (defined as fitted log odds) of reaching the service class are not different for those with foreign qualifications from those with British qualifications. In the case of West Indians, however, we do detect a reduction in the size of the ethnic effect on class for those West Indians with foreign qualifications, compared to West Indians with British qualifications. This is to say that the odds of a Briton reaching the service class as against not reaching it is one and a quarter times those of a West Indian of the same age and with the similar British qualification. But the odds of a Briton are three times those of a West Indian of the same age but with a similar foreign qualification. In other words, the ethnic penalty is worse for the foreign educated than for the British educated West Indian at all educational levels. In the case of Irish, there are simply too few people with foreign highest qualifications to form any meaningful contrast with Irish holding British qualifications.

[12]The bump in the Chinese curve at O-level is probably caused by a small number of people who fit into this category.

[13]The parsimonious model which comes closest to the existing full model, both in terms of goodness of fit and the sociological story told, is the one where education is collapsed into 1 = degree and A-level, 2 = O-level, CSE and no-qualification, and ethnicity is collapsed into 1 = Chinese, 2 = Indians and Pakistanis, 3 = African Asians, West Indians, Irish, and Whites. After fitting the interaction effect of ethnicity by education thus recoded, the change in G2 is 9 for 2 degrees of freedom. The interaction effect is considered statistically significant at the 0.05 level. Since the interaction effect of ethnicity by education is also found to remain constant across age cohorts, I have selected one age cohort, i.e. those between the age of 35 and 39, and presented the fitted probabilities of reaching the service class by education for various ethnic groups as in Appendix 5.5.a. Compared to Figure 5.1, the graph in Appendix 5.5.a is much simplified.

137

In the second part of this section, I shall examine ethnic differences in risks of unemployment, in particular, ethnic differences between Chinese and other ethnic groups. The results of hypothesis testing are presented in Table 5.9 and parameter estimates for the best fitting model in Appendix 5.2.

First, it can be seen from Table 5.8 that the baseline model does not fit very well, with deviance $G^2=533$ and d.f=257 and the Index of Dissimilarity equal to 21.78. We can improve the fit of the model by adding the effect of ethnicity. In fitting the ethnicity model, the change in G^2 is 213 for 4 degrees of freedom. This reduces deviance by 40% and the Index of Dissimilarity by 6.41. It shows that when age and education are held constant, there is a statistically significant difference between various ethnic groups in risks of unemployment. Therefore, the null hypothesis of the ethnicity model is rejected. Yet the ethnicity by education model provides an even better fit.[14] With a change in G^2 equal to 42 for 24 degrees of freedom, the ethnicity by education model reduces deviance by 71% and the Index of Dissimilarity by 11.39, compared to the baseline model.

Table 5.8 Modelling Male Immigrants Risk of Unemployment (N=11,466)

	G^2	d.f	ΔG^2	Δd.f	p-value	$rG^2(\%)$	ID
Baseline	532.8	257			0.0000		21.78
Ethnicity	320.1	251	213	4	0.0021	40	15.37
Control	195.8	181	89	42	0.1162	63	11.59
Ethn.Educ	153.4	157	42	24	0.3599	71	10.39

In Appendix 5.2, parameter estimates are presented for the final model. To illustrate the ethnic differences in risk of unemployment, in particular the interaction effect of ethnicity by education in that respect, a graph is presented in Figure 5.2, where the vertical axis stands for the predicted probabilities of risks of unemployment and the horizontal axis stands for five educational levels in descending order. The curves stand for the fitted

---

[14]The interaction effect of age by education is not statistically significant at the 0.05 level and has been excluded from the control model.

138

probabilities of risk of unemployment at different educational levels for all ethnic groups.[15]

On the whole, the curves indicate a rather weak but positive linear relationship between the predicted probability of being unemployed and decreasing educational levels.[16] The curve for Chinese lies below those of other ethnic groups, except at CSE, where the predicted probability is higher than those of all other ethnic groups.[17]

It is particularly noticeable from Figure 5.2, that compared with other ethnic groups, unqualified Chinese have a very low percentage of unemployment, at 5.7%. Their fitted percentage unemployed is about 27% lower than that of unqualified Indians and 18% lower than that of unqualified Pakistanis. Even compared with whites with similar education, unqualified Chinese are still better at avoiding unemployment. The answer seems to lie with the family oriented Chinese catering business, which gives jobs to members, relatives, and friends of the family, even when it is sometimes not economically viable to do so. Perhaps due to the monopolistic nature of the Chinese catering trade, even the poorly educated Chinese have an edge over unqualified people from other ethnic backgrounds in avoiding unemployment.[18]

---

[15]Any age cohort may be selected because the interaction effect of ethnicity by education is found to be constant across age cohorts. The change of G^2 is 191 with 185 degrees of freedom, when the three way interaction of age by ethnicity by education is fitted.

[16] To check if foreign qualifications and British qualifications of the same level have different rates of translation into avoidance of unemployment for male immigrants, we fit the ethnicity model to all male groups, splitting up into two parts, according to the place where the qualification was received. We have found, as in Appendix 5.4.b, that possession of foreign qualifications reduces the chance (defined as fitted log odds) of avoiding unemployment for Chinese, Indians, and the West Indians. It does not affect Pakistanis.

[17]The obvious bump in the Chinese curve at the level of CSE might be caused by the fact that there are only a small number of people in this category.

[18]I have made several efforts to fit a more parsimonious model for male immigrants, with regard to risks of unemployment, by collapsing categories of ethnicity and education. No unique superior model to the existing one has been identified. The model which comes closest in goodness of fit to the full model is one in which ethnicity and education have both been made binary variables, dichotomizing between Chinese and non-Chinese, and, degree plus A-level and the rest. When the interaction term is added to the model, the change in G^2 is 6 for 2 degrees of freedom. Thus, the fit of the final model is $G^2=267$ and d.f=235. A graphic representation of the interaction effect is given in Appendix 5.5.b. As the interaction of ethnicity by education thus defined is found to remain constant across age cohorts, only those between the age of 35 and 39 have been selected for the sake of illustration.

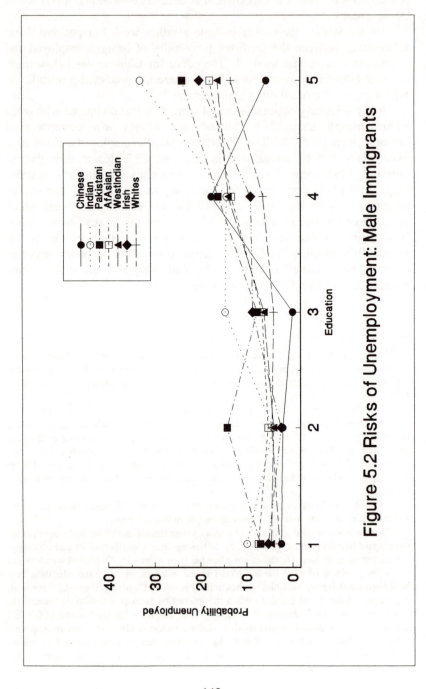

Figure 5.2 Risks of Unemployment: Male Immigrants

In this section, we have found that Chinese male immigrants have rather better chances than other non-white immigrant groups of reaching the service class. The ethnic advantage seems even greater at the higher educational levels. Therefore, with regard to access to the service class, Chinese display a polarized pattern in favour of the well educated. We have also found that Chinese enjoy a greater ethnic advantage in avoidance of unemployment than other ethnic groups. The ethnic advantage seems greater at lower educational levels. Thus, in avoidance of unemployment, Chinese display a less polarized pattern than other ethnic groups in favour of the unqualified.

Female immigrants

In this section, we shall look at ethnic differences in class attainment for female immigrants, in particular, differences between Chinese women and women of other ethnic minorities, as well as British white women. The analysis is divided into two parts, hypothesis testing and explaining the parameter estimates of the best fitting model.

Table 5.9 Modelling Female Immigrants Access to the Service Class (N=7,936)

Model	G2	d.f	ΔG2	Δd.f	p-value	rG^2(%)	ID
Baseline	494.5	217			0.0000		10.90
Ethnicity	302.0	211	192.5	6	0.0000	39	8.01
Control	244.0	172	57.8	39	0.0000	51	7.11
Ethn.Educ	219.0	170	25	2	0.0066	56	6.86

Listed in Table 5.9 are measures of goodness of fit for access to the service class among the female immigrants. It can be seen that the ethnicity model provides a better fit than the baseline model, with the change in G^2 equal to 193 for 6 degrees of freedom, with a reduction in deviance of 39% and a reduction in the Index of Dissimilarity of 2.89. This implies that, age and education being equal, the chances of reaching the service class as against not reaching it vary with ethnic origin. Furthermore, the interaction effect of ethnicity by education is also found to be statistically significant, with the change in G^2 being 25 by a loss of 2 degrees of freedom. By fitting the ethnicity by education model, we reduce deviance by 70% and the Index of Dissimilarity by 4.04. It shows that, other things being equal, the chances of various ethic groups reaching the service class as against not reaching it vary with educational levels. Thus, the null hypotheses of both the ethnicity model and the ethnicity by education model are rejected.

Note, the final model as presented in Table 5.9 is not a full model, in that the interaction of ethnicity by education is fitted after both variables are collapsed. Ethnicity is made into a three category variable, where 1=Chinese, 2=Indians and Pakistanis and 3=African Asians, West Indians, Irish, and Whites. Education is transformed into a binary variable dichotomizing between first-degree and above and all qualifications below the level of first-degree. This is a more parsimonious model than the full model. By saving a few degrees of freedom, we have gained a fit fairly close to that of the full model.[19]

In Appendix 5.3, parameter estimates for the final model are presented. A graphic representation of service class by education for the age cohort of 35-39 is presented in Figure 5.3. The vertical axis stands for predicted probability of reaching the service class and the horizontal axis stands for educational levels in descending order. The three curves represent Chinese, Indians and Pakistanis, and other ethnic groups.

On the whole, the curves show a negative relationship between the probability of reaching the service class and a decreasing level of education.[20] However, the curves are more spread out at degree level rather than at non-degree levels, indicating bigger ethnic differences in the probability of reaching the service class among the qualified than among the unqualified.

It can be seen, for instance, that the curve for Chinese nearly coincides with the curve for Indians and Pakistanis. At both educational levels, Chinese have a similar fitted probability as South Asians of reaching the service class, but Chinese and South Asians have significantly lower fitted

---

[19]In fitting the interaction effect of ethnicity by education, the change in G^2 is 56 for 24 degrees of freedom before both variables are collapsed. The fit of the full model is $G^2=150$ and d.f=120. In addition, in the full model, the interaction effect of ethnicity by education is also found to vary with age cohort. This will make presentation rather difficult. In our preferred final model, the interaction effect of ethnicity by education remains constant across age cohorts. This makes presentation easier. For instance, when the three-way interaction of age by ethnicity by education is fitted, the change in G^2 is 15 for 9 degrees of freedom.

[20]To check if the place where qualifications are obtained makes any difference to occupational returns to education for ethnic minorities, we split up each ethnic minority group into two parts, those receiving the highest qualification in the UK and those receiving it abroad. We find in Appendix 5.4.c that, given the same age and education, chances for reaching the service class are reduced for all ethnic minorities (except Chinese and Irish).

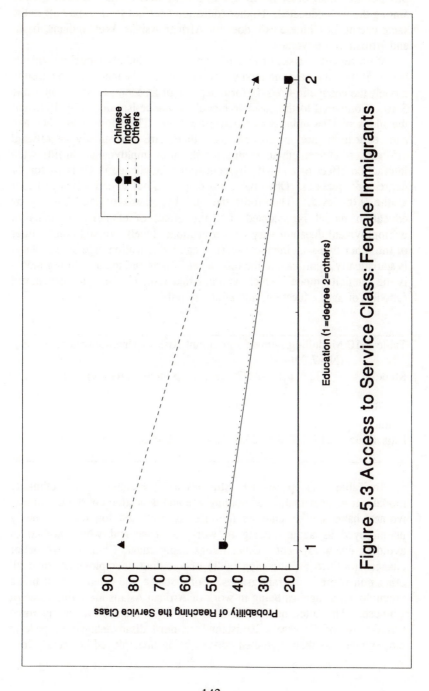

Figure 5.3 Access to Service Class: Female Immigrants

probabilities than other ethnic groups. The discrepancy is even greater among the well educated. Higher education does not seem to pay off to the same extent for Chinese as it does for African Asians, West Indians, Irish, and British white women.

With regard to risks of unemployment, the ethnicity model provides a better fit than the baseline model. When ethnicity is added to the baseline model, the change in G^2 is 43 for 6 degrees of freedom, as shown in Table 5.10. Compared to the baseline model, deviance is reduced by 15% and the Index of Dissimilarity is reduced by 2.39. This shows that when age and education are controlled for, there are statistically significant differences between ethnic groups in risks of unemployment. In fitting the interaction effect of ethnicity by education, the change in G^2 is 24 for 24 degrees of freedom. Obviously, this change is not statistically significant at the 0.05 level. Therefore, the null hypothesis of the ethnicity by education model is accepted, i.e. the effect of ethnicity on risks of unemployment does not vary with educational levels. In addition, neither of the other two-way interactions (i.e. age by education, age by ethnicity) is statistically significant at the 0.05 level. Therefore the best fitting model is the ethnicity model, which assumes that risks of unemployment are a function of age, education, and ethnicity only.

Table 5.10 Modelling Female Immigrant Risk of Unemployment (N=7,936)

Model	G2	d.f	ΔG2	Δd.f	p-value	rG^2(%)	ID
Baseline	284.3	217			0.0015		21.55
Ethnicity	241.1	211	43.3	6	0.0762	15	19.16
Ethn.Educ	217.3	187	23.8	24	0.0636	24	18.11

In Table 5.11, parameter estimates are presented for the ethnicity model. It is clear that, after holding age and education constant, Chinese women have similar chances (defined as predicted log odds of being unemployed as against being in work) as Irish and white women of avoiding unemployment. Other things being equal, Chinese have better chances (defined as fitted log odds) of avoiding unemployment than all other non-white immigrant groups. For instance, the fitted odds of being unemployed as against being in work of African Asians are twice those of Chinese. The fitted odds of Indians and West Indians are nearly three times those of Chinese. Pakistanis are most disadvantaged in seeking employment, as their predicted odds of being unemployed are nearly four times those of Chinese.[21] As the interaction effect of ethnicity by education is found to be statistically insignificant at the 0.05 level, we may conclude that the ethnic advantage enjoyed by Chinese women over all other non-white immigrant women in avoidance of unemployment remains constant at all educational levels.

Table 5.11 Risks of Unemployment: Female Immigrants

	Estimate	s.e.	Parameter
1	-2.984	0.3604	1
2	-0.09736	0.1251	AGE(2)
3	-0.3490	0.1296	AGE(3)
4	-0.6712	0.1421	AGE(4)
5	-0.8186	0.1582	AGE(5)
6	-1.131	0.1834	AGE(6)
7	-0.6036	0.1810	AGE(7)
8	-0.1425	0.3726	AGE(8)
9	-0.1079	0.1907	EDUC(2)
10	0.2311	0.1720	EDUC(3)
11	0.5979	0.1726	EDUC(4)
12	0.7575	0.1596	EDUC(5)
13	**1.096(2.9)[22]**	**0.3462**	**ETHN(2)**
14	**1.469(4.3)**	**0.4277**	**ETHN(3)**
15	**0.807(2.2)**	**0.3472**	**ETHN(4)**
16	**1.028(2.8)**	**0.3658**	**ETHN(5)**
17	0.4650(1.6)	0.3443	ETHN(6)
18	0.4835(1.6)	0.3322	ETHN(7)

---

[21] To check if female immigrants with foreign qualifications have worse chances of avoiding unemployment than female immigrants with British qualification, we fit the ethnicity model to the sample split between those receiving the highest qualification overseas and those receiving it in Britain. We have found, as in Appendix 5.4.d, that only among Indians and Pakistanis are foreign qualifications a disadvantage.

[22] The value in bracket is the fitted odds ratio. It is obtained by exponentiating the parameter to its left.

In this section, we have found that female Chinese immigrants suffer an ethnic penalty with reference to access to the service class, compared with majority whites, Irish, West Indians, and African Asians. The degree of ethnic penalty seems greater at higher educational levels. Among the unqualified, Chinese are not sharply differentiated from other ethnic groups, although they are better placed to avoid unemployment than other non-white immigrants. The ethnic advantage of Chinese in avoiding unemployment is probably because of the existence of the Chinese enclave economy.

These findings have shown similarities and differences between male and female Chinese. With regard to access to the service class, Chinese male immigrants seem to enjoy a much greater ethnic advantage than Chinese female immigrants do. They also display a much more sharply differentiated pattern of class attainment between the well educated and the poorly educated. However, both male and female Chinese immigrants seem to have lower risks of unemployment than their counterparts from most other ethnic backgrounds. Therefore, Chinese immigrants on the whole seem to be protected from unemployment.

The enclave economy

In the above three sections, we studied Chinese class attainments with regard to access to the service class and avoidance of unemployment, given individual characteristics, such as sex, country of birth, age, ethnicity, and education. We have learnt that qualified Chinese, men in particular, have better chances of reaching the service class than other ethnic groups. With regard to risks of unemployment, we have found that both qualified and unqualified Chinese enjoy a certain amount of ethnic advantage in seeking employment.

It has been suggested that the Chinese enclave economy in catering provides a channel for upward mobility and a safety net against unemployment.[23] These statements seem to give support to mounting arguments in favour of comparable economic returns to human capital in the enclave economy as in the wider labour market.[24] In this section, I

---

[23] Runnymede Trust, *The Chinese Community in Britain: The Home Affairs Committee Report in Context* (London: Runnymede Trust, 1986).

[24] R. Waldinger, "Immigrant Enterprise and the Structure of the Labour Market," in R. Finnegan and D. Gallie ed. *New Approaches to Economic Life* (Manchester: Manchester University Press, 1984); S. Model, "A Comparative Perspective on the Ethnic Enclave," *International Migration Review* XIX (1): 64-81, 1986; A. Portes and A. Stepick, "Unwelcomed Immigrants: The Labour Market Experiences of 1980 (Mariel) Cuban and Haitian Refugees in South Florida," *American Sociological Review* 50 (1985) 493-514; K.

shall do a comparative analysis of occupational attainments between Chinese working inside the enclave economy and those working outside it. We shall conduct statistical analysis to test this hypothesis after a brief introduction to the Chinese enclave economy in Britain.

Over more than a century, Chinese established a large ethnic enclave economy by monopolizing restaurants and take-aways serving Chinese cuisine in Britain. Chinese businesses are dispersed all over Britain, although clusters of Chinese businesses, popularly known as "Chinatown", are found in large urban centres, such as London, Manchester, Birmingham, Liverpool and Glasgow. Of today's Chinese working population in Britain, the LFS sample informs us that 57% work in catering and related service jobs.

Chinese migration to the U.K. can be dated back to the middle of the 19th century. In 1851, seventy-eight Chinese from China were recorded living in London. Since then, Chinese immigration history can be divided into two phases: from the mid-nineteenth century to World War II, and from the end of World War II to the present time.[25]

In the nineteenth century, Chinese living in Britain were mainly seamen, who had been recruited to work for the British East India Company from poverty stricken southern China, although there were also small groups of diplomats and students. With the coming of the seamen, a Chinatown began to form in the 1880s in the Limehouse District bordering the West India Docks in London. Streets such as Limehouse Causeway and Pennyfields had Chinese grocery stores, eating houses, and meeting places. Names of Chinese cities were given to the streets, such as "Pekin", "Nanking", and "Canton". All these enhanced the physical and cultural visibility of the Chinese community in Limehouse. At a later date, similar communities of sailors and illegal immigrants (who jumped ship to look for jobs) also emerged in Liverpool and Cardiff.

Towards the turn of the century, Chinese gradually shifted away from dockland occupations to start laundries, which required hard work yet little capital. By 1931, there were 800 Chinese laundries in Britain. A decline in the laundry business set in after the Second World War, largely because of the introduction of washing machines and launderettes. It was during this time that some of the Chinese went into the restaurant business.

After WWII, Britain experienced a resurgence of Chinese immigration. Mainland China ceased to be the major source of migrant workers and the

Wilson and A. Portes, "Immigrant Enclaves: An Analysis of the Labour Market Experiences of Cubans in Miami," *American Journal of Sociology* 86 (1980) 295-319.

[25] A. Shang, *The Chinese in Britain* (London: Batsford Academic and Educational, 1984).

majority of migrants now came from Hong Kong, especially the rural New Territories, to work in the booming post-war catering industry. Jerald Street in Westminster evolved into a new "Chinatown" and today, in the midst of cinemas, restaurants, bingo halls, shops, newspaper stands, and various other establishments of good and ill repute, it still remains the centre of Chinese communal life.[26]

One possible reason for so many Chinese immigrants being directly recruited into the Chinese catering industry might be the voucher system, the legal procedure by which most of the New Territories Chinese migrated. The 1962 Immigration Act demanded that all prospective Commonwealth immigrants be issued with an employment voucher for a specific job for a single employer in Britain before being allowed to enter the country. Moreover, a work permit holder cannot transfer to another employer without permission from the Department of Employment.[27] Voucher holders from the New Territories were mostly relatives of people already settled down in the U.K.. As many their sponsors had already established Chinese restaurants, catering seemed the automatic choice for many newcomers, both as a means of immigration and as a means of making a living. Thus, the existing Chinese enclave economy expanded.

In the following, we shall investigate whether the enclave economy really does bring positive returns to human capitals for immigrants. Hypothesis testing will be done through logit analysis. The independent variables consist of age, education and enclave:

Age:

1=25-29
2=30-34
3=35-39
4=40-44
5=45-49
6=50-54
7=55-59
8=60-64

Education:

1=degree
2=A-level

[26] Linda Yeuk Lin Lai, *Chinese Families in London: A Study into Their Social Needs* (M.A. thesis, Brunell University, 1975) 17.

[27] Susan Baxter, *A Political Economy of the Ethnic Chinese Catering Industry* (Ph.D thesis, University of Aston, 1988) 103.

3 = O-level
4 = CSE
5 = no qualification

Enclave:

1 = enclave
2 = non-enclave.

The enclave is so defined as to include the Chinese working in restaurants and take-aways.[28] It is a division purely based on industrial sector.[29] About 67% of male immigrants and 53% of female immigrants work in the enclave.

We shall test three hypotheses. First, we assume that access to the service class[30] is a function of age and education only. This implies that the effect of sector is independent of access to the service class and risks of unemployment. This model, which we call the baseline model, is written:

$$\text{Ln } (P/1\text{-}P) = \theta_1 + \theta_2(\text{AGE}) + \theta_3(\text{EDUC}).$$

Secondly, the newly developed theory of the enclave economy asserts that economic returns to human capital for people working inside the enclave actually reach parity with those of people working outside it. Therefore, the ethnic enclave economy may serve as an alternative channel for upward mobility to the wider labour market. I shall test this hypothesis for Chinese engaged in traditional catering and those working outside the catering business. This will be done by looking at the effect of the enclave on occupational success, holding age and education constant. This model, which we call the enclave model, looks like this:

---

[28] The enclave is defined as the catering business where Chinese are most likely to be found. It is derived from the variable of "industry", i.e. Standard Industry Code, where category 233 (restaurants, snack bars, cafes and other eating places, eating places supplying food for consumption on the premises) and 234 (take-away food shops) are recoded as the enclave and the rest as non-enclave.

[29] In Zhou and Logan's study of the Chinese enclave economy in New York City, they used three definitions of enclave: place of work, place of residence and industrial sector. The results obtained by using three definitions are found to be similar. See M. Zhou and Logan, "Returns on Human Capital in Ethnic Enclaves: New York City's Chinatown," *American Sociological Review* 54 (1989) 809-820.

[30] Of course, we would like to examine the case of unemployment. However, in LFS, the unemployed are automatically deprived of an "industry of main job". As a result, we can conduct analysis only for access to the service class.

149

$$\text{Ln } (P/1-P) = \delta_1 + \delta_2(AGE) + \delta_3(EDUC) + \delta_4(ENCL).$$

Lastly, we shall test the hypothesis which assumes that, other things being equal, the effect of sector on class varies with education. This hypothesis implies that people with different levels of educational qualification may look for jobs in different labour markets. Those with relatively better education will have expectations higher than catering, not just because many jobs outside the enclave entail higher socio-economic rewards, but also because they do not want to be stigmatized by association with the catering trade. This model, which we call the enclave by education model, is written:

$$\text{Ln } (P/1-P) = \delta 1 + \delta 2(AGE) + \delta 3(EDUC) + \delta 4(ENCL) \\ + \delta_5(AGE*EDUC) + \delta_6(AGE*ENCL) \\ + \delta_7(EDUC*ENCL).^{31}$$

We have found from Table 5.12 that, although the baseline model gives a fairly good fit, with $G^2 = 69$ and d.f=42, the ethnicity model provides an even better fit. The change in G^2 is 28 for 1 degree of freedom, with the percentage reduction in deviance being 39%. The index of dissimilarity is also reduced by 6.49. Moreover, none of the two-way interactions is found to be statistically significant at 0.05 level. Therefore, the enclave model is the best fitting model, with $G^2 = 42$ and d.f=41.

Table 5.12 Modelling Chinese Males Access to the Service Class:
Enclave vs Non-enclave (N=246)

	G^2	d.f	ΔG^2	Δd.f	p-value	$rG^2(\%)$	ID
Baseline	69.0	42			0.0055		22.82
Enclave	41.5	41	27.5	1	0.4487	40	16.33

It can be seen from Table 5.13 that after controlling for age and education, working outside the enclave economy entails better chances (defined as fitted log odds) of reaching the service class than working inside the enclave economy. For instance, age being equal, the fitted odds of a male immigrant working outside the enclave reaching the service class (as against not reaching it) are nearly eleven times those of a male immigrant

---

[31] To conduct a conservative test, we have controlled for two other two-way interactions before adding the interaction of "education by enclave" into the model.

working in the enclave economy. The difference is the same for the qualified as it is for the unqualified.

Next, we shall look at chances of reaching the service class for female immigrants working inside and outside the enclave economy. In Table 5.14, measures of goodness of fit are provided for hypothesis testing. When enclave is added to the baseline model, the change in G^2 is 7 with 1 degree of freedom. This shows that, age and education being equal, chances of reaching the service class vary with sector. Furthermore, we fit the interaction effect of enclave by education. To do a conservative test, we included two other two-way interactions in the model, i.e. age by education and age by enclave. As the interaction effect of enclave by education is not statistically significant at 0.05 level, we take the enclave model as the final model.

Table 5.13 Parameter Estimates for Enclave Economy: Male
        Immigrants

	Estimates	s.e.
Constant	0.2804	0.6850
Age		
25-29	0	
30-34	0.2887	0.5906
35-39	-0.3908	0.5997
40-44	0.3070	0.8075
45-49	-1.557	0.9951
50-54	1.270	0.9207
55-59	0.9259	1.091
60-64	-4.759	19.04
Education		
Degree	0	
A-level	-0.9376	0.6691
O-level	-3.510	0.7711
CSE	-2.859	0.7123
None	-4.204	0.8240
Enclave		
Enclave	0	
Non-enclave	2.368(10.7)	0.4870

$G^2 = 42$ d.f $= 41$

151

Table 5.14 Modelling Chinese Female Access to the Service Class: Enclave vs Non-enclave (N=190)

	G^2	d.f	ΔG^2	Δd.f	p-value	$rG^2(\%)$	ID
Baseline	51.3				0.0169		24.4
Enclave	44.4	31	6.8	1	0.0561	13	21.6

Table 5.15 Parameter Estimates for Enclave Economy: Female Immigrants

	estimate	s.e.	parameter
1	-0.9585	0.7533	1
2	0.4570	0.5539	AGE(2)
3	-0.4727	0.6229	AGE(3)
4	-0.1815	0.7962	AGE(4)
5	0.7686	0.9644	AGE(5)
6	-0.8955	1.427	AGE(6)
7	2.212	1.245	AGE(7)
8	0.000	aliased	AGE(8)
9	0.2165	0.5240	GRAD(2)
10	-0.5734	0.6562	GRAD(3)
11	-1.989	0.9036	GRAD(4)
12	-2.918	0.9082	GRAD(5)
13	**1.482(4.4)**	**0.5929**	**ENCL(2)**

In Table 5.15, parameter estimates are presented for the final model. Other things being equal, women working outside the enclave enjoy better chances (defined as fitted log odds) of reaching the service class. For instance, the predicted odds of a 30-year-old Chinese female graduate working outside the enclave reaching the service class (as against not reaching it) are over 4 times those had she worked inside the enclave. The advantage of working outside the enclave is the same for the well educated as it is for the unqualified.

To summarize, given the same age and education, Chinese working outside the catering trade have an advantage over Chinese working inside the enclave in reaching the service class. The sector difference in terms of fitted odds is constant across all educational levels. This is true for both males and females.

Native-born males and females

In studying the class attainment of native-born males and females, we are confronted with the small N problem, especially in the case of ethnic minorities with a relatively young mean age. Chinese, with a mean age of 7 (the youngest among all ethnic groups), have a sample size of only 18. The Ns for other ethnic groups are 219 for Indians, 58 for Pakistanis, 598 for West Indians, and 8186 for British whites.

In spite of the small N, I did try to fit logit models to compare native-born Chinese with other native-born ethnic groups with regard to chances of reaching the service class and risks of unemployment. All parameter estimates for ethnicity have huge standard errors, so none of the coefficients for ethnicity is statistically significant. The same pattern is found among males and females; a highly unlikely result. Therefore, the results of this statistical analysis are not considered appropriate for report and discussion in this section. More sensible analysis will be conducted when a bigger sample of working British-born Chinese is made available in years to come. Similar analysis of American-born Chinese can already be conducted as a much bigger sample of working American-born Chinese is available (as presented in Chapter 7).

Conclusions

In this chapter, I tried to test hypotheses with regard to ethnic differences in occupational returns to education, in particular the relative level of occupational attainment of Chinese in access to the service class and avoidance of unemployment.

First, polarization seems to be characteristic of Chinese male immigrants (but not Chinese female immigrants) when it comes to access to the service class, where highly qualified Chinese males have better chances than similar males from other ethnic backgrounds.

Secondly, both Chinese male and female immigrants seem to enjoy an ethnic advantage in avoidance of unemployment, in comparison with other ethnic groups, including British whites. On the whole, male Chinese immigrants seem to have a comparatively higher level of class attainments relative to other ethnic groups, than female Chinese immigrants do.[32]

Last, at all educational levels, Chinese working outside the traditional catering trade are more likely to reach the service class than those working inside the enclave. The advantage enjoyed by those working in the wider labour market over those working in the enclave economy is constant at all educational levels. Thus, the enclave economy brings negative returns to class attainment for working Chinese in Britain.

---

[32] As a final note, we have found that among non-white ethnic minorities, especially Afro-Caribbeans and South Asians, people with highest qualifications received outside Britain experience disadvantage in access to the service class and avoidance of unemployment, even compared with people from their own groups and with equivalent British qualifications.

6 Demographic profile of Chinese in the United States

Introduction

In the previous three chapters, I have studied the demographic profile, education and class attainments of Chinese in Britain. In this chapter and the following one, I will present results on similar topics for Chinese in the USA. I have two purposes in this chapter. First, I will draw a demographic profile of Chinese in the USA, i.e. a static picture of such demographic characteristics as population composition and population distribution in 1980. The purpose is to bring out Chinese demographic potentials, which may positively or negatively contribute to their level of occupational success,[1] through comparisons with majority whites and major ethnic minorities in contemporary America. Secondly, where possible, I will draw parallels in demographic potentials between Chinese in the USA and Chinese in Britain. The purpose is to pave the way for the final comparative analysis of Chinese class attainments in the two countries.

With regard to demographic characteristics, I will examine ethnic composition, country of birth, year of arrival, sex composition, age composition, and regional distribution. In addition, I will look at two indicators which affect subsequent occupational integration, the level of English speaking and the highest year of school attended.

---

[1]Robert Jiobu, *Ethnicity and Assimilation: Blacks, Chinese, Filipinos, Japanese, Koreans, Mexicans, Vietnamese and Whites* (Albany: State University of New York Press, 1988).

155

Ethnic composition

The present data file contains two parts, namely, Asian Americans, who consist of Japanese, Chinese, Koreans, Filipinos, Indians and Vietnamese, and the others, who consist of whites, blacks and Hispanics. The Asian Americans have been extracted from the 1980 census 5% Public Use Microdata Sample (PUMS A), by including all households containing at least one Asian American. This procedure eliminates households not containing Asian Americans. So a smaller sample of whites, blacks and Hispanics has been extracted from a 0.1% Public Use Microdata Sample (PUMS A). Thus, the present data represent 5% of the population of Asian Americans and 0.1% of the population of whites, blacks and Hispanics.

The variable "race" is used to classify groups of different origins. According to the U.S. Census Bureau, "race" reflects self-identification by respondents and does not denote any clear-cut scientific definition of biological stock. Thus the information on "race" in the 1980 US census represents self-classification by people according to the race with which they identify themselves.[2]

People of Spanish origin have been placed in the "white" racial group,[3] with a separate indicator showing origin as "Mexican", "Puerto Rican", "Cuban", and "other Spanish", etc. Thus the Hispanics included in this study are defined as those whose race is "white" and whose origin is "Mexican", "Puerto Rican", "Cuban", or "other Spanish". The other racial groups, such as whites, blacks, and Asian Americans, are selected in such a way that there are no overlaps between them and Hispanics.

Listed in Table 6.1 are Ns for all individual racial groups included in the analysis. Among the Asians, Chinese appear to be the largest group, closely followed by Japanese and Filipinos. Asian Indians and Koreans have a similar group size, which is about half that of Chinese, Japanese, and Filipinos. Vietnamese have a smaller group size, which is only about one third that of Chinese, Japanese, and Filipinos. The group size of blacks is about 15% that of whites, and the group size of Hispanics is about 5% that of whites.

---

[2] Inter-university Consortium for Political and Social Research. *Census of Population and Housing, 1980 (Unites States): Public Use Microdata Samples* (Ann Arbor: ICPSR, 1984) K-37.

[3] Robert Jiobu, *Ethnicity and Assimilation: Blacks, Chinese, Filipinos, Japanese, Koreans, Mexicans, Vietnamese and Whites* (Albany: State University of New York Press, 1988) 61.

It is difficult to compare directly the group sizes of Asian Americans with those of other groups, as the sample sources are different. To obtain a picture of racial and ethnic composition, we have constructed a pie chart as Figure 6.1. The percent distribution of racial groups is obtained from the 0.1% Public Use Microdata Sample (PUMS A).

Group size forms an important demographic potential, which has been found to affect the level of occupational integration of an ethnic minority. Previous studies on American blacks, Hispanics and whites, for instance, showed that the larger the relative size of an ethnic minority, the greater the majority-minority disparities in income.[4] Similar results have also been obtained for occupational disparity.[5] The premise seems to be that a smaller ethnic minority tends to incur less racial hostility in the pursuit of socio-economic success.

Table 6.1 Sample Sizes for All Ethnic Groups

Racial Group	N
Japanese	35,625
Chinese	40,253
Filipino	34,159
Korean	17,954
Asian Indian	19,400
Vietnamese	12,508
Hispanics	8,414
Blacks	26,378
White	180,392
Total	375,083

[4] Hubert M. Blalock, "Economic Discrimination and Negro Increase," *American Sociological Review* 22 (October, 1956) 584-588; Hubert M. Blalock, "Percent Nonwhite and Discrimination in the South," *American Sociological Review* 22 (December, 1957) 677-682; W. Frisbie and L. Neidert, "Inequality and the Relative Size of Minority Populations: A Comparative Analysis," *American Journal of Sociology* 82 (1977) 1007-1030.

[5] David Brown and Glenn V. Fuguitt, "Percent Nonwhite and Racial Disparity in Nonmetropolitan Cities in the South," *Social Science Quarterly* 53 (December, 1972) 573-582.

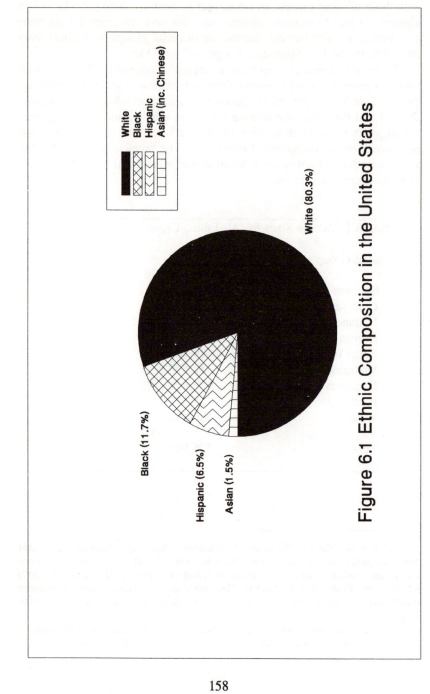

Figure 6.1 Ethnic Composition in the United States

Compared with blacks and Hispanics, American Asians altogether share a much smaller piece of the pie. If the connection between group size and socio-economic disparity is correct, we would expect Asian Americans to face less opposition than blacks and Hispanics and to achieve greater socio-economic attainments.

A notable fact revealed by the 1980 census is that the Chinese population has superseded the Japanese for the first time and become the most populous Asian American group.[6] This may increase the visibility of Chinese in America. Whether it is going to increase the amount of hostility to Chinese and subsequently affect their level of socio-economic success is yet to be seen.

Country of birth

In Figure 6.2, a pie chart has been created to show the country of origin of Chinese. It can be seen that about 34% of Chinese were born in America. Forty-two percent immigrated from China and Taiwan, nearly 14% from Hong Kong and nearly 3% from Vietnam, with the rest from other parts of the world.

One noticeable difference between the country of origin of Chinese in the USA and that of Chinese in Britain is that, while Hong Kong contributes the great majority of Chinese immigrants in Britain, mainland China and Taiwan seem to contribute the great majority of Chinese immigrants in the USA. Hong Kong's colonial connection with Britain and its status as a member of the British Commonwealth may explain why Britain was a preferred country of destination, especially during the post-war years.

It ought to be noted that other ethnic minorities also consist of people born in the U.S. and people born in the country of origin. In the former case, they are second or subsequent generations, and in the latter case, they are immigrants. By allowing distinctions between American-born and foreign-born, the ethnic minorities are further distributed as in Table 6.2.

[6]Shi-shan Henry Tsai, *The Chinese Experience in America* (Bloomington: Indiana University Press, 1986).

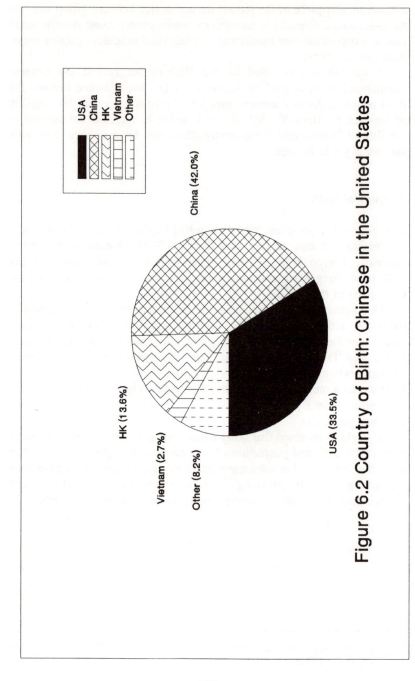

Figure 6.2 Country of Birth: Chinese in the United States

Table 6.2 Percent Country of Birth: Ethnic Minorities in USA

Ethnic/Country	Number	% of Own Ethnic Group Total
Japanese/foreign	10,906	30.6
Japanese/USA	24,719	69.3
Chinese/foreign	26,103	64.8
Chinese/USA	14,150	35.2
Filipino/foreign	23,393	68.5
Filipino/USA	10,766	31.5
Korean/foreign	14,988	83.5
Korean/USA	2,966	16.5
Indian/foreign	13,833	71.3
Indian/USA	5,567	28.7
Vietnamese/foreign	11,416	91.3
Vietnamese/USA	1,092	8.7
Black/foreign	750	2.8
Black/USA	25,801	97.2
Hispanics/foreign	4,837	33.9
Hispanics/USA	9,448	66.1

The ratio of foreign-born to American-born may be an important indicator of cultural assimilation. With many migrant groups, an American-born second generation, who absorb the English language and adopt the American customs via school, may be effective in helping their foreign-born parents to adopt the American way of life and become acculturated.[7]

Moreover, it has also been argued by some researchers that the degree of cultural assimilation bears a positive relationship to the level of socio-

---

[7]Standford Lyman, *Chinese Americans* (New York: Random House, 1974) 112-115.

economic success.[8]   Therefore, a connection between a greater proportion of native-born and a higher level of socio-economic success may be established, though we are aware that cultural assimilation is only a necessary, and not a sufficient, condition for subsequent occupational integration.[9]

Of all ethnic minorities, blacks have the highest proportion of American-born, at 97%. Among Asian Americans, Japanese have the greatest proportion of American-born, at 69%. Chinese, Filipinos, and Asian Indians each have around 30% American-born, their percentages being about half that of Japanese. Koreans and Vietnamese have the lowest percentage of native-born, with 17% and 9% respectively. This finding is no surprise, because the last two groups are the most recent immigrant groups.

Year of arrival

It is suggested that duration in the country of destination is positively related to the degree of cultural assimilation. According to Gordon, this is because "cultural assimilation or acculturation is likely to be the first of the types of assimilation to occur when a minority group arrives on the scene".[10] So, year of arrival, which directly affects duration in the host country, may be useful in establishing the level of cultural assimilation. Of course, for those people who choose non-assimilation through conscious effort, the link may be weak.

In Figure 6.3, cumulative percentages by year of arrival are displayed for Asian Americans, blacks and Hispanics. The percentage shows what proportion of an ethnic group had already immigrated by a given year, i.e. not just the people arriving in that year, but also those who came before.

Three patterns are readily discernable in Figure 6.3. First, over the three decades from 1950 to 1980, Hispanics had the most even increase of immigration. Among Asian Americans, Japanese experienced the most even increase, despite a sharp percentage increase in the mid-1970s. The duration of these two groups also seems to be the longest of all immigrant groups. By 1950, over 40% of Hispanics had already arrived in the USA,

---

[8] D. Montero and R. Tsukashima, "Assimilation and Educational Attainments: the Case of the Second Generation Japanese American," *Sociological Quarterly* 18 (1977) 490-503.

[9] Milton Gordon, *Assimilation in American Life: The Role of Race, Religion and National Origin* (New York: Oxford University, 1964) 80-81.

[10] Gordon, p.77.

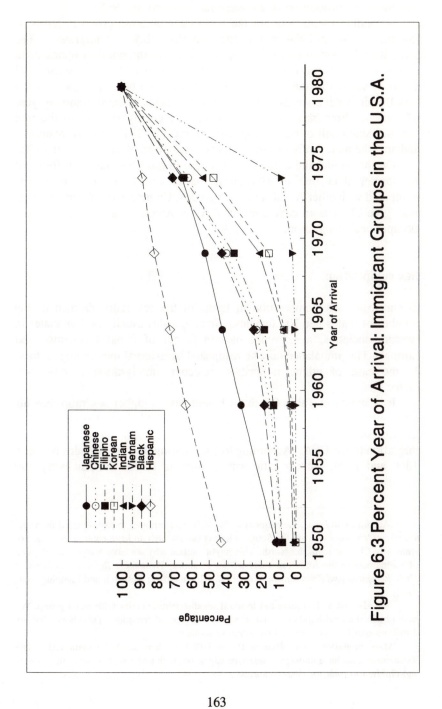

Figure 6.3 Percent Year of Arrival: Immigrant Groups in the U.S.A.

and the same proportion of Japanese had arrived by 1965.

Secondly, Vietnamese are the youngest immigrant group in terms of duration. Up until the mid 1970s, less than 10% had migrated. The majority migrated after 1974, presumably due to the political upheaval in Vietnam. Like Great Britain, America also participated in the international effort to settle Vietnamese refugees.[11] Among the other groups, Chinese and Filipinos have similar cumulative percentages of immigrants by year of arrival. Both saw immigration increase greatly starting in the mid 1960s. About half of both groups had migrated by 1970. For Koreans and Indians, the major influx of immigrants did not take place until after 1970.

On the whole, the duration of Chinese in the USA has been found to be shorter than that of Hispanics, blacks and Japanese. However, compared with other Asian American groups, Chinese arrived earlier. This may give Chinese an edge over most Asian American groups in terms of occupational integration.

Sex composition

We measure sex composition in terms of the sex ratio, defined as the number of males per 100 females. Since females usually outlive males in western societies, a sex imbalance in favour of females is considered normal. This imbalance may be readjusted by external intervening factors. In the case of ethnic minorities, selective immigration is one such factor.[12]

It is shown in Table 6.3 that Chinese have a higher sex ratio than all other ethnic groups, except Vietnamese.[13] An imbalanced sex ratio with a male surplus was already noted during the early phase of Chinese migration to the USA. According to Tsai, during the four decades between 1860 and 1900, the sex ratio was as high as 1,963, i.e. for every 100

---

[11] According to Jones, the majority of the Veitanese refugees to have entered the U.K. are ethnic Vietnamese from the South, whereas the majority to have entered the U.K are ethnically Chinese from the North. This might explain why we have a separate category of Vietnamese in the American analysis. See P. Jones, *Vietnamese Refugees: A Study of Their Reception and Resettlement in the U.K.* (Home Office: Research and Planning Unit, 1982).

[12] We also did a chi-square test to see if sex distribution varies with racial group. We have obtained a likelihood ratio of 1,468 with 8 degrees of freedom. This shows that sex distribution differs from one ethnic group to another.

[13] Mass migration took place in the mid-1970s, when South Vietnam fell. The Vietnamese must have undergone selective migration, with males sent ahead of the females and children to look for chances abroad.

164

Chinese women, there were 1,963 Chinese men. This was considered a direct consequence of the early immigrants being primarily male bonded labourers, and later the notorious Chinese Exclusion Act of 1882 prevented the replenishment of the female Chinese population from abroad.[14]

Table 6.3 Sex Ratio by Ethnic Group

Ethnic group	Sex ratio
Japanese	84
Chinese	101
Filipino	91
Korean	72
Asian Indian	100
Vietnamese	105
Whites	94
Blacks	88
Hispanics	98

Filipinos, Indians, and Hispanics have similar normal sex ratios, compared with whites. But blacks, Japanese and Koreans have lower sex ratios. In the case of blacks, differential infant mortality against black male babies may be the explanation. Japanese and Koreans were by tradition male dominated immigrant groups. War brides after WWII and the Korean war then eased the situation, and, up until 1965, a lot more Japanese and Korean women than men entered the country.[15] The different patterns of sex distribution for different ethnic groups may also be observed from the ethnic population pyramids in the next section.

Age composition

In this section, two measures will be used to describe the age structure of ethnic groups. First, group mean age will be calculated to summarize the

---

[14] S. Lyman, *Chinese Americans* (New York: Random House, 1974) 80-81.
[15] Hyung-chan Kim, "Koreans," *Harvard Encyclopedia of American Ethnic Groups* ed. Thernstrom and Almond (Cambridge: Massachusetts, 1980) 604.

level of seniority. Then, population pyramids will be constructed to show the age structure of different ethnic groups.

Table 6.4 Mean Age of Ethnic Groups

Ethnicity	Mean Age	s.d.
Japanese	35	20
Chinese	31	20
Filipino	30	20
Korean	26	17
Asian Indian	30	20
Vietnamese	23	16
Whites	35	22
Blacks	29	21
Hispanics	27	20

It can be seen in Table 6.4 that Japanese and whites display the highest mean age of 35. Vietnamese have the lowest mean age of 23, a gap of 12 years. Chinese are at an intermediate level, with an average age of 31. In general, Chinese are younger than whites and Japanese but older than all other ethnic minority groups.

A group mean age in the twenties indicates that the group under discussion entered the labour market only a short time ago and, in a society where seniority counts in occupational success, the group might only be starting to get established. A group with a mean age in the mid thirties may be in a higher socio-economic position than a group ten years younger. In this respect, Chinese may be in a slightly less advantageous position than Japanese and whites in regard to occupational success.

In Figures 4-12, population pyramids have been constructed for each ethnic group. A population pyramid is a bar chart used to display the sex and age composition of a population or group. It has two parts, males on the left and females on the right. The middle axis stands for age categories, ten-year intervals in our case, and the length of the horizontal bars displays the population of a particular age-sex subgroup. Note, the data used in Figures 4-12 are numbers of people in the sample; strictly speaking, total populations should be used. The shape of the pyramid provides information not only on the long term population trajectory, but

Figure 6.4 Age by Sex: Japanese

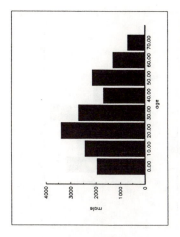
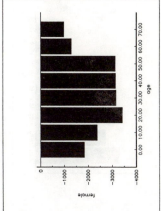

Figure 6.5 Age by Sex: Chinese

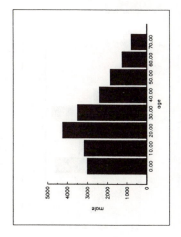
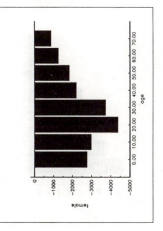

Figure 6.6 Age by Sex: Filipino

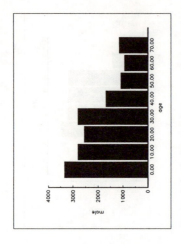

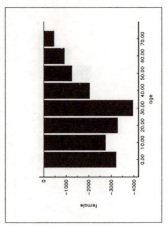

Figure 6.7 Age by Sex: Korean

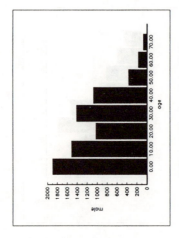

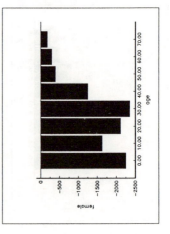

Figure 6.8 Age by Sex: Indian

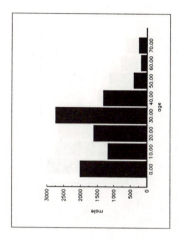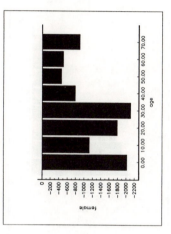

Figure 6.9 Age by Sex: Vietnamese

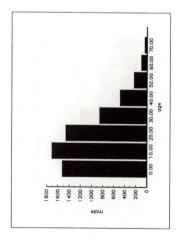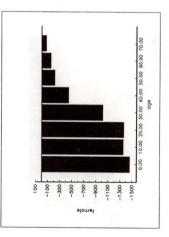

Figure 6.10 Age by Sex: Hispanic

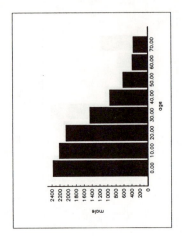
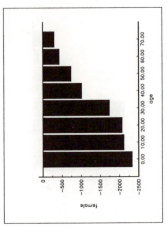

Figure 6.11 Age by Sex: Black

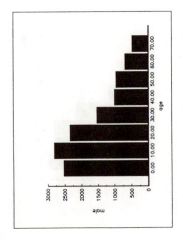
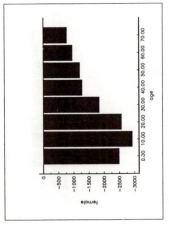

Figure 6.12 Age by Sex: White

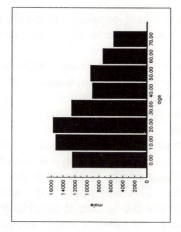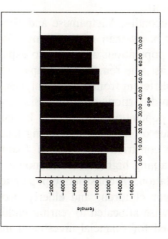

also on the level of dependency, a non-negligible factor in studying inter-racial group socio-economic differentials.

The population pyramids in Figures 4-12 may be classified into three types. First, Chinese, like Japanese, whites and blacks, have a population pyramid with a base narrower than the mid-portion. This means that they have a constrictive population and do not have large number of young children.

Secondly, Vietnamese and Hispanics have population pyramids with wider bases than mid-portions. With a big reserve of younger people, these populations are going to expand.

Last, the remaining groups, such as Indians, Filipinos, and Koreans, look different from both prototypes. Their population pyramids have bases and mid-portions of similar size and taper off quickly at the top. Thus, their population growth will be fairly stationary in the long run, in the absence of external intervening factors.

A constrictive population, like the Chinese, may have some advantage in attaining higher socio-economic status than an expansive or stationary population. A constrictive population has a smaller number of dependents, younger children, and elderly people. This may imply that resources otherwise allocated to rearing children and taking care of the elderly can be used for financial investment instead. In addition, such a population profile may be beneficial to young people entering the labour market, because they face less competition from their own cohort. Finally, with a big mid-portion and a smaller base, a constrictive population may have greater earning power than an expansive one and thus be able to invest more in younger generation in terms of education and training conducive to a good start in working life.

Geographical distribution

The study of ethnic geographical distribution in America can be conducted at different levels, such as census tract, SMSA (Standard Metropolitan Statistical Area), and state. For instance, a conventional approach deals with the level of ethnic spatial or residential assimilation. The analysis is normally done within the census tract.

Ethnic spatial compactness and contiguity have become established fact in America, in the form of black ghettos and Chinatowns, and have long been associated with socio-economic deprivation. However, this association remains hypothetical. Empirically, spatial segregation (normally measured by the index of dissimilarity, i.e. the percentage of a group that would have to change census tracts in order to be equally

172

distributed across the city), has been found to bear little relation to socio-economic status.[16] Although Chinese have higher income than blacks, for instance, their degree of segregation is about the same.[17] Because of this weak link, spatial segregation may be considered to possess little value in accounting for ethnic socio-economic differentials, or vice versa. Therefore, it will not be pursued further in this thesis.

SMSA, which separates metropolitan areas from surrounding areas, may be a useful indicator for studying ethnic geographical distribution. It may be particularly effective in identifying ethnic enclave economies, which tend to form in the centre of large metropolitan areas. Unfortunately, the data set on which this secondary analysis is based does not identify all SMSAs. Therefore, it may not be appropriate to use this indicator for studying various ethnic minorities, who may have concentrations in SMSAs that are not picked up.[18]

In this section, we deal with the geographical distribution of Chinese at state level only. As in the analysis of Chinese in Britain, we take ethnic geographical distribution to be indicative of, among other things, job availability in the wider labour market and the existence of the ethnic enclave economy.

In Figure 6.13, ethnic geographical distribution at state level is presented. It takes the form of cumulative percentage. The X-axis stands for any ten most densely populated states ranked in descending order. For different ethnic groups, these states may be different either in name or in ranking order. In the case of Chinese, for instance, about 37% live in the first most densely populated state and 20% in the second most densely populated state. Thus, around 57% live in the first two states, nearly 70% live the first five states, and over three quarters in the first ten states.

As far as inter-group comparison is concerned, whites and blacks have the lowest degree of concentration at state level, perhaps because both groups have resided in the country for a long time. Slightly over half of whites and nearly 60% of blacks reside in the first ten states. Filipinos, Japanese, Chinese, and Hispanics are at the other end of the spectrum, all with over 80% concentrated in the first ten states.

---

[16] Douglas Massey and Nancy Denton, "Trends in the Residential Segregation of Blacks, Hispanics, and Asians: 1970-1980," *American Sociological Review* 52 (December, 1988) 802-825.

[17] Jiobu, 1988. p.115.

[18] See U.S. Department of Commerce, Bureau of the Census, *Census of Population and Housing, 1980 (United States) Public Use Microdata Samples* (Ann Arbor: ICPSR, 1984) Appendix B1.

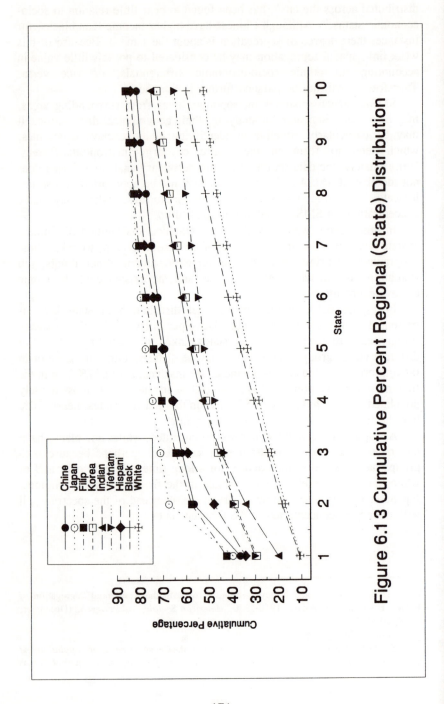

Figure 6.13 Cumulative Percent Regional (State) Distribution

Asian American groups with a shorter duration in the USA, such as Indians, Koreans, and Vietnamese, nevertheless appear to be more dispersed geographically.

Recency of immigration seems unable to explain ethnic geographical distribution at state level. Longer duration in the country of destination does not necessarily bring about gradual dispersion of the ethnic group. Cultural elements may help shape the choice of place of residence.[19] In the case of Chinese, for instance, states with large residential concentrations, such as New York and California, have major metropolitan centres, where the Chinese enclave economy is likely to exist. In 1980, 70% of Chinese reported to reside in an identified SMSA live in city centre.

Level of English speaking

Immigrants may differ in their English speaking level according to their exposure to English before and after arrival. Proficiency in any language, other than the mother tongue, depends on such factors as country of birth, length of duration in the host country in the case of immigrants, schooling, motivation, and, when language becomes a political issue, external pressure.

It should be mentioned that English speaking ability, as measured by the U.S. census bureau, may not serve as a clear indicator of cultural assimilation. At the methodological level, the variable has been constructed from the responses given by the people who answered the questionnaire. Answers from an untrained observer may introduce bias to an unknown extent. In addition, at the conceptual level, good English is hard to define, as the immigrants may come from bilingual countries where the English commonly spoken is but a deviation of proper English.

It can be seen from Table 6.5 that, among Asian American immigrants, Indians and Filipinos have the highest percentage of people who claim to speak English very well. In both groups, the overwhelming majority speak English well, probably due to colonial legacy of Britain in India and America in the Philippines.

Compared with Indians and Filipinos, other Asian American groups have lower proportions of people speaking English well or very well. Chinese have the highest percentage of people not speaking English well at all, at 11%. These may be uneducated labourers surviving in the enclave economy, where Chinese is the major means of communication.

---

[19] Jiobu, p. 115.

Because of this, we conjecture that Chinese may be more differentiated in terms of education received than other ethnic groups.

Table 6.5 English Speaking Level by Ethnic Origin[20]

Level	Japanese	Chinese	Filipino	Korean	Indian	Vietnam	Hispanic
Very Well	30.0	31.6	56.1	29.3	66.2	20.6	49.0
Well	39.4	33.2	34.4	39.0	24.3	37.3	28.0
Not Well	26.2	23.7	8.5	25.9	7.4	31.9	15.4
Not Well at All	4.5	11.4	1.0	5.8	2.0	10.2	7.6
Total	100.0	100.0	100.0	100.0	100.0	100.0	100.0
N	35625.0	40253.0	34159.0	17954.0	19400.0	12508.0	21160.0

Education

In America, universal education is claimed to have provided equal opportunities for occupational success. "Virtually everyone favours equality, but at the same time everyone feels comfortable in the face of great inequality. Evidently it is not unequal wealth that people object to, but unequal opportunity. As long as people can believe that everyone has a fair chance, then success or failure can produce morally acceptable inequality".[21] In this section, I shall examine the relative level of educational attainments of Chinese. The purpose is to see whether Chinese enter the competition for occupational success on an equal basis with other ethnic groups.

The variable used as an indicator of education is "grade", or "the highest year of school attended". It has 22 categories coded as follows:

    0=never attended school   High School:
      or N/A if under 3   11=ninth grade
      years of age   12=tenth grade

---

[20] The whites and Blacks are not included because the question does not apply to 97% of the Blacks and 95% of the whites, mainly because English is the only language spoken by these people.

[21] Jiobu, *Ethnicity and Assimilation*, p.180.

176

| 1 =nursery school | 13 =eleventh grade |
| 2 =kindergarten | 14 =twelfth grade |

Elementary	College:
3 =first grade	15 =first year
4 =second grade	16 =second year
5 =third grade	17 =third year
6 =fourth grade	18 =fourth year
7 =fifth grade	19 =fifth year
8 =sixth grade	20 =sixth year
9 =seventh grade	21 =seventh year
10 =eighth grade	22 =eighth year or more.[22]

It can be seen that this variable is measured in terms of years. For instance, those finishing nursery school are considered as attending school for one year, those finishing kindergarten are considered as attending school for two years. It follows that those finishing elementary school are regarded as attending school for ten years, those finishing high school fourteen years, etc.

Table 6.6 Mean Highest Year of School Attended

	Mean Year	s.d.
Whites	12.0910	5.5916
Blacks	10.3704	5.2640
Hispanic	9.5622	5.5916
Chinese	13.2536	6.0942
Japanese	13.6195	4.9207
Filipino	13.7448	5.3800
Koreans	12.2438	5.8671
Indians	15.1825	6.1292
Vietnamese	10.5669	5.5154

Listed in Table 6.6 are the mean highest year of school attended for all Asian Americans, blacks, Hispanics, and whites. It can be seen that

[22] U.S. Department of Commerce, *Census of Population and Housing*, p.80.

177

Chinese have a mean of 13 years schooling, which is equivalent to reaching the eleventh grade. They have
a similar average level of education as Japanese and Filipinos. Indians, however, have a much higher mean year of school attended than Chinese. The average Indian American has an educational level equivalent to finishing the first year at college. All other ethnic groups, whites, blacks, Hispanics, Koreans, and Vietnamese have lower mean scores than Chinese. Thus, compared with non-Asian American groups, Chinese have longer years of schooling on average. Compared to most other Asian Americans, Chinese have an intermediate level of school duration.

In the next section, I will explore the relationship between education and demographic characteristics, such as sex, age, and ethnicity. The dependent variable is the educational level, a four category variable obtained from the highest year of school attended, where 1 =postgraduate, 2 =college, 3 =high school completion, and 4 =not completing high school.[23] The independent variables include age, coded as 1 =25-29, 2 =30-34, 3 =35-39, 4 =40-44, 5 =45-49, 6 =50-54, 7 =55-59, 8 =60-64; sex, coded as 1 =male, 2 =female; and ethnicity, coded as 1 =Chinese, 2 =Japanese, 3 =Filipino, 4 =Korean, 5 =Indian, 6 =Vietnamese, 7 =whites, 8 =blacks, and 9 =Hispanics. The logit model looks like this:

$$\text{Ln } (P/1\text{-}P) = \delta_1 + \delta_2(\text{age}) + \delta_3(\text{sex}) + \delta_4(\text{ethnicity})$$

and the parameter estimates are in the form of fitted log odds ratios, expressed by:

$$\text{Ln}[(F_{ij}{:}F_{0j}) \, / \, (F_{i0}{:}F_{00})]$$

in the simple case with no control variables, where i refers to education, j refers to ethnic group, i =0 represents not completing high school, and j =0 represents Chinese. Therefore, we compare the fitted log odds of the jth ethnic group with those of Chinese.

Listed in Table 6.7 are parameter estimates for ethnicity after controlling for the age and sex of the immigrants.[24] First, given the same age and sex, Japanese have a similar chance (defined as fitted log odds) as

---

[23] In recoding the highest year of school attended into the four category educational level, I combined codes 19 to 22 into 1 =post-graduate, 15 to 18 into 2 =college, 14 into 3 =completing high school and 1 to 13 into 4 =not completing high school.

[24] It can be seen from the deviance and degrees of freedom that the model presented is not a best fitting model. However, the purpose of this analysis is simply to see the ethnic differences in educational attainments given the same age and education, therefore, modelling the data has not been given priority.

Chinese to pursue post-graduate education as against not even completing high school. The fitted log odds of Chinese having postgraduate education as against not even completing high school are higher than the fitted log odds of Koreans, Vietnamese, Hispanics, blacks, and whites. In other words, the fitted odds of Chinese pursuing post-graduate education as against not completing high school are about 1.3 times those of Koreans, 1.6 times those of whites, around 5 times those of Vietnamese and Hispanics, and nearly 9 times those of blacks. But Filipinos and Indians have rather greater fitted log odds than Chinese of doing so.

Where access to college education is concerned, all other Asian American immigrant groups, except Vietnamese, have better chances than Chinese of receiving college education as against not completing high school. Whites also have much better chances than Chinese of doing so. Their predicted odds of having college education versus not completing high school are 1.6 times those of Chinese. Finally, Chinese have worse chances (defined as fitted log odds) than all other ethnic groups, except Vietnamese and Hispanics, of completing high school versus not completing high school.

Table 6.7 Parameter Estimates for Qualification by Ethnicity: Foreign-born

	Postgrad.	College	High School	Below High.
Chinese	0.	0.	0.	0.
Japanese	.0299	**1.1790**	**1.4703**	0.
	(.0538)	(.0440)	(.0448)	
Filipino	**.3716**	**.9210**	**.1534**	0.
	(.0347)	(.0321)	(.0381)	
Korean	-.2781	.5966	.7956	0.
	(.0451)	(.0385)	(.0407)	
Indian	**1.1794**	**.6255**	**.1634**	0.
	(.0407)	(.0421)	(.0497)	
Vietnam	**-1.6518**	**-.3057**	**-.0287**	0.
	(.0615)	(.0425)	(.0454)	
Hispanic	**-1.5169**	**-.5012**	**-.1272**	0.
	(.0452)	(.0348)	(.0366)	
Black	**-2.1684**	**-.6465**	**.2510**	0.
	(.0530)	(.0340)	(.0329)	
Whites	**-.5063**	**.4933**	**1.1650**	0.
	(.0257)	(.0238)	(.0256)	
likelihood ratio=3496	d.f=126			

These patterns clearly indicate that Chinese immigrants are polarized in terms of educational attainment. A portion of Chinese have better chances to be highly qualified, compared with many other ethnic groups. But there are certainly Chinese whose chances of attaining even the minimum educational level are worse than those of other ethnic groups.

Listed in Table 6.8 are parameter estimates for qualification by ethnicity for native-born Asian Americans and three non-Asian American control groups. At all educational levels, native-born Chinese seem to have better chances (defined as fitted log odds) of avoiding poor education than all other ethnic groups. Only in one case do Japanese have better chances than Chinese of achieving a higher educational level. The fitted odds of Japanese completing high school as against not completing it are nearly three times those of Chinese.

Table 6.8 Parameter Estimates for Qualification by Ethnicity: Native-born

	Postgrad.	College	High School	Below High
Chinese	0.	0.	0.	0.
Japanese	-.5799	-.2392	.2528	0.
	(.0712)	(.0667)	(.0692)	
Filipino-	2.5686	-1.4392	-.4276	0.
	(.1142)	(.0866)	(.0859)	
Korean	-.8738	-.6464	-.1598	0.
	(.1886)	(.1677)	(.1679)	
Indian	-1.6718	-1.6575	-.8727	0.
	(.1270)	(.1092)	(.1030)	
Vietnam	-2.2690	-1.8956	-.9507	0.
	(.4465)	(.3523)	(.3277)	
Hispanic	-3.0067	-2.4121	-1.7821	0.
	(.0738)	(.0656)	(.0684)	
Black	-3.6554	-2.5558	-1.4064	0.
	(.0788)	(.0651)	(.0664)	
White	-1.9534	-1.3831	-.4794	0.
	(.0636)	(.0602)	(.0630)	

likelihood ratio=2058 d.f=126

Inter-generational difference in the relative level of educational attainments is clear in the case of Chinese. Compared to foreign-born

Chinese, native-born Chinese seem more qualified than all other ethnic groups, when age and sex are held constant. Polarization in the level of education, which characterizes immigrant Chinese does not exist among native-born Chinese. Instead, native-born Chinese seem to enjoy ethnic advantage over all other groups, including majority whites, at (nearly) all educational levels.

Conclusions

Chinese do not possess the most favourable demographic profile among Asians American. Their group size being the largest, their percentage of native-born is less than half that of Japanese. It is true that they have a constrictive population pyramid, but the mean age of Chinese is four years younger than that of Japanese. In addition, males still outnumber females, a result of selective immigration in the past. Geographically, with over half of the population living in two states, Chinese are more concentrated than many Asian groups.

Regarding indicators of assimilation, the length of duration of Chinese in the U.S. is shorter than that of Japanese but similar to that of Filipinos. Their level of English proficiency is equivalent to that of Koreans and Vietnamese and falls behind that of other Asian groups. This shows that ties with the country of origin are still close for Chinese, and this might serve as a barrier to cultural assimilation.

On the educational level, Chinese share with Japanese the same mean years of schooling, but fall behind Indians by a big gap of three years. They occupy an intermediate level in terms of mean years of schooling. However, when age and sex are held constant, Chinese immigrants exhibit a pattern of polarization between the extremely well-qualified and the poorly qualified, a pattern reminiscent of that of Chinese immigrants in Britain. American-born Chinese enjoy an ethnic advantage over all others in attaining better education.

To summarize, compared with other Asian groups (except Japanese), Chinese seem to have more favoured demographic characteristics. In losing ties with the past and gaining new identities, Chinese immigrants significantly lag behind Japanese, Indians, and Filipinos. The extraordinary educational attainments of American-born Chinese, however, may indicate a strong desire for occupational success and an effort to overcome the demographic handicap and educational disadvantage faced by many immigrant Chinese.

7 Occupational attainments of Chinese in the United States

Introduction

In 1980, the U.S. Commission for Civil Rights published a report entitled "Success of Asian Americans: Fact or Fiction?". Based on the 1970 U.S. Census of Population and Housing, it stated that, while many Asian Americans, including Chinese, were in high-paying occupational categories, a disproportionately large number of Asian Americans were also in low-paying jobs. With regard to Chinese Americans, in particular, researchers found that although the proportion of Chinese in the professional and technical occupations was large compared with majority Americans, and although their proportion in managerial and administrative occupations was equivalent to that of majority Americans, Chinese were yet over-represented among the several lowest paying occupations.[1]

In this chapter, I study the relative level of occupational attainments of Chinese in the 1980s through comparisons with majority American whites and other major ethnic minorities. The purpose is to see whether the occupational polarization of Chinese in America still persists a decade later for Chinese in America.

Through logistic regression analysis, I intend to identify and describe ethnic differences in translating the education into occupational attainments. Specifically, I intend to bring out the complexity with which ethnic differences interact with education in determining occupational success. The statistical analysis itself is the same as that conducted on the British data in Chapter Five.

---

[1]U.S. Commission for Civil Rights, *Success of Asian Americans: Fact or Fiction?* (Washington: Clearinghouse Publication 64, 1980).

The data file used for this secondary analysis is extracted from the combined 1980 U.S. Census of Population and Housing 5% PUMS A Asian American Data File and PUMS A 0.1% samples. The extracted sample is restricted to ages 25-64, a convention enabling us to include persons who had presumably completed formal education by the time of interview.

This chapter is divided into four parts. In part one, I conduct simple cross-tabular analysis to examine ethnic distributions in industry and occupation. Preliminary results are presented for Chinese in comparison with other ethnic groups. The second part describes how the indicator of occupational attainment is obtained, i.e. the process by which I translate the American occupation data into Goldthorpe's class categories. In part three, logistic regression analysis is undertaken to test a series of hypotheses concerning ethnic differences in occupational success. Parameter estimates for the best fitting models are also discussed. The research findings are summarized in part four.

Industry and occupation: preliminary results

Industry

The indicator of "industry" refers to the "kind of business or industrial activity in which the person was employed during the reference week, or, if not employed, in which the person was most recently employed since 1975".[2] Unlike the coding of "industry" in the British Labour Force Survey, it is not coded in the form of Standard Industrial Classification. Its 231 industry categories do not reflect the full SIC detail in categories.

Distribution in industry is important for the study of the occupational attainments of ethnic minorities. This is because concentration of an ethnic minority in a certain industry or industries is likely to create an enclave economy, which by monopolizing resources and outlets for products, may provide a separate and insular labour market for the minority. A self contained process of recruitment and promotion is likely to be formed sheltering ethnic minority members from external competition. An interesting hypothesis to test is whether the enclave economy is able to help ethnic minority members to achieve occupational returns to education to the same extent as the wider labour market.

---

[2]U.S. Department of Commerce, Bureau of the Census, *Census of Population and Housing, 1980 (United States): Public Use Microdata Samples* (Ann Arbor: ICPSR, 1984) K-24.

Table 7.1 Percent Ethnic Distribution in First Ten Most
          Concentrated Industries (N=140,160)

Industry	percent
Chinese	
eating & drinking places	16.7
apparel & accessories manuf.	7.8
hospitals	5.4
college and university	4.8
elementary & secondary school	3.0
banking	2.7
grocery store	2.6
construction	1.9
electrical mach. equip. supplies	1.8
engineering, architectural & survey	1.8
total	48.5
Japanese	
elementary and secondary school	6.7
eating and drinking places	5.1
construction	4.4
hospitals	4.0
college and university	3.2
agricultural production	2.3
banking	2.3
grocery stores	2.2
general government	2.1
hotels and motels	2.0
total	34.3
Filipino	
hospitals	18.1
banking	3.7
hotels & motels	3.6
construction	3.3
electrical mach. equip. supplies	2.8
eating and drinking places	2.8
elementary & secondary school	2.6
office of physician	2.3
nat. security & intern. affairs	2.1
agricultural production	2.0
total	43.3

	Industry	percent
Korean		
	eating & drinking places	8.3
	hospitals	7.8
	apparel & accessories manuf.	5.4
	grocery stores	4.2
	college & university	2.7
	apparel & accessory store	2.6
	electrical mach. equip. manuf.	2.4
	hotel and motel	2.3
	construction	2.2
	banking	1.4
	total	39.3
Indian		
	hospital	14.9
	college & university	6.6
	engineering, architectural, survey	4.0
	office of physician	3.7
	construction	2.9
	banking	2.8
	electrical mach. equip.	2.7
	eating and drinking places	2.6
	elementary and secondary school	2.3
	hotel & motel	2.1
	total	44.6
Vietnamese		
	eating & drinking place	6.5
	electrical mach.equip.&supplies	5.8
	hospitals	3.7
	apparel & accessories	3.7
	electronic & computer equip.manu.	3.3
	elementary & secondary school	2.9
	college and university	2.6
	grocery stores	2.5
	not specified elec. mach. equip.	2.4
	construction	2.3
	total	35.7

Industry	Percent
Hispanics	
hospital	7.2
construction	5.0
elementary & secondary school	4.0
eating and drinking places	3.9
apparel & accessories manuf.	3.2
agricultural production	2.4
hotel and motel	2.1
banking	2.1
general government	1.9
electrical mach. equip and supplies	1.8
total	33.6
Blacks	
hospital	8.5
elementary & secondary school	7.6
construction	5.0
private household	3.1
motor vehicles and equipment	2.6
nursing and personal care	2.3
eating and drinking place	2.2
general government	2.1
U.S. postal service	1.9
apparel accessories manuf.	1.7
total	37.1
Whites	
elementary & secondary school	6.9
construction	6.7
hospital	4.0
eating and drinking places	2.7
insurance	2.0
college and university	1.9
trucking service	1.7
banking	1.7
justice, public order and safety	1.7
grocery store	1.5
total	30.9

Thus, in studying industrial distribution, our focus is not on ethnic distribution in all industries, but on the ethnic concentration in a certain industry or industries and the degree of concentration. For this purpose, we have listed the top ten most populous industries for each ethnic group in Table 7.1.

It can be seen that Chinese have the highest degree of concentration, with 48.5% working in the top ten industries. Chinese also have a high degree of concentration in a single industry, i.e. 16.7% of all Chinese work in eating and drinking places. Although catering is also listed as the most popular trade among Koreans and Vietnamese, degrees of concentration for these groups are far lower. Therefore, we have identified a Chinese enclave economy, which centres around catering and which hires one out of every five Chinese in the U.S.. How their occupational status varies within the enclave economy will be examined in the next section.

Occupation

The variable for occupation identifies "the kind of work the person was doing at a job or business during the reference week, or if not at work, at the most recent job or business if employed since 1975". The 503 occupation categories are based on the Standard Occupational Classification, issued by the Office of Federal Statistical Policy and Standards in 1977.[3]

To help simplify the analysis, I have recoded the variable into 12 occupational levels. In general, these occupational levels correspond to the occupational group titles defined in the census, but occupations of particular interest to us have been recoded in more details. For example, food preparation is considered an economic niche for Chinese, and has therefore been singled out as one occupational category.

As shown in Table 7.2, 13.7% of Chinese are in executive, administrative and managerial occupations. This percentage is similar to that of Japanese and greater than all other ethnic groups, including majority whites. Chinese are over represented in professional specialty occupations. Nearly 22% of Chinese work in professional jobs. The percentage is not only the second highest among Asian Americans, but it is also much higher than those of Hispanics, blacks and majority whites.

---

[3]U.S. Department of Commerce, Bureau of the Census, *Census of Population and Housing, 1980 (United States): Public Use Microdata Samples* (Ann Arbor: ICPSR, 1984).

Table 7.2 Percent Ethnic Distribution in Occupational Groups
(N=140,198)

Group	Chine	Japan	Filipino	Korea	Indian	Vietnam	Hispanic	Black	White
1	13.7	13.8	8.4	10.5	12.6	5.8	8.1	5.2	12.8
2	21.8	17.6	20.6	15.9	39.8	9.7	10.4	9.4	14.7
3	6.5	4.4	6.3	3.7	7.4	7.8	3.1	3.1	3.1
4	7.6	9.0	4.5	13.1	6.1	4.2	5.7	4.1	10.0
5	13.5	18.6	20.8	8.6	11.9	12.4	16.1	15.7	16.6
6	.5	.6	.5	.2	.3	.2	1.0	2.7	2
7	.4	.6	.9	.2	.4	.2	1.1	1.9	16
8	13.8	5.4	4.2	7.9	2.1	6.9	4.3	3.8	29
9	3.1	5.2	9.2	6.7	3.9	6.1	9.1	13.5	4.7
10	.5	4.3	2.5	1.0	1.0	1.1	3.6	1.9	25
11	5.9	10.7	8.5	10.5	5.1	16.1	13.0	9.7	14.3
12	12.8	9.7	13.6	21.6	9.2	29.4	24.5	29.0	16.6
Tota	100.0	100.0	100.0	100.0	100.0	100.0	100.0	100.0	100.0

1. executive, administrative, and managerial occupations
2. professional specialty occupations
3. technical, sales, and administrative support occupations
4. sales occupations
5. administrative support occupation, including clerical
6. private households occupations
7. protective service occupations
8. food preparation and service occupations
9. other service occupations
10.farming, forestry and fishing occupations
11.precision production, craft and repair occupations
12.operators, fabricators and labourers

It is discernible that Chinese are relatively over-represented in technical, administrative, and sales support occupations, and in service occupations, particularly, catering, such as food preparation and private households. Fourteen percent alone work in food preparation and service occupations alone. On the other hand, Chinese are under-represented in farming, forestry and fishing occupations. Comparatively lower proportions of Chinese are also found in occupations requiring skilled or non-skilled manual labour such as in precision production and as operators, fabricators and labourers.[4]

In Table 7.3, Chinese working in food preparation and service occupations are selected. They are further cross-tabulated in more detailed occupational categories. Of the catering Chinese, the majority work in restaurants, with 47% working as cooks, and 25% as waiters and waitresses. These figures confirm the existence of a Chinese catering trade, mainly in the form of restaurants serving Chinese cuisine.

Table 7.3 Percent Chinese Distribution in Food Preparation
Occupations (N=2,277)

Occupation	Percent
supervisor, food preparation	10.5
bar-tenders	3.1
waiters & waitresses	25.4
cooks	46.7
short order cooks	0.4
food counter and related	0.9
kitchen workers	0.8
assistants of waiter & waitress	2.5
miscellaneous	9.6
Total	100.0

Employment status

The original variable from which employment status is derived is "class of worker", which is classification of workers according to the type of ownership of the employing organization.[5] In the 1980 U.S. census, class of worker is coded into seven categories, 1=private wage and salary

---

[4]This finding seems to contradict that of the U.S. Commission for Civil Rights. However, the Commission's report did not specify the four lowest paying occupations. Hence, the suspicion that the Commission used different measures of occupation from the author. Another possible explanation might be discrepancy over time as the Commission's report is based on the 1970 census data and this thesis uses the 1980 census data.

[5]Ibid., K-10.

worker: employee of private company, 2=federal government worker, 3=state government worker, 4=local government worker, 5=self-employed worker - business not incorporated, 6=employee of own corporation, and 7=unpaid family worker.

Our concern in this section, is to see what proportion of working Chinese are engaged in self-employment (a major form of employment in the enclave economy), and how this compares to the proportion of self-employed among workers from other ethnic backgrounds. Therefore, we recode the class of worker into a binary variable called "employment status" by combining categories 5 and 6 into 1=self-employed, and 1,2,3,4 and 7 into 2=employee. The cross-tabulation of employment status by ethnicity is presented in Table 7.4.

Table 7.4 Percent Ethnic Distribution in Employment Status
        (N=140,198)

Status	Chin	Japan	Filip	Korea	India	Vietn	Hisp	Black	White
self-emp.	11.6	11.5	4.6	17.7	9.5	3.8	6.0	3.0	11.1
employee	88.4	88.5	95.4	82.3	90.5	96.2	94.0	97.0	88.9
total	100.0	100.0	100.0	100.0	100.0	100.0	100.0	100.0	100.0

It can be seen that of all working Chinese, 11.6% are self-employed, the rest are employees. The percentage of self-employed workers is lower than that of Koreans with 17.7%, but it is higher than those of all other ethnic groups. This finding, again, supports the existence of a Chinese enclave economy.

Measuring occupational attainments: class

In developing measures of occupational attainment, we are primarily concerned with achieving comparability between these measures and those used in the previous study of Chinese in Britain. Our ultimate goal is to compare the relative level of occupational success of Chinese Americans with that of Chinese in Britain. Therefore, we adopt a research strategy in which statistical analysis on the British data will be replicated for the American data.

190

Previously, in the analysis of British data, the dependent variable took the form of two binary contrasts: service class versus non-service class and the unemployed versus those in work. The service class was obtained by following Goldthorpe's class schema. For purposes of comparison, the same two binary contrasts will be used as dependent variables in the analysis of American data. In this section, I shall discuss the process by which Goldthorpe's class categories are obtained from the American data.

According to Erikson and Goldthorpe, the Class Schema attempts to "differentiate positions within labour markets and production units, or more specifically...to differentiate such positions in terms of the employment relations they entail". Thus, the purpose of the schema is to provide a high degree of differentiation in terms of both occupational function and employment status. In fact, the associated employment status is treated as part of the definition of a class position.[6]

In transforming the American census data into Goldthorpe's sevenfold class categories, I have selected the two variables, which are closest in meaning to "occupational function" and "employment status", i.e. "occupation" and "class of worker".

The recoding format, which has been presented in Appendix 7.1, involves a two dimensional diagram, where the column displays occupation and the row shows the class of worker. While the original 503 occupational categories maintain as they are, the seven categories of "class of worker" are aggregated into a binary variable, which consists of "employee" and "the self-employed".[7]

The actual process of transforming American data into Goldthorpe's seven class categories takes five steps. First, for each American occupation listed in the column of Appendix 7.1, we find the code number in the Alphabetical Index for Classifying Occupations.[8] Note, however, that these codes are intended for coding purposes only.

Secondly, we find out the relationship between these codes and the 1980 occupational groups by combining the code number with the employment status, such as self-employed, managers, foreman, or

---

[6] Robert Erikson and John Goldthorpe, *Constant Flux: A Study of Class Mobility in Industrial Societies* (Oxford: Clarendon Press, 1992).

[7] In recoding "class of worker", the employee consists of "private wage and salary worker: employee of private company", "federal government workers", "state government worker", "local government worker" and "unpaid family worker"; the self-employed include "self-employed worker-business not incorporated" and "employee of own corporation".

[8] Office of Population Censuses and Surveys, *Classification of Occupations* (London: Her Majesty's Stationary Office, 1980) 6-109.

employee in order to find a new code number, called the operational code.[9] Note, some occupations have all four types of employment status, others do not. This is therefore a useful procedure to filter out any employment status that is irrelevant for the occupation specified. In such cases, no operational codes are usually obtained.

Thirdly, the operational codes are used in Goldthorpe's Revised Class Schema (1983) to produce the eleven category numerical version of the schema.[10] Fourthly, the numerical codes are translated into the seven category Goldthorpe class schema, indicated by Roman letters:

I   Higher-grade professionals, administrators, and officials; managers in large establishments; large proprietors

II   Lower-grade professionals, administrators and officials; higher grade technicians; managers in small business and industrial establishments; supervisors of non-manual employees

IIIa Routine non-manual employees in administration and commerce
IIIb Personal Service Workers

IVa Small proprietors, artisans, etc., with employees
IVb Small proprietors, artisans, etc., without employees
IVc Farmers and small holders; self-employed fishermen

V   Lower grade technicians, supervisors of manual workers

VI   Skilled manual workers

VIIa Semi-skilled and unskilled manual workers (not in agriculture)
VIIb Agricultural workers.[11]

---

[9]Ibid., 111-114.

[10]John Goldthorpe, *Revised Class Schema Based on OPCS Classification of Occupations*. Provided by John Goldthorpe, 2-21.

[11]John Goldthorpe and Clive Payne, *Social Mobility and Class Structure in Modern Britain* (Oxford: Clarendon Press, 1987) 40-43.

Finally, the seven class categories can be further aggregated into three classes of service, intermediate, and working class. The service class consists of I and II, the intermediate class IIIa to V, and the working class VI to VIIb. It is this last three category class schema that is useful to our analysis, because it makes distinctions between the service class and the rest.[12]

It should be pointed out that in translating the American data, the author has been confronted with some serious flaws in the original occupational groupings. First, the basic occupational categories and the major occupational groups, which were originally intended to capture status divisions, are sometimes determined on sectoral lines.

This problem was addressed by Erikson and Goldthorpe, when they recoded the occupation variable in the 1960 U.S. Census to be used in the CASMIN (Comparative Analysis of Social Mobility in Industrialized Nations) project. They were so irritated by it that they rated the American occupational groupings the least coherent of all the national occupational classifications they had ever encountered.[13]

Unfortunately, some of these problems remain. Two decades after the 1960 U.S. census data were released, we are in no better position to cope with what the authors called "disturbing cases". For instance, in "professional specialty occupations", we are unable to distinguish, authentic scientists and engineers from those whose work entails routine laboratory assistance. Among "sales occupations", those requiring professional training cannot be separated from the helping staff. We cannot tell for instance real estate agents from those requiring door-to-door visits, such as insurance salesmen. As a result, we have to adopt the same strategy as Erikson and Goldthorpe, namely, in cases of problematic occupational categories, we give class codings to those constituent occupations in which we estimate that the largest number of people are employed.[14]

Another problem, perhaps of minor importance, is that we are unable to distinguish higher service class jobs from the lower service class jobs. In the British case, the criterion is usually the size of the firm. Those working as administrators or managers in firms with 25 and more employees are generally coded as higher service class, whereas those working in firms with fewer than 25 people are coded as lower service class. Information on the size of the firm is not available in the American

---

[12] The recoding is executed in SPSSX following the format laid out in Appendix 7.2.

[13] Robert Erikson and John Goldthorpe, *Constant Flux* (Oxford: Clarendon Press, 1992) 14.

[14] Ibid., 17.

census data, so people with service class jobs must be treated as one single class.

In spite of these problems, we have translated the 1980 U.S. Census data into Goldthorpe's Class Schema by following the procedure in Appendix 7.2. The total combined data set has 387,863 cases, and excluding missing cases, 217,781, or 56% of the sample, have been assigned one of the Goldthorpe class categories.[15] Class frequencies are presented in Appendix 7.3. Furthermore, class frequencies for males and females are also presented separately in Appendices 7.4 and Appendix 7.5. It can be seen that a substantial gender difference exists in class distribution. The males are typically over-represented in classes I&II and VI, i.e. service and skilled manual classes, and the females are over-represented in class IIIa, i.e. routine non-manual employees in administration and commerce. These differences inspire a certain degree of confidence in the class categories so strenuously constructed from the American data.

Hypothesis testing

Preliminary analysis of the demographic potentials and levels of cultural and socioeconomic assimilation of various ethnic groups in the U.S. has led us to the postulation that Chinese may rank as one of the more occupationally successful Asian American groups. Among possible causes, Chinese are better educated than many other Asian groups. This may give them an edge in achieving occupational success. In this section, we test a series of hypotheses with regard to ethnic differences in occupational returns to education by conducting logit analysis.

The response variable class, as in the case of the British analysis, takes the form of two binary contrasts, the service class versus the rest, and the unemployed versus those in work. The service class, defined as in Goldthorpe's class schema, consists of higher-grade professionals, administrators, and officials; managers in large establishments; large proprietors and lower-grade professionals, administrators, and officials; higher grade technicians; managers in small business and industrial establishments (excluding the self-employed) and supervisors of non-manual employees. The unemployed refer to "civilians 16 years old and over who were neither 'at work' nor 'with a job, but not at work' and who were a) looking for work during the last four weeks, and b) available to accept a

---

[15]The missing cases are people who have no entry in occupation or employment status in the 1980 U.S. census data.

job".[16]   As in the British case, we have deliberately selected the most advantaged and the most disadvantaged classes for the study of class differentiation.

Among explanatory variables, both sex and place of birth are dummy variables, with sex dichotomized between male and female, and place of birth between foreign country and U.S.A..   Instead of regressing them directly on class, we shall control these variables by splitting the sample into four sub-samples according to sex and place of birth, i.e. foreign-born males, foreign-born females, native-born males, and native-born females. Logistic regression analysis will then be conducted separately for the four different sub-samples, with regard to access to the service class and risks of unemployment.   The explanatory variables are age, education, and ethnicity, all of which are multinomial:

age:	1	25-29
	2	30-34
	3	35-39
	4	40-44
	5	45-49
	6	50-54
	7	55-64

education:	1	postgraduate
	2	college
	3	high school completion
	4	below high school completion

ethnicity:	1	Chinese
	2	Japanese
	3	Filipino
	4	Korean
	5	Indian
	6	Vietnamese
	7	Hispanic
	8	Black
	9	White.

---

[16]U.S. Department of Commerce, Bureau of the Census, *Census of Population and Housing, 1980 (United States): Public Use Microdata Samples* (Ann Arbor: ICPSR, 1984) k-25.

The same three hypotheses tested in the British case will be tested for the American data. First, we test whether a meritocratic situation applies to class attainments. The null hypothesis assumes that ethnic origin make no difference to achieving a certain class position. Class is a function of age, which serves as a proxy for labour market duration and education. This model, which we call the "baseline model", is written as:

$$Ln(P/1-P) = \beta_0 + \beta_1(AGE) + \beta_2(EDUC).$$

Of course, our experience tells us that this model rarely fits. Therefore, the next model we fit is one which suggests that when age and education are held constant, class varies with ethnicity. This model, which we call the "ethnicity model" is written as:

$$Ln(P/1-P) = \beta_0 + \beta_1(AGE) + \beta_2(EDUC) + \beta_3(ETHN).$$

While in the "ethnicity model", we assume that ethnic difference is the same at all educational levels, we next postulate that ethnic difference varies with educational levels. For reasons discussed in Chapter 5, we expect the ethnic effect to differ between the qualified and the unqualified. Therefore, we add the interaction term of ethnicity by education into the model. To conduct a conservative test, we control for two other two-way interactions, age by education and age by ethnicity, should either or both of them be statistically significant at 0.05 level. We therefore compare the fit of the following two models, which we call the "control model" and the "ethnicity by education" model:

$$Ln(P/1-P) = \beta_0 + \beta_1(AGE) + \beta_2(EDUC) + \beta_3(ETHN)$$
$$+ \beta_4(AGE*EDUC) + \beta_5(AGE*ETHN);$$
$$Ln(P/1-P) = \beta_0 + \beta_1(AGE) + \beta_2(EDUC) + \beta_3(ETHN)$$
$$+ \beta_4(AGE*EDUC) + \beta_5(AGE*ETHN) + \beta_6(EDUC*ETHN).$$

Male immigrants

In this section, I test the three hypotheses stated in the above models, i.e. the baseline model, the ethnicity model, and the ethnicity by education model. I test the three hypotheses separately with regard to access to the service class and risks of unemployment.

It can be seen in Table 7.5 that, with regard to access to the service class, the baseline model does not fit well, with $G^2 = 1368$ for 277 degrees of freedom and the index of dissimilarity, otherwise known as the percentage of misclassified cases, equal to 5.52. There is certainly room for improvement. Next we fit the ethnicity model. We notice that when ethnicity is added to the baseline model, the change in G^2 is 815 for 8 degrees of freedom. This implies that when age and education are held constant, the effect of ethnicity on class is statistically significant at the 0.05 level. Therefore, the null hypothesis of the ethnicity model is rejected. It is clearly discernable that the ethnicity by education model provides an even better fit than the ethnicity model, with a further reduction of G^2 by 96 for 24 degrees of freedom. It shows that, other things being equal, the effect of ethnicity on class varies with education.[17] Because of this, the null hypothesis stated in the ethnicity by education model is also rejected.[18]

Parameter estimates for the ethnicity by education model are presented in Appendix 7.6.[19] They are in the form of fitted log odds ratios and are therefore not straightforward for explanation. To overcome this difficulty, we adopt the strategy of transforming the fitted log odds ratios into fitted probabilities, presented in percentage forms in Figure 7.1.

The process of transformation was described in Chapter Two. In addition, not all 120 coefficients in Appendix 7.6 are of theoretical concerns to us. Therefore, we concentrate only on the effect of ethnicity and the interaction effect of ethnicity by education. For convenience of presentation, we select one age cohort of 35-39. This is because, in Western countries, a man's occupation is likely to mature in this age band.[20]

---

[17]In fitting the ethnicity by education model, we obtain a p-value of 0.0425, which is not a perfect fit. However, the only other term we may put into the model is a three-way interaction term of ethnicity by education by age, in which case we fit a saturated model. We may have a perfect fit, but may not obtain theoretically interesting associations. The fact that the Index of Dissimilarity is equal to 1.32, which is a very small value, suggests that the ethnicity by education model is a good fitting model, given a huge sample of 68,805.

[18]The fit of the ethnicity by education model is $G^2 = 201$ and d.f $= 168$. I tried to fit a more parsimonious model by collapsing the categories for ethnicity and/or education, but failed to obtain a unique superior model. Thus the ethnicity by education model is taken as the final model. In all following analyses, the model presented will be the accepted final model, which is theoretically interesting, unless otherwise pointed out.

[19]In subsequent analysis, where the ethnicity by education model is accepted as the best fitting model, we shall report parameter estimates for that model in the Appendix. We shall present the interaction effect by selecting the age cohort of 35-39 for the sake of illustration.

[20]We can select only one age cohort because the interaction effect of ethnicity by education (defined as fitted odds), as defined by the present model, does not vary with age.

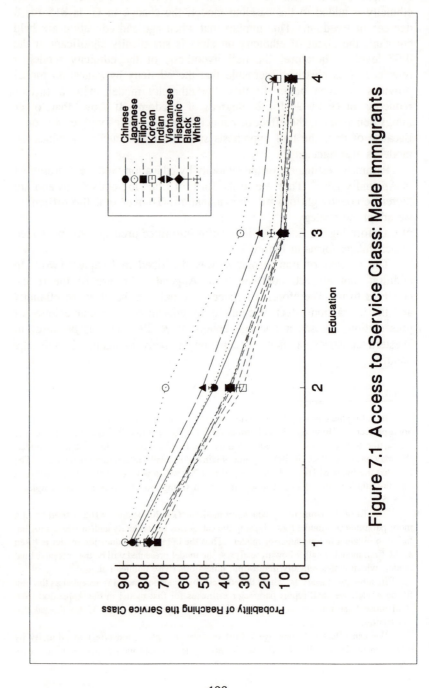

Figure 7.1 Access to Service Class: Male Immigrants

Table 7.5 Goodness of Fit: Male Immigrants (N=68,805)

Access to Service Class

Model	G^2	d.f	ΔG^2	Δd.f	p-value	$rG^2(\%)$	ID
Baseline	1368	277			0.0000		5.52
Ethnicity	553	269	815	8	0.0000	60	3.21
Control	297	192	256	77	0.0000	78	1.75
Educ.Ethn	201	168	96	24	0.0425	85	1.32

Risks of Unemployment

Model	G^2	d.f	ΔG^2	Δd.f	p-value	$rG^2(\%)$	ID
Baseline	519	277			0.0000		12.58
Ethnicity	373	269	146	8	0.0000	28	10.54
Control	274	213	99	56	0.0029	47	8.92
Educ.Ethn	204	189	70	24	0.2089	61	6.84

In Figure 7.1, the fitted probabilities of reaching the service class are shown for all male immigrant groups of Asian origin and the three non-Asian control groups.

The vertical axis stands for the fitted probability of reaching the service class in percentage form, with the value ranging from 0 to 100, and the horizontal axis stands for educational levels in descending order, where 1=degree and above, 2=college, 3=high school completed and 4=high school not completed.

The curves generally show a negative linear relationship between the probability of reaching the service class and decreasing level of education. The curve for Chinese lies below those for Japanese and Indians, coincides with that for whites, and most of the time, lies above those for other ethnic groups.

Compared to Japanese and Indians, Chinese have lower fitted probabilities of reaching the service class at all educational levels. Yet the absolute difference in fitted probability, as indicated by the vertical difference between any two curves is different at different educational levels. Chinese with degrees and above actually have quite a similar fitted probability as Japanese and Indians of reaching the service class, with the fitted probabilities for these three groups being 0.85 for Chinese, 0.89 for Japanese, and 0.87 for Indians. However, the gap in fitted probability widens as we go down the scale of education.

In similar vein, compared with other ethnic groups, except whites, Chinese with college education and above enjoy an ethnic advantage (defined as fitted probability) in access to the service class. Yet the advantage decreases for Chinese whose education did not extend beyond high school. Therefore, compared with all other non-white ethnic groups, Chinese male immigrants display a pattern of polarization in the predicted probability of reaching the service class.

Next, we examine the relative risks of unemployment of Chinese in comparison with other ethnic groups. With regard to hypothesis testing, we find in Table 7.5 that the baseline model does not provide a very good fit, with $G^2=519$ and d.f$=277$, and ID$=12.58$. So we fit the ethnicity model, where we add the effect of ethnicity into the baseline model. The change in G^2 is 146 for 8 degrees of freedom, with a percentage reduction of G^2 of 28%. The index of dissimilarity is reduced to 10.54. This implies that, age and education being equal, risks of unemployment vary with ethnicity. However, it is the ethnicity by education model which gives a better fit still. The change in G^2 is 70 for 24 degrees of freedom compared with the control model.[21] This entails a 61% reduction in the deviance G^2 and a reduction of 5.74 in the index of dissimilarity, compared with the baseline model.

In Figure 7.2, we present the fitted probabilities of unemployment for the ethnicity by education model, again selecting the age cohort of 35-39.[22] It can be seen that at the level of degree and above, Chinese have a lower fitted probability of unemployment than all other ethnic groups except Japanese. However, the ethnic advantage of Chinese (defined as fitted probability) is weaker at levels below university degree.

It is noticeable that, despite an overall positive linear relationship between the fitted probability of being unemployed and decreasing educational levels, the curve for Chinese grows rather flatter as it moves towards the unqualified end. This shows that compared to many other ethnic groups, Chinese male immigrants are less differentiated in their risks

[21]Although we would like to fit a conservative model, the interaction effect of age by education is not statistically significant at 0.05 level. So, we take it off the final model.

[22]Parameter estimates for the ethnicity by education model, from which the fitted probabilities are obtained, are presented in Appendix 7.7.

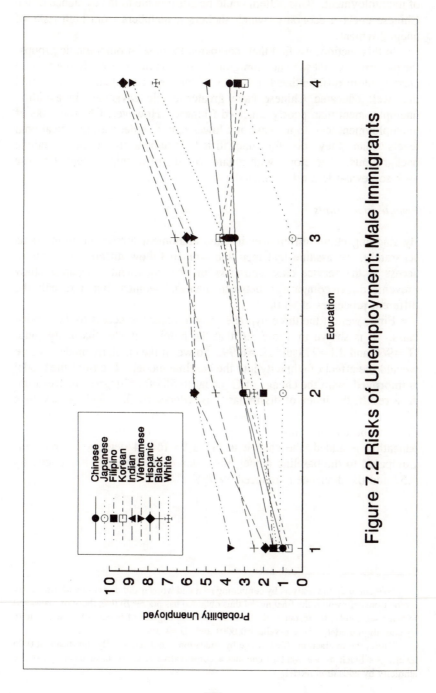

Figure 7.2 Risks of Unemployment: Male Immigrants

of unemployment. This pattern could be attributable to the existence of the Chinese enclave economy, which shelters it members from high risks of unemployment.

In this section, we find that, compared to those of other ethnic groups, the pattern of Chinese male immigrants with regard to access to the service class is more differentiated in favour of the well educated. We also find that well educated Chinese have greater ethnic advantage in avoiding unemployment than poorly educated Chinese. However, Chinese risks of unemployment tend to increase at a lower rate with decreasing educational levels than they do for unqualified members from other ethnic backgrounds. Therefore, with regard to risks of unemployment, Chinese look somewhat less differentiated.

Female immigrants

By studying ethnic differences in class attainment for female immigrants separately, we assume that men and women follow different patterns in access to the service class and risks of unemployment. Separate study prevents direct comparison between men and women, but it reveals the different processes at work.[23]

First, we test the three hypotheses with regard to access to the service class. It is shown in Table 7.6 that the baseline model fits badly, with $G^2=960$ and d.f$=273$ and ID$=6.99$. So we fit the ethnicity model, where we add the effect of ethnicity into the baseline model. The fit of the model is improved, with the change of G^2 equal to 564 for 8 degrees of freedom. As a result, the index of dissimilarity is reduced by 3.13 and the deviance of the baseline model G^2 is reduced by 59%. Of course, this does not yet give the best fitting model. When the interaction effect of ethnicity by education is added, the change in G^2 is 95 for 24 degrees of freedom. Compared to the baseline model, the index of dissimilarity is reduced by 4.57 and the deviance is reduced by 79%.[24]

---

[23]We could do the analysis by combining men and women and dispense with fitting sex interactions. However, the final model thus obtained has poorer fit than those of males and females separately, for instance, the G^2 is 258 for 180 degrees of freedom for the ethnicity by education model, where p-value$=0.0001$ and ID$=1.39$.

[24]Note, the interaction effect of age by education is not statistically significant at 0.05 level. As much as we want to conduct a conservative test, we have taken it off the ethnicity by education model.

Table 7.6 Goodness of Fit: Female Immigrants (N=53,316)

Access to Service Class

Model	G^2	d.f	ΔG^2	Δd.f	p-value	$rG^2(\%)$	ID
Baseline	960	273			0.0000		6.99
Ethnicity	395	265	564	8	0.0000	59	3.86
Control	301	209	95	56	0.0000	69	3.04
Educ.Ethn	206	185	95	24	0.1431	79	2.42

Risks of Unemployment

Model	G^2	d.f	ΔG^2	Δd.f	p-value	$rG^2(\%)$	ID
Baseline	492	273			0.0000		14.94
Ethnicity	379	265	113	8	0.0000	23	12.78
Control	273	209	106	56	0.0020	45	10.42
Educ.Ethn	213	185	60	24	0.0758	57	8.76

In Figure 7.3, fitted probabilities of reaching the service class by educational levels are presented again for the age cohort of 35-39.[25] Curves representing different ethnic groups do not fall parallel but coincide with each other, although the spectrum of curves indicates a rather negative linear relationship between the probability of reaching the service class and decreasing education.

The curve for Chinese lies somewhere in the middle of the spectrum of curves for all ethnic groups. However, we do notice that the fitted probability of reaching the service class is lower for Chinese than for any other ethnic group among the unqualified. At other educational levels, the relative position of Chinese is better. Therefore, Chinese female immigrants look slightly differentiated in access to the service class.

With regard to risks of unemployment, we find that the baseline model does not fit very well, so we go on fitting the ethnicity model. With a change of G^2 equal to 113 for 8 degrees of freedom, we reject the null hypothesis of the ethnicity model. This is to say that, controlling for age

---

[25]The parameter estimates for the ethnicity by education model are presented Appendix 7.8.

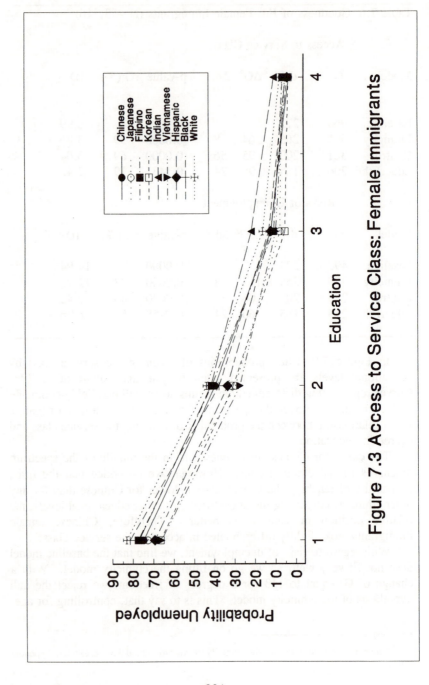

Figure 7.3 Access to Service Class: Female Immigrants

and education, chances of reaching the service class vary with ethnicity. We then fit the ethnicity by education model. Compared with the control model, the ethnicity by education model provides a superior fit.[26] Deviance is reduced by 60 for 24 degrees of freedom. This implies that risks of unemployment do not only vary only with ethnicity, but also with education.

To illustrate the interaction effect of ethnicity by education, Figure 7.4 has been constructed with the vertical axis standing for probability of unemployment (in percentage form) and the horizontal axis representing educational level in descending order.[27] Again, the age cohort of 35-39 is presented. On the whole, the spectrum of curves for all ethnic groups displays a weak positive relationship between probability of unemployment and decreasing education. It is discernible that the curves are more spread out among the unqualified than among the qualified. The pattern shows that well educated females are more alike in risks (defined as fitted probability) of unemployment than the unqualified.

Compared with women from other ethnic groups, the relative ethnic advantage (defined as fitted probability) of Chinese is somewhat greater at levels below degree, as indicated by the relative position of the curve for Chinese at four different educational levels. For example, other things being equal, Filipino women with college education have better chances than Chinese women of avoiding unemployment. Filipino women with high school diploma or lower, however, also have a higher probability of unemployment.

In this section, we have found that qualified Chinese female immigrants do not display an ethnic advantage over qualified members from other ethnic backgrounds in occupational success. This is the most striking difference between male and female immigrants of Chinese origin with regard to access to the service class. Moreover, unqualified foreign-born Chinese women seem to suffer from greater ethnic penalty in access to the service class than their unqualified counterparts from other ethnic origins. In avoidance of unemployment, however, poorly educated Chinese seem to enjoy greater ethnic advantage than qualified Chinese, probably due to the existence of the enclave economy. This finding is similar to that for male Chinese immigrants. We thus find that Chinese immigrants as a whole are much protected from unemployment.

---

[26]Much as we want to fit a conservative model, we have to take off the interaction effect of age by education from the final model, because it is not statistically significant at 0.05 level.

[27]Parameter estimates for the ethnicity by education model, from which the probabilities are obtained for female immigrants with regard to unemployment, are presented in Appendix 7.9.

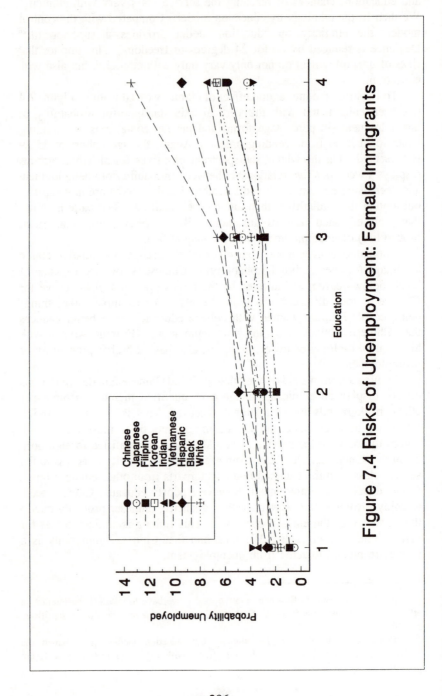

Figure 7.4 Risks of Unemployment: Female Immigrants

In this section, we test similar hypotheses as we did for male immigrants with regard to ethnic differences in access to the service class and risks of unemployment. The results of the modelling are presented in Table 7.7.

Table 7.7 Goodness of Fit: Native-Born Males (N=54,920)

Access to Service Class

Model	G^2	d.f	ΔG^2	Δd.f	p-value	$rG^2(\%)$	ID
Baseline	661	253			0.0000		4.10
Ethnicity	379	245	283	8	0.0000	43	2.96
Control	232	169	147	76	0.0010	65	1.70
Educ.Ethn	206	145	26	24	0.0007	69	1.52

Risks of Unemployment

Model	G^2	d.f	ΔG^2	Δd.f	p-value	$rG^2(\%)$	ID
Baseline	359	253			0.0000		9.76
Ethnicity	208	245	152	8	0.9601	42	7.44
Educ.Ethn	179	221	28	24	0.9816	50	6.49[29]

With regard to access to the service class, the baseline model provides a poor fit, with deviance $G^2=661$ and d.f=253. Thus, we fit the ethnicity model, by adding the effect of ethnicity into the baseline model. The change in G^2 is 283 for 8 degrees of freedom. By doing this, we reduce deviance by 43% and the index of dissimilarity by 1.14. As a result, access to the service class is found to vary with ethnic background. However, when we fit the ethnicity by education model, the interaction effect is found to be statistically insignificant at 0.05 level. This implies that, other things being equal, the effect of ethnicity remains constant on

---

[28]Since there is no variable indicating the country of birth of parents, we can not distinguish second generation from third generation native-born.

[29]The other two-way interactions are not controlled for int his case as neither is statistically significant at the 0.05 level.

all educational levels. In this case, the ethnicity model is taken as the best fitting model.

In Table 7.8, parameter estimates are presented for the ethnicity model. After controlling for age and education, we find that native-born Chinese males share similar chances (defined as fitted log odds) of reaching the service class as Koreans

Table 7.8 Native-Born Males: Access to Service Class[30]

	Estimate	s.e.	Parameter
1	1.394	0.05851	1
2	0.2245	0.03473	AGE(2)
3	0.4306	0.03767	AGE(3)
4	0.4279	0.04053	AGE(4)
5	0.5216	0.04128	AGE(5)
6	0.6403	0.04107	AGE(6)
7	0.4368	0.04369	AGE(7)
8	0.3945	0.05273	AGE(8)
9	-1.683	0.03225	EDUC(2)
10	-3.100	0.03551	EDUC(3)
11	-4.060	0.04907	EDUC(4)
12	**-0.1977(.82)**	0.05805	ETHN(2)
13	**-0.5489(.58)**	**0.09565**	**ETHN(3)**
14	-0.002541	0.1797	ETHN(4)
15	**-0.4826(.62)**	**0.1881**	**ETHN(5)**
16	-0.9770	0.5746	ETHN(6)
17	-0.7224(.49)	0.06921	ETHN(7)
18	-0.8750(.42)	0.07107	ETHN(8)
19	-0.2785(.76)	0.05156	ETHN(9)

only.[31] Compared with other Asian American groups, the fitted odds of Chinese reaching the service class are 1.2 times those of Japanese, 1.6

---

[30]The value in bracket is the fitted odds ratio, i.e. the exponentiated value of the parameter estimate to its left.

[31]The parameter estimate for Vietnamese has a big standard error probably caused by a small sample size.

times those of Indians and 1.7 times those of Filipinos. Compared with non-Asian Americans, the fitted odds of Chinese reaching the service class are twice those of Hispanics, 2.4 times those of blacks and 1.3 times those of whites. Moreover, the ethnic advantage of native-born Chinese males is the same among the qualified as among the unqualified.

Secondly, we test hypotheses with regard to ethnic differences in risks of unemployment. Measures of goodness of fit are reported in Table 7.7. Compared to the baseline model, the ethnicity model provides a better fit, with the change in G^2 equal to 152 for 8 degrees of freedom. It reduces the deviance by 42% and the index of dissimilarity by 2.32. Furthermore, we find the interaction effect of ethnicity by education to be statistically insignificant at the 0.05 level. Therefore, the ethnicity model is taken as the best fitting model.

Table 7.9 Native-Born Males: Risks of Unemployment

	Estimate	s.e.	Parameter
1	-4.296	0.1861	1
2	-0.3959	0.06450	AGE(2)
3	-0.6387	0.07350	AGE(3)
4	-0.7881	0.08057	AGE(4)
5	-0.8370	0.08331	AGE(5)
6	-0.9263	0.08269	AGE(6)
7	-0.7339	0.08111	AGE(7)
8	-0.8552	0.1008	AGE(8)
9	0.7276	0.1040	EDUC(2)
10	1.201	0.1015	EDUC(3)
11	1.761	0.1038	EDUC(4)
12	-0.01182	0.1893	ETHN(2)
13	**0.7979(2.2)**	**0.2163**	**ETHN(3)**
14	0.3368	0.4842	ETHN(4)
15	**1.613(5.0)**	**0.3060**	**ETHN(5)**
16	-5.005	9.324	ETHN(6)
17	0.6455(1.9)	0.1825	ETHN(7)
18	1.139(3.1)	0.1760	ETHN(8)
19	0.6399(1.9)	0.1671	ETHN(9)

It is observed from Table 7.9 that after controlling for age and education, native-born Chinese males share similar chances (defined as fitted log odds) as Japanese and Koreans in risks of unemployment.[32] They have better chances (defined as fitted log odds) than Filipinos, Indians, Hispanics, blacks and whites of avoiding unemployment. For instance, the fitted odds of a 35-39 year old Indian being unemployed rather than employed are 5.0 times those of Chinese. The fitted odds of Hispanics, whites and Filipinos being unemployed are twice those of Chinese, and the fitted odds of blacks three times those of Chinese. The extent of the ethnic advantage (defined as fitted log odds ratio) of Chinese is the same for those with degrees as it is for those without any qualifications.

In this section, we have found that at the same age and educational level, native-born Chinese share similar chances of reaching the service class and avoiding unemployment as most Asian American groups. However, compared to Hispanics, blacks and whites, Chinese enjoy an ethnic advantage in both aspects at all educational levels.

Native-born females

It is shown in Table 7.10 that the baseline model does not fit well, with deviance $G^2=471$ and d.f=257. The fit of the model is much improved when the effect of ethnicity is added to the baseline model. With a change in G^2 equal to 143 for 8 degrees of freedom, deviance is reduced by 30%, and the index of dissimilarity is reduced by 1.2. Moreover, the interaction effect of ethnicity by education is also statistically significant. By fitting the ethnicity by education model, we reduce deviance by 43% and the index of dissimilarity by 1.42, compared to the baseline model. As a result, the null hypotheses stated in both the ethnicity model and the ethnicity by education model have been rejected. This is to say that, other things being equal, ethnicity makes difference to access to the service class. The effect of ethnicity on class is also different at different educational levels.

In Figure 7.5, the fitted probabilities of service class by education are presented for the age cohort of 35-39.[33] The vertical axis stands for the

---

[32]The coefficient for Vietnamese is not statistically significant at 0.05 level, because it has a very big standard error. This might be a result of small N for Vietnamese.

[33]Parameter estimates for the ethnicity by education model, which are in the form of predicted log odds ratios and from which the fitted probabilities are obtained, are presented in Appendix 7.10.

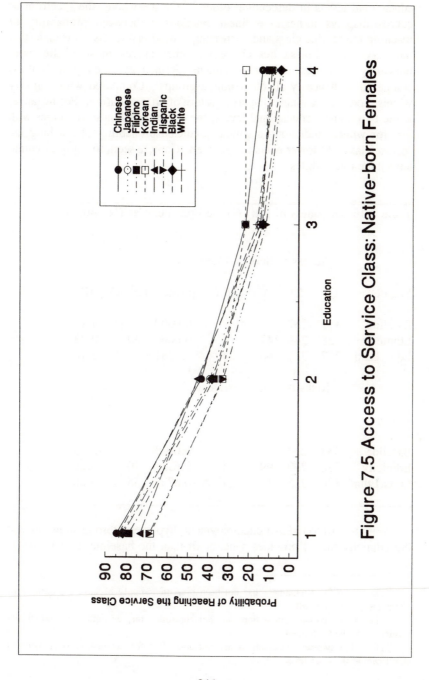

Figure 7.5 Access to Service Class: Native-born Females

fitted probability of reaching the service class and the horizontal axis shows educational levels in descending order.[34] On the whole, the spectrum of curves displays a negative linear relationship between probability of reaching the service class and decreasing educational levels. It is clear that the curve for Chinese lies above the other curves most of the time, indicating a Chinese ethnic advantage (defined as fitted probabilities) compared with nearly all other ethnic groups. Compared with majority whites, however, Chinese display a pattern of differentiation. For instance, at the two highest educational levels, the curve for Chinese coincides with that for whites, indicating a similar predicted probability of reaching the service class. At lower educational levels, Chinese seem to enjoy an ethnic advantage over whites.

Table 7.10 Goodness of Fit: Native-Born Females (N=40,658)

Access to Service Class

Model	G^2	d.f	ΔG^2	Δd.f	p-value	$rG^2(\%)$	ID
Baseline	471	257			0.0000		4.18
Ethnicity	328	249	143	8	0.0006	30	2.98
Educ.Ethn	267	225	60	24	0.0281	43	2.76[35]

Risks of Unemployment

Model	G^2	d.f	ΔG^2	Δd.f	p-value	$rG^2(\%)$	ID
Baseline	338	257			0.0005		13.25
Ethnicity	238	249	99	8	0.6736	30	10.26
Educ.Ethn	220	225	18	24	0.6736	35	10.26[36]

With regard to risks of unemployment, hypothesis testing shows us that the ethnicity model provides a better fit than the baseline model. After

[34]The curve for Vietnamese has not been presented simply because the number of Vietnamese is very small.

[35]The other two-way interactions are not controlled for, as neither is statistically significant at the 0.05 level.

[36]The other two-way interactions are not controlled for, as neither is statistically significant at the 0.05 level.

adding the effect of ethnicity into the baseline mode, the change in G^2 is 99 for 8 degrees of freedom. This reduces deviance by 30% and the index of dissimilarity by 2.99. Therefore, we reject the null hypothesis and accept the alternative hypothesis that, age and education being equal, ethnicity affects risks of unemployment. Since the ethnicity by education model fails to provide a superior fit, we take the ethnicity model as the best fitting model.

Listed in Table 7.11 are parameter estimates for the ethnicity model. After controlling for age and education, Chinese have worse chances (defined as fitted log odds) than Japanese of avoiding unemployment. The fitted odds of Japanese being unemployed rather than being in work are 63% those of Chinese. On the other hand, Chinese have better chances (defined as fitted odds) than Hispanics and blacks of avoiding unemployment. For instance, the fitted odds of Hispanics being unemployed as against otherwise are nearly 1.7 times those of Chinese, and the fitted odds of blacks in this respect are 1.9 times those of Chinese. Moreover, given the same age, ethnic differences remain constant at all educational levels.

Table 7.11 Native-Born Females: Risks of Unemployment

	Estimate	s.e.	Parameter
1	-3.824	0.1819	1
2	-0.2232	0.07761	AGE(2)
3	-0.4421	0.08679	AGE(3)
4	-0.5664	0.09464	AGE(4)
5	-0.6162	0.09892	AGE(5)
6	-0.5302	0.09511	AGE(6)
7	-0.8306	0.1102	AGE(7)
8	-0.6657	0.1240	AGE(8)
9	0.4177	0.1220	EDUC(2)
10	0.8764	0.1183	EDUC(3)
11	1.473	0.1235	EDUC(4)
12	**-0.4680(.63)**	**0.1858**	**ETHN(2)**
13	-0.07110	0.2538	ETHN(3)
14	0.09489	0.4804	ETHN(4)
15	0.1395	0.3217	ETHN(5)
16	-5.404	9.579	ETHN(6)
17	**0.5531(1.74)**	**0.1712**	**ETHN(7)**
18	**0.6152(1.85)**	**0.1652**	**ETHN(8)**
19	0.2311	0.1544	ETHN(9)

213

In this section, we have found that native-born Chinese women have better chances than most non-white ethnic groups of gaining access to the service class. With regard to risks of unemployment, native-born Chinese women suffer an ethnic penalty only in comparison with native-born Japanese women.   Generally, native-born Chinese seem to enjoy an ethnic advantage over non-Asian groups, while having similar chances as most Asian Americans. Therefore, we have found the native-born Asian Americans as a whole achieving relatively greater levels of class attainment than non-Asian Americans.

Enclave economy: the Chinese case

In this section, we address the enclave economy hypothesis with special reference to Chinese occupational attainments in the U.S.. At this stage, we postulate, in line with hypotheses advanced by Portes et al,[37] that being employed in the enclave economy does not entail a lower rate of occupational returns to education. Occupational attainment is measured by two indicators, access to the service class and petit-bourgeoisie combined, and risks of unemployment. The analysis is conducted on the sample of Chinese only, since the Chinese enclave economy in catering and related industries is well established.   It ought to be pointed out that the first response variable, which indicates the more advantaged class is a combination of Goldthorpe's classes I, II, IVa, IVb and IVc. It includes not only higher and lower grade professionals, administrators, and managers, but also small proprietors, with or without employees.   The reason for including petit-bourgeoisie in the service class is to give a fair chance to those ethnic minority members who become employers and managers through self-employment.   They may not be included in Goldthorpe classes I and II, because the data are coded in such a way that self-employed non-professionals are given the status of petit-bourgeoisie. By limiting the service class to employee managers, we might have missed many ethnic entrepreneurs who prosper through self-employment in the enclave economy.[38]

---

[37]A. Portes and A. Stepick, "Unwelcomed Immigrants: The Labour Market Experiences of 1980 (Mariel) Cuban and Haitian Refugees in South Florida," *American Sociological Review* (1985) 50: 493-514; K.L.Wilson and A. Portes, "Immigrant Enclave: An Analysis of the Labour Market Experiences of Cubans in Miami," *American Journal of Sociology* 86 (1980) 295-319.
[38]The whole matter would be easier if we knew the number of people working in the firm, as we did in the British case. In statistical analysis of the first four sections, we used a rather restricted measure of the service class, excluding self-employed people working in firms with even more than 25 people. In this section, we use a less restricted measure

Age, education and industrial sector will be treated as explanatory variables. As age and education remain unchanged, industrial sector is introduced for the first time as a dummy variable dichotomizing between enclave and non-enclave economy.[39]

We shall test three hypotheses with regard to sector differences in occupational success. First, we assume that chances of reaching the service class and risks of unemployment depend on age and education. Sector has no effect on class. This model which we call the baseline model, is written:

$$Ln \ (P/1\text{-}P) = \beta_0 + \beta_1(AGE) + \beta_2(EDUC).$$

Secondly, we assume that, at the same age and education, a Chinese person's class depends on whether he/she works inside the Chinese enclave economy or outside the enclave in the wider labour market. This model, which we call the enclave model, is written:

$$Ln \ (P/1\text{-}P) = \beta_0 + \beta_1(AGE) + \beta_2(EDUC) + \beta_3(ENCL).$$

Thirdly, we postulate that the effect of sector on class varies with education. For instance, our previous analyses indicated that unqualified Chinese had an edge over unqualified members of other ethnic groups in avoiding unemployment. Could this be attributable to the Chinese enclave economy, which provides sufficient employment opportunities for its own members? At this stage, we postulate that working within the enclave economy entails a greater pay-off for the unqualified rather than the qualified Chinese. Therefore we shall compare the fit of the following two models, which we call the control model and the enclave by education model:[40]

---

of the service class, including self-employed people working in firms with even less than 25 people.

[39]In dividing the industrial sector into enclave and non-enclave economies, we have, in general, followed the definition of Zhou and Logan. Thus the enclave industry include the 1980 PUMS standard industry codes 132-152, 500-532, 540-542, 550-571, 580-691, 771-780, and 812-830. The non-enclave industry include all the other industrial codes except 991-992. The non-enclave industry is more broadly defined than Zhou and Logan by adding into it the occupational categories of "public administration".

[40]To do a conservative test, we control for two other two-way interaction effects of age by education and age by enclave before adding the interaction effect of enclave by education.

215

$$\text{Ln } (P/1\text{-}P) = \beta_0 + \beta_1(\text{AGE}) + \beta_2(\text{EDUC}) + \beta_3(\text{ENCL})$$
$$+ \beta_4(\text{AGE.EDUC}) + \beta_5(\text{AGE.ENCL});$$
$$\text{Ln } (P/1\text{-}P) = \beta_0 + \beta_1(\text{AGE}) + \beta_2(\text{EDUC}) + \beta_3(\text{ENCL})$$
$$+ \beta_4(\text{AGE.EDUC}) + \beta_5(\text{AGE.ENCL}) + \beta_6(\text{EDUC.ENCL}).$$

Table 7.12 Goodness of Fit: Chinese Enclave Economy

Access to Service Class (Male Immigrants N=7,218)

Model	G^2	d.f	ΔG^2	Δd.f	p-value	$rG(\%)^2$	ID
Baseline	155	46			0.0000		3.90
Enclave	116	45	39	1	0.0000	25	3.13
Control	92	39	24	6	0.0000	41	2.75
Educ.Encl	49	36	43	3	0.0703	68	2.18

Risks of Unemployment (Male Immigrants N=7,218)

Model	G^2	d.f	ΔG^2	Δd.f	p-value	$rG(\%)^2$	ID
Baseline	72	46			0.0084		20.94
Ethnicity	72	45	0.1	1	0.0066	0	20.86
Educ.Encl	62	42	10	3	0.0231	14	20.22

Access to Service Class (Female Immigrants N=5,397)

Model	G^2	d.f	ΔG^2	Δd.f	p-value	$rG(\%)^2$	ID
Baseline	93	46			0.0001		5.79
Enclave	73	45	20	1	0.0049	22	4.90
Educ.Encl	46	42	27	3	0.2975	51	4.22

Risks of Unemployment (Female Immigrants N=5,397)

Model	G^2	d.f	ΔG^2	Δd.f	p-value	$rG(\%)^2$	ID
Baseline	77	46			0.0026		21.80
Enclave	63	45	14	1	0.0366	18	19.11
Control	32	27	31	18	0.2206	58	11.18
Educ.Encl	23	24	10	3	0.5479	70	9.77

(to be continued)

(continued)

Access to Service Class (Native-Born Males N=2,157)

Model	G^2	d.f	ΔG^2	Δd.f	p-value	$rG(\%)^2$	ID
Baseline	66	46			0.0299		4.12
Enclave	65	45	0.2	1	0.0249	1.5	4.06

Risks of Unemployment (Native-Born Male N=2,157)

Model	G^2	d.f	ΔG^2	Δd.f	p-value	$rG(\%)^2$	ID
Baseline	34	46			0.8982		33.80
Enclave	33	45	1	1	0.8989	2.9	33.00

Access to Service Class (Native-Born Female N=1,733)

Model	G^2	d.f	ΔG^2	Δd.f	p-value	$rG(\%)^2$	ID
Baseline	63	44			0.0308		5.82
Enclave	56	43	7	1	0.0865	11	5.06

Risks of Unemployment (Native-Born Female N=1,733)

Model	G^2	d.f	ΔG^2	Δd.f	p-value	$rG(\%)^2$	ID
Baseline	47	44			0.3334		35.77
Enclave	42	43	5	1	0.5023	11	32.14

As far as Chinese male immigrants are concerned, we find that chances of reaching the service class and risks of unemployment not only vary working inside or outside the enclave economy, but the effect of sector on class also varies with educational levels. As indicated in Table 7.12, the null hypotheses of the enclave model and the enclave by education model are both rejected.

To illustrate the interaction effect of enclave by education, a graphical representation has been provided in Figure 7.6[41] for the age cohort of 35-39.[42] The vertical axis stands for probability of reaching the service class in percentage form, with the value ranging from 0 to 100, and the horizontal axis stands for education, where 1=postgraduate, 2=college, 3=high school completed and 4=high school not completed. It is shown that among people with postgraduate and college education, chances of reaching the service class are better if working outside the enclave economy, that is, holding other things constant. However, the advantage (defined as fitted probability) associated with working in the wider labour market is not constant at all educational levels. At levels of high school completion and below, the advantage lies with the enclave workers. The advantage associated with working outside the enclave economy seems to favour the well educated rather than the poorly educated.

With regard to risks of unemployment, the interaction effect of enclave by education is presented for the age cohort of 35-39 in Figure 7.7.[43] At postgraduate and college level, those working outside the ethnic enclave enjoy an advantage (defined as fitted probability) in avoidance of unemployment. However, the effect of the enclave on risks of unemployment is found to vary with the level of education. At levels of high school completion and below, the fitted probabilities of unemployment are somewhat lower for the enclave workers. This implies that the advantage in avoiding unemployment which is associated with working in the wider labour market favours the well educated only, a similar finding as in respect of reaching the service class.

For female Chinese immigrants, we find similar patterns in access to the service class and risks of unemployment as for male Chines immigrants, i.e. working outside the enclave has a better pay-off for the qualified rather than the unqualified. The interaction effects of enclave by education are illustrated in Figure 7.8 for access to the service class and in Figure 7.9 for risks of unemployment.[44]

---

[41]The parameter estimates for the enclave by education model, from which the fitted probabilities are calculated, are presented in Appendix 7.11.

[42]We select this age cohort not only because occupation tends to mature in this this age band, but also because age cohort does not vary with the interaction effect of ethnicity by education, given the present model.

[43]The parameter estimates of the enclave by education model, from which the fitted probabilities are obtained, are presented in Appendix 7.12.

[44]The parameter estimates for the enclave by education model are presented in Table 7.13 for access to the service class and Table 7.14 for avoidance of unemployment.

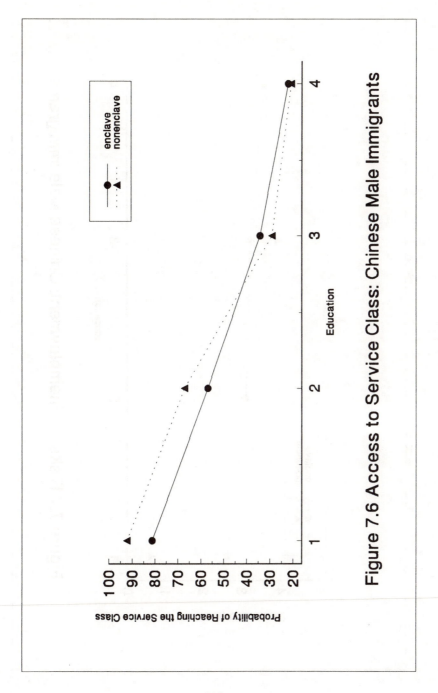

Figure 7.6 Access to Service Class: Chinese Male Immigrants

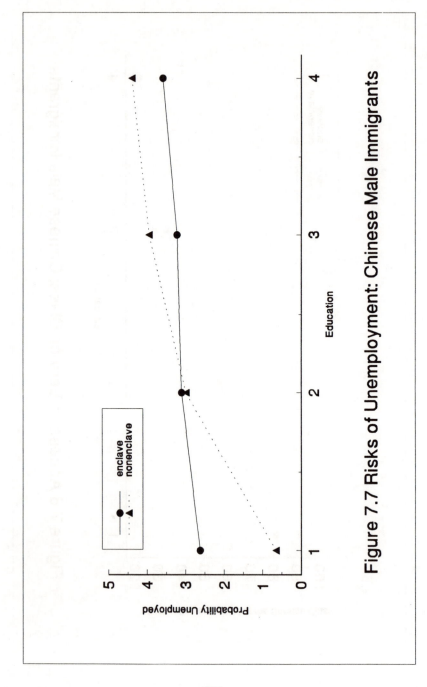

Figure 7.7 Risks of Unemployment: Chinese Male Immigrants

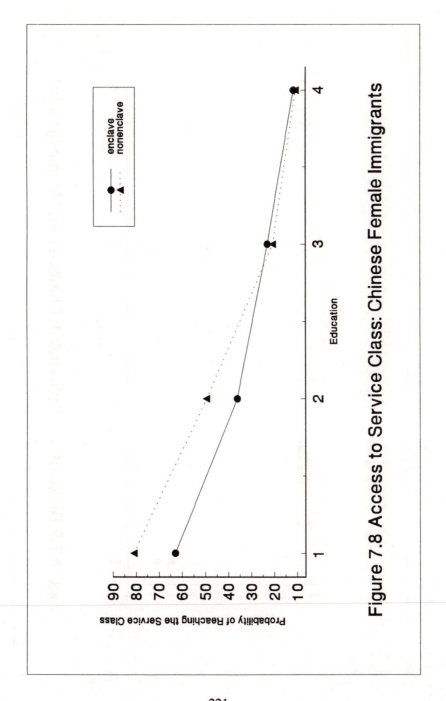

Figure 7.8 Access to Service Class: Chinese Female Immigrants

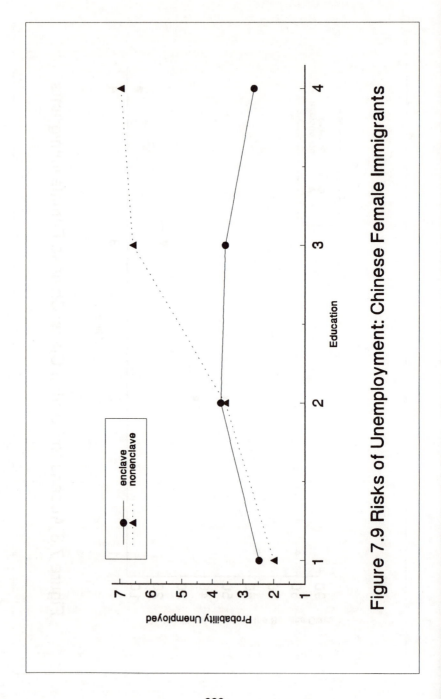

Figure 7.9 Risks of Unemployment: Chinese Female Immigrants

As far as native-born Chinese males are concerned, we test the three hypotheses stated in the baseline model, the enclave model, and the enclave by education model. The measures of goodness of fit are reported in Table 7.12. With regard to access to the service class, we find the enclave model giving no better fit than the baseline model. Nor does the enclave by education model give a better fit than the enclave model. Therefore, we fail to reject the null hypotheses of both the enclave model and the ethnicity by education model. As a result, the baseline model is taken as the best fitting model. In Table 7.13, parameter estimates are presented for the baseline model, where class is a function of age and education.

Table 7.13 Chinese Native-Born Males: Access to Service Class

	Estimate	s.e.	Parameter
1	1.402	0.1297	1
2	0.4125	0.1414	AGE(2)
3	0.7344	0.1779	AGE(3)
4	0.5306	0.2082	AGE(4)
5	0.5962	0.1803	AGE(5)
6	1.154	0.1881	AGE(6)
7	1.159	0.1866	AGE(7)
8	-1.491	0.1287	EDUC(2)
9	-2.745	0.1673	EDUC(3)
10	-3.384	0.2553	EDUC(4)

With regard to risks of unemployment, too, we fit the enclave model and the enclave by education model. The effect of enclave and enclave by education are both found to be statistically insignificant at the 0.05 level, i.e. the effect of working in or out of the enclave economy is independent of access to the service class. As a result the final model is one which assumes that risks of unemployment are a function of age and education only. The parameter estimates of this final model are presented in Table 7.14.

As far as native-born Chinese females are concerned, we find in Table 7.12 that chances of reaching the service class vary with sector. The null hypothesis of the enclave model is rejected. As shown in Table 7.15, after controlling for age and education, the fitted odds of people working outside the enclave economy reaching the service class, rather than not, are one and half times those of enclave workers. Because the interaction effect of enclave by education is not statistically significant at 0.05 level, the advantage associated with working in the wider labour market is considered the same at all educational levels.

Table 7.14 Chinese Native-Born Males: Risks of Unemployment

	Estimate	s.e.	Parameter
1	-4.510	0.4716	1
2	0.03931	0.4347	AGE(2)
3	-1.144	0.7732	AGE(3)
4	-0.6667	0.7753	AGE(4)
5	-1.073	0.7743	AGE(5)
6	-0.7773	0.6668	AGE(6)
7	-0.05653	0.5168	AGE(7)
8	0.8043	0.4757	EDUC(2)
9	**1.587**	**0.5254**	**EDUC(3)**
10	0.08189	1.109	EDUC(4)

Table 7.15 Chinese Native-Born Females: Access to Service Class

	Estimate	s.e.	Parameter
1	1.298	0.1974	1
2	0.1384	0.1497	AGE(2)
3	0.3365	0.2037	AGE(3)
4	0.2172	0.2123	AGE(4)
5	0.2496	0.2025	AGE(5)
6	-0.01813	0.2313	AGE(6)
7	0.3729	0.1953	AGE(7)
8	**-1.937**	**0.1553**	**EDUC(2)**
9	**-2.757**	**0.1888**	**EDUC(3)**
10	**-3.021**	**0.3006**	**EDUC(4)**
11	**0.3546(1.4)**	**0.1349**	**ENCL(2)**

Risks of unemployment, too, are found to vary with sector but not with the interaction effect of enclave by education, controlling for other things. Therefore, we reject the null hypotheses stated by the enclave model but not the hypothesis stated by the enclave by education model. As shown in Table 7.16, the fitted odds of people working inside the enclave being unemployed are nearly twice those of people working outside the enclave. Such sector difference is the same at all educational levels.

Table 7.16 Chinese Native-Born Females: Risks of Unemployment

	Estimate	s.e.	Parameter
1	-3.249	0.5032	1
2	-0.1350	0.3953	AGE(2)
3	0.03954	0.4947	AGE(3)
4	-0.5701	0.6411	AGE(4)
5	-0.8331	0.6496	AGE(5)
6	-0.8815	0.6694	AGE(6)
7	**-1.378**	**0.6686**	**AGE(7)**
8	0.4433	0.4429	EDUC(2)
9	0.7861	0.5090	EDUC(3)
10	1.423	0.6436	EDUC(4)
11	**-0.7599(.47)**	**0.3225**	**ENCL(2)**

To summarize, we have found that, among Chinese immigrants, both access to the service class and risks of unemployment vary according to whether one works inside or outside the enclave economy. Working outside the enclave economy entails greater occupational pay-offs only for the well educated, whereas working inside the enclave economy benefits the poorly educated to a greater extent. Because of this, we may conclude that the enclave economy serves, to a certain extent, as a safety net which softens the disadvantage in occupational attainments associated with unfavourable educational backgrounds. For native-born Chinese, working in the wider labour market seems to have an advantage over working in the enclave economy for the females only. For males, sector seems to make no difference either to access to the service class or risks of unemployment.[45]

Conclusions

First, it can be readily stated that different processes are at work for immigrants and native-born Chinese. Compared with other ethnic groups, Chinese immigrants, both male and female, display more differentiated patterns of reaching the service class varied by educational level, and less differentiated patterns in risks of unemployment. Although native-born Chinese exhibit a certain ethnic advantage over non-Asian groups in occupational returns to education, the ethnic difference is constant among people of all educational backgrounds. Secondly, the Chinese enclave economy helps poorly qualified Chinese enter the service class and avoid unemployment. However, the advantage associated with working in the enclave economy seems restricted to first generation Chinese only. For the second and subsequent generations, in particular females, greater occupational success is undoubtedly achieved by breaking away from the traditional enclave economy.

---

[45]This finding about the gender difference seems to be in agreement with the earlier finding by Zhou and Logan on the New York City Chinatown.

8 Occupational attainments of Chinese in Britain and the United States: A comparison

Introduction

Recently, there has been a revival of interest in the old topic of American exceptionalism, which was first proposed by de Tocqueville more than a century ago.[1] In spite of studies by American scholars in favour of American exceptionalism in general,[2] scholars outside America have argued on the basis of empirical evidence that, in certain aspects of social life, America is no different from other industrial societies under comparison.[3]

In this chapter, we compare the experience of Chinese in Britain with the experience of Chinese in the U.S. with regard to occupational attainment, relative to non-Chinese in each country. The significance of this comparison displays itself at three related levels.

First, by providing the most up-to-date quantified comparative material on the relative chance of Chinese occupational success in two advanced industrialized societies, we may answer a broader sociological question as to whether there is country disparity in the level of relative occupational success of an ethnic minority.

Secondly, from the perspective of rigorous empirical inquiry, the comparative evidence obtained may be used to confirm or refute common perceptions of the relative occupational levels of Chinese in the two

---

[1]Alexis de Tocqueville, *Democracy in America* (New York: Random House, 1990).

[2]Byron E. Shafer, ed. *Is America Different: A New Look at American Exceptionalism* (Oxford: Clarendon Press, 1991).

[3]Robert Erikson and John Goldthorpe, "Are American Social Mobility Rates Exceptionally High? New Evidence on an Old Issue," *European Sociological Review* 1 (1985)1-22; A.C. Kerckhoff, R.T. Campell and I. Wingfield-Laird, "Social Mobility in Great Britain and the United States," *American Journal of Sociology* 91 (1985) 281-308.

countries. For instance, it may support or oppose the so called "American exceptionalism" and its implied impact on the occupational success of Chinese in the U.S. In this chapter, American exceptionalism is taken to mean that there are greater opportunities for Chinese immigrants to succeed occupationally in the U.S. than in Britain.

Finally, from a policy perspective, it may be appropriate to ask whether lessons can be learnt from the past experience of these countries with regard to the immigration and subsequent integration of Chinese into the dominant occupational structure. This could be of assistance to those involved in making policy on immigration and community relations.

"As a sociological tool, the comparative method is useful as a means of establishing characteristics of social systems that are universal, or at least common to the societies and periods of time compared, and those which are unique, or particular to the time and place in question".[4]

The immigration of Chinese into Britain and the U.S. started at approximately the same time, and was more or less motivated by aspirations common to most immigrants to the Western world, i.e. opportunities for better occupational status and greater economic success. What has been noticeable about Chinese, however, is the tradition of placing high value on education.[5] This promotes the pursuit of academic and technical qualifications in order to achieve relatively high level of occupational success.

This seems to be true of foreign-born and native-born Chinese in both Britain and the U.S., as seen from their relatively higher proportions of people holding university degrees and above, when compared with other ethnic minorities. Nevertheless, educational achievements only provide partial underlying conditions for occupational success in these countries. Intervening variables, such as the unique occupational structure in each country, different educational systems, and, more importantly, varying mechanisms through which education is transformed into occupational success constitute the remaining underlying conditions. Variations in any of these conditions might affect the chance of Chinese attaining a similar level of relative occupational attainment in the two countries.

Previously, in Chapters V and VII, we investigated the relative level of occupational attainment for Chinese immigrants in Britain and the U.S.. In conducting statistical analysis, we operationalized occupational

---

[4]Anthony Richmond, "Race Relations and Immigration: A Comparative Perspective," *International Journal of Comparative Sociology* XXXI (1990) 156-176.

[5]Charles Hirschman and Morris Wong, "The Extraordinary Educational Attainments of Asian Americans: A Search for Historical Evidences and Explanations," *Social Forces* 65 (1986) 1-27.

attainment into chances of reaching the service class and risks of unemployment. We assumed that chances of reaching the service class and risks of unemployment vary with ethnicity. Moreover, we assumed that ethnic effects on occupational attainment differ for people with different levels of education. We therefore fitted three models according to three hypotheses with regard to ethnic difference in class. These three models, which we called the baseline model, the ethnicity model, and the ethnicity by education model, are written as follows:

Baseline Model:

$$\text{Ln } (P/1-P) = \beta_0 + \beta_1(AGE) + \beta_2(EDUC)$$

Ethnicity Model:

$$\text{Ln } (P/1-P) = \beta_0 + \beta_1(AGE) + \beta_2(EDUC) + \beta_3(ETHN)$$

Ethnicity by Education Model:

$$\text{Ln } (P/1-P) = \beta_0 + \beta_1(AGE) + \beta_2(EDUC) + \beta_3(ETHN)$$
$$+ \beta_4(AGE.EDUC) + \beta_5(AGE.ETHN) + \beta_6(EDUC.ETHN).$$

Results obtained on the relative level of Chinese occupational attainment have indicated that Chinese in both countries enjoy a similar ethnic advantage over many other ethnic groups. This is especially true of male immigrants. More rigorous comparative analysis is therefore required.

In the next section, we shall summarize similarities and differences emerging from previous analysis. The purpose is to extract what is common to Chinese immigrants in Britain and the U.S. and to derive the comparative hypothesis. Later, we shall test the comparative hypothesis by fitting logit models.

Previous findings: summary

Male immigrants: a comparison

Previous analysis indicates that both British and American Chinese males are in a relatively advantageous position to reach the service class, compared with other non-white ethnic minorities. Both groups reached parity with majority whites in this respect. American Chinese, however,

229

while doing better than most non-white groups, still lagged behind Japanese and Indians. British Chinese do as well as Irish and are better off than all other non-white minority groups. Therefore, the relative ethnic advantage for Chinese male immigrants in access to the service class in Britain appears to be somewhat greater than that of their counterparts in the U.S.

As for risks of unemployment, the ethnic advantage is confirmed for Chinese in both countries. Chinese Americans break even with Japanese, but have better chances than nearly all other groups of avoiding unemployment, including American whites. Chinese in Britain have better chances of doing so than all other non-white minority groups and share similar chances with British whites. In both cases, however, the ethnic advantage of Chinese is greater among the unqualified than among the qualified.

Female immigrants: a comparison

Compared with their male counterparts, Chinese female immigrants have a relatively lower degree of ethnic advantage in access to the service class and avoidance of unemployment, compared to other ethnic groups. This is true of foreign-born Chinese women in both Britain and the U.S.

As far as access to the service class is concerned, British Chinese women have similar chances as Indians and Pakistanis at all educational levels. Compared with all other ethnic groups, they suffer an ethnic penalty in reaching this class. The American Chinese, however, display ethnic advantage over four non-white groups (Japanese, Koreans, Vietnamese, and Hispanics) at higher educational levels. Among the unqualified, Chinese have a lower propensity to reach the service class than all other ethnic groups.

With regard to unemployment, what is common to foreign-born Chinese women in both countries is that they share similar chances as majority white women of avoiding unemployment. Compared with other non-white ethnic minorities, Chinese women in the U.S. have better chances than all except Filipinos of avoiding unemployment. Similarly, compared with other non-white female minorities, Chinese in Britain have better chances of avoiding unemployment than all except Irish.

Comparative hypotheses

The common perceptions of the occupational attainments of the Chinese community in Britain is one of occupational segregation. Chinese are considered to be concentrated in the enclave economy, which is centred around the single industry of catering and geographically dispersed over the country. This gives rise to the stereotype of Chinese keeping a low profile in the wider society.

Previous studies of Chinese occupational attainment focused mainly on the catering communities in Britain and neglected Chinese participating in the wider labour market. Although studies were conducted to compare the occupational attainments of ethnic minorities, such as South Asians and Afro-Caribbeans, in relation to majority whites, it was not customary among British researchers to include Chinese in the comparison. Consequently, common perceptions of Chinese occupational levels passed unchecked.

On the other hand, American literature on the occupational attainments of ethnic minorities over the past three decades seems to have reached a consensus on the relatively successful occupational experience of Chinese in American society, and particularly, the role of educational success in leading to prestigious occupations. This empirical research helps strengthen the idea of American exceptionalism, in defence of which Temin wrote, "The United States none the less remains somewhat open to the immigration of Asians and Latin Americans. These new Americans are being absorbed into the economy and society of the United States in a free wheeling fashion reminiscent of frontier settlement. Individuals are free to go their own way, and the success of individuals is celebrated. American education is very open and inclusive, providing an avenue for immigrants of all sorts to make their way into the higher levels of the economy in a very few generations".[6]

Temin may be right in saying that immigrants achieve high levels of occupational attainment, as our own research indicates. It is less clear, however, whether America is exceptional in this respect. We suspect that the notion of America being exceptional arises less from real differences in immigrant occupational attainment than from a lack of knowledge of what immigrants achieve in other industrialized societies.

Our earlier separate analyses showed patterns of similarity with regard to the relative level of occupational success for Chinese in Britain and the U.S.. This similarity is less evident among female than among male immigrants. Nevertheless, our results concerning British Chinese, obtained for the first time from a nationally representative sample, displayed patterns contrary to the common perception. This gives rise to the hypothesis that the occupational attainment level of Chinese in relation to others in Britain

---

[6]Peter Temin, "Free Land and Federalism: American Economic Exceptionalism," *Is America Different*, ed. Byron E. Shafer (Oxford: Clarendon Press, 1991) 92-93.

is actually not significantly different from that of Chinese in the U.S..

Hypothesis testing

To test the comparative hypothesis that Chinese in Britain and the U.S. have similar relative chances of access to the service class and avoiding unemployment, we need to find out the interaction effect of "ethnicity by country" over class. In conducting the statistical analysis, we operationalize the variable of "ethnicity" into 1 = "Chinese" and 2 = "non-Chinese",[7] and the variable of "country" into 1 = "Britain" and 2 = "the U.S.A.". Therefore, the interaction term implies that the effect on class of being Chinese or not varies with whether one lives in Britain or the U.S.. It follows that the null hypothesis suggests that chances of Chinese reaching the service class or being unemployed, as against otherwise, are the same in both countries.

In testing the comparative hypothesis, logistic regression analysis is conducted over a pooled data set comprising of a sub-sample of the 1983 to 1989 British Labour Force Surveys and a sub-sample of the 1980 American Population Census.[8] An important question arising from the use of a cross-nationally combined data set is whether measures of the response and explanatory variables are comparable. It is important to note that, in comparative analysis, differences in the final result may not be caused by difference in the relationship of variables as much as by the incomparability of the variables.

In this secondary analysis, the response variable is class. In one case, it takes the form of a dichotomy between the service and the rest, and, in the other case, a dichotomy between the unemployed and those in work. As discussed earlier, in the British case, the class variable was first derived from two variables of "socio-economic status" and "employment status" by following Goldthorpe's class schema. Then the American data were

---

[7]Non-Chinese refers to all other ethnic groups included in the previous analysis of relative occupational attainments of Chinese in Britain and the U.S.A.. In the case of Britain, non-Chinese refers to immigrant groups with Indian, Pakistani, West Indian, and Irish origin, and British-born whites. In the case of the U.S., non-Chinese refers to immigrant groups with Japanese, Korean, Filipino, Indian and Vietnamese origins, Hispanics, blacks, and whites.

[8]Note the difference in the dates of British and American data. This is expected to cause difference in the constant of the model. The structural differences are controlled for in the model. For the British data, the interaction effect of class and ethnicity has been found constant over years. Therefore, no opposing evidence is present for pooling the LFS data from 1983 to 1989.

translated into the same class schema to make the measures of class as comparable as possible.

The explanatory variables include age, ethnicity, country, and education. Age is a multinomial variable, where 1=25-29, 2=30-34, 3=35-39, 4=40-44, 5=45-49, 6=50-54, 7=55-60, and 8=60-64. Ethnicity is a dummy variable, with 1=Chinese and 2=non-Chinese. Country, too, is a dummy variable, with 1=Britain and 2=the U.S.A..

Of the explanatory variables, education, in particular, involves the question of comparability. Complications arise, as the American school system is one of overall incremental progress, whereas Britain has various school systems for even the same age cohort. Thus, in earlier separate analyses, we used different educational predictors: "the highest qualification" for Britain and "the highest grade attended" for the U.S.. In carrying out the comparative study, we cannot employ two separate indicators for the same factor, i.e. education. Therefore we shall adopt a strategy of recoding the variable of education of one country at one time to make it comparable to that of the other country.

As a first step, we keep the variable of "the highest qualification". As it is our preferred indicator for the British data, we recode the American variable of education, i.e. "the highest grade attended", and make it as comparable as we can to the British variable. In this way, we obtain a four category measure of the highest educational qualification as follows:

1. first degree and above
2. A-level and equivalent
3. O-level, CSE and equivalent
4. no qualification.[9]

As a second step, we keep the American variable of education, i.e. the "highest grade attended". As it is our preferred indicator for the American educational level, we recode the British variable of education to make it as comparable as we can to the American one. In the British Labour Force Survey, the variable, which is the closest in meaning to the American variable of "the highest grade attended" is "terminal age of continuous full-time education". To achieve maximum comparability, we recode both the American and the British variable into the International Standard

---

[9]The American equivalent of the four British qualifications are listed as follows:
Degree and Higher: fourth-year college and above
A-level: 12th grade and 1st, 2nd and 3rd year college
O-level: 9th, 10th and 11th grade
no qualification: nursery, kindergarten, 1st to 8th grade.

Classification of Education.[10] What we obtain subsequently is a four category indicator of education:

1. pre-first level
2. first level
3. second level
4. post-secondary level.[11]

In subsequent statistical analyses, we shall use the two educational indicators interchangeably. If the results we obtain from a logistic regression using one education variable are not different from those obtained when the other education variable is used, we may conclude that the indicators have reached a sufficient degree of comparability to provide us with reliable information on the relationship between education and class.

We fit the model where we assume that chances of reaching the service class or risks of unemployment depend on age, education, ethnicity, country, education by country, and ethnicity by country. We therefore compare the fit of the following two models, which we call the baseline model, corresponding to the null hypothesis, and the comparative model:

---

[10]UNESCO, *Statistical Year Book*, 1990, p.3-7 to 3-12.

[11] Pre-first level refers to the ISCED (International Standard Classification of Education) categories 1 and 2, i.e. "no schooling" applying to those who have completed less than one year of education, and "incompleted first level" referring to those who completed at least one year of education at the first level, but who did not complete the final grade at this level.

First level refers to those who completed the final grade of education at the first level but did not go on to second level studies.

Second level comprises those whose level of educational attainment was limited to the lower stage of education at the second level, and those who moved to the higher stage of second level of education from the lower stage but did not proceed to studies at the third level.

Post-secondary level refers to anyone who undertook third level studies. Whether or not they completed the full course, they would be counted in this category.

To transform the American data into the ISCED categories, I first added 3 to the "highest year of school attended" to obtain the age of attending the highest year of school specified. Then, I collapsed the new variable into the equivalent of the ISCED categories, where $1 = 5,6$; $2 = 7$ to 14; $3 = 15$ to 18 and $4 = 19$ to 26 and over.

To transform the British data, I recoded the age terminating continuous fulltime education into $1 = 5$; $2 = 6$ to 11; $3 = 12$ to 18; $4 = 19$ to 29 and over.

234

Baseline Model:

$$Ln(P/1-P) = \beta_0 + \beta_1(age) + \beta_2(education) + \beta_3(ethnicity) + \beta_4(country) + \beta_5(education*country);[12]$$

Comparative Model:

$$Ln(P/1-P) = \beta_0 + \beta_1(age) + \beta_2(education) + \beta_3(ethnicity) + \beta_4(country) + \beta_5(education*country) + \beta_6(ethnicity*country).[13]$$

Access to the service class

We fit the comparative model separately for males and females, first using "the highest qualification" as the indicator for education, in which case the better variable is preserved for the British case, and then using "the highest grade attended", which suits the American data better, to check the results.

Table 8.1 Goodness of Fit: Access to the Service Class

Males (N=80,271)

Model	G^2	d.f	ΔG^2	Δd.f	p-value	rG^2(%)	ID
Baseline	261.13	109			0.0000		1.837
Comparative	260.64	108	0.495	1	0.000 0	0.2	1.832

Females (N=61,252)

Model	G^2	d.f	ΔG^2	Δd.f	p-value	rG^2(%)	ID
Baseline	136.53	102			0.0128		1.534
Comparative	136.47	101	0.064	1	0.0108	0.04	1.530

---

[12]We could control for other interaction terms in the model. The reason we have not done so is to give "ethnicity by country" maximum chance to be statistically significant at the 0.05 level.

[13]The results based on the American variable of education are presented in Appendices 8.1-8.6.

It can be seen from Table 8.1 that after adding the interaction effect of ethnicity by country into the baseline model, the change in G^2 is 0.495 for 1 degree of freedom for males. This implies that, other things being equal, the effect of ethnicity on access to the service class does not vary with country. Similarly, in the case of females, the change of G^2 is 0.064 for 1 degree of freedom. These results imply that ethnic difference in reaching the service class remains constant across countries. Therefore, we fail to reject the null hypothesis as stated in the baseline model for both males and females.

It ought to be noted that in addition to our efforts to make response and explanatory variables comparable, there are structural differences between the two societies for which we have controlled. For instance, American Chinese may be more likely to enter the service class than British Chinese, simply because a higher proportion of service class jobs are available in the U.S. than in Britain. Therefore, a greater proportion of Americans (Chinese or non-Chinese), may hold service class jobs. Such speculations are supported by the large positive regression coefficient on "country", with $B_{4[COUN(2)]}=0.8231$ and s.e=0.1875 for males in Table 8.2 and $B_{4[COUN(2)]}=2.166$ and s.e=0.3148 for females in Table 8.3. Compared with the British in general and other things being equal, Americans are much more likely to reach the service class.[14]

Another country difference concerns the link between certain qualifications and occupational prospects. Generally speaking, the U.S. has developed a large and diverse system of colleges and universities catering

---

[14]To check the level of comparability of education variables, we fit the same model while keeping the American variable of education and converting the British variable of education. We find in Appendix 8.1 that in the case of males, after adding the interaction effect of ethnicity by country into the model, the change in G^2 is 14.36 for 1 degree of freedom. This change is statistically significant at the 0.05 level. In Appendix 8.2, after controlling for other things, the parameter estimate $b_{6[ETHN(2)COUN(2)]}=-0.5828$ and s.e=0.1603. Therefore, Chinese males are better placed to reach the service class relative to non-Chinese in the U.S. than Chinese males in Britain. Of course, we may argue that the sample used for this analysis is as big as 82,482. By fitting the comparative model, we have only improved the Index of Dissimilarity by 0.038%. Therefore, the interaction effect of ethnicity by country is not considered very important, although it is statistically significant. We also tried to fit the model by controlling for other two-way or even three-way interactions, such as age by ethnicity, age by country, age by education, age by education by country. Yet the interaction effect of ethnicity by country is still statistically significant at the 0.05 level. Therefore, the result we obtained failed to reject the American exceptionalism in this particular test. In the case of females, the change in G^2 is 0.037 with 1 degree of freedom. In this case the change in G^2 is statistically insignificant at the 0.05 level. Therefore, country difference in access to the service class disappears for female Chinese immigrants.

for students of nearly all abilities, ages, and interests, whereas Britain has created a system of universities, polytechnics, and colleges for academically gifted students only. As a result, the function of American undergraduate education, especially in the first two years, is largely remedial. It brings students with widely varying ability and preparation up to a standard level. By contrast, in Britain the whole idea of general education, the introduction to the main branches of learning, is already completed in secondary schools.[15]

Table 8.2 Access to the Service Class: Males

	Estimate	s.e.	Parameter
1	-0.1313	0.1859	1
2	0.2371	0.02894	AGE(2)
3	0.3846	0.03036	AGE(3)
4	0.3810	0.03241	AGE(4)
5	0.3387	0.03478	AGE(5)
6	0.3958	0.03685	AGE(6)
7	0.3156	0.04023	AGE(7)
8	0.2338	0.04965	AGE(8)
9	-0.8470	0.08230	EDUC(2)
10	-2.067	0.07182	EDUC(3)
11	-3.512	0.1040	EDUC(4)
12	-0.02974	0.1818	ETHN(2)
13	0.8231	0.1875	COUN(2)
14	-1.266	0.08467	EDUC(2).COUN(2)
15	-1.227	0.08575	EDUC(3).COUN(2)
16	-0.2875	0.1194	EDUC(4).COUN(2)
17	-0.1288	0.1844	ETHN(2).COUN(2)

[15]Martin Trow, "American Higher Education: Exceptional or Just Different?" *Is America Different* ed, Byron E. Shafer (Oxford: Clarendon Press, 1991) 162.

It might be assumed that people with first degrees in Britain are a much smaller proportion of post-secondary school graduates, and thus have a greater propensity than the average American college graduate to enter the service class, compared with those without college degrees. For both British and American data, however, we have combined college graduates with those possessing higher degrees, postgraduate, and professional. In America, where professional education is very strong in the universities (quite unlike British universities where professional education was largely excluded[16]), the link between professional degrees and service class jobs may be tremendously strengthened. Therefore, the country difference at the highest level of education may be dampened.

Table 8.3 Access to the Service Class: Females

	Estimate	s.e.	Parameter
1	-1.805	0.3133	1
2	**0.1268**	**0.03301**	**AGE(2)**
3	**0.1250**	**0.03536**	**AGE(3)**
4	**0.09004**	**0.03821**	**AGE(4)**
5	0.03080	0.04209	AGE(5)
6	0.06565	0.04488	AGE(6)
7	0.07119	0.05083	AGE(7)
8	-0.08397	0.06731	AGE(8)
9	-0.7233	0.1281	EDUC(2)
10	**-1.635**	**0.1294**	**EDUC(3)**
11	**-3.036**	**0.2073**	**EDUC(4)**
12	0.2209	0.3096	ETHN(2)
13	**2.166**	**0.3148**	**COUN(2)**
14	**-1.339**	**0.1302**	**EDUC(2).COUN(2)**
15	**-1.550**	**0.1413**	**EDUC(3).COUN(2)**
16	**-0.9291**	**0.2239**	**EDUC(4).COUN(2)**
17	-0.07839	0.3120	ETHN(2).COUN(2)

[16]Ibid., 155.

At the level of secondary education, the American students normally follow the uniform high school system, which serves as an extension of the primary school in the structure and content of teaching.[17] British students, however, are provided with a variety of choices between academically oriented secondary schools, public or private, and vocational schools. Therefore, among those with intermediate qualifications, the average British student may have received more specialized education or training. Moreover, in Britain, professional guilds rather than universities dominate professional training, providing a part of it themselves through a form of apprenticeship. Therefore, even among those with intermediate school qualifications, the average Briton may be more likely than his American counterpart to find a skilled job, given that he may be able to translate his occupation specific qualifications more readily into employment. This speculation is confirmed to some extent by the parameter estimates taking the form of large negative values at the middle two qualifications for Americans (see $\beta_{5[EDUC(2)COUN(2)]}$ and $\beta_{5[EDUC(3)COUN(2)]}$).

It is true that, other things being equal, workers in the U.S. are more likely than those in Britain to reach the service class, and that Chinese have a greater propensity than others to do so in general. Nonetheless, this does not necessarily imply that Chinese in America are bound to have better chances of reaching the service class than British Chinese. It is readily discernible from the coefficient for ethnicity by country that, after holding structural differences constant, there is no country difference in Chinese chances (defined as fitted log odds ratio) of reaching the service class as against not reaching it, with $\beta_{6[ETHN(2)COUN(2)]}=-0.1288$ and s.e$=0.1844$ for males, and $\beta_{6[ETHN(2)COUN(2)]}=-0.0784$ and s.e$=0.3120$ for females. It may be concluded therefore that immigrants of Chinese origin in Britain and America share similar chances (defined as fitted odds) of reaching the service class. The common perception that Chinese are more successful in the U.S. than in Britain is therefore inaccurate.

Avoidance of unemployment

In studying risks of unemployment, we compare the fit of the same two models, i.e. the baseline model and the comparative model. We find in Table 8.4 that, after controlling for age, education, ethnicity, and education by country, the effect of ethnicity by country is not statistically significant at the 0.05 level for either males or females. After adding the interaction term of ethnicity by country into the model, the change in G^2 is 0.507 for 1 degree of freedom for males, and the change in G^2 is 1.013 for 1 degree

---

[17]Ibid., 163.

of freedom for females.[18] These results imply that the effect of ethnicity (being Chinese or not) on unemployment does not vary with country, holding other variables constant. Therefore, we fail to reject the null hypothesis.[19]

Table 8.4 Goodness of Fit: Risks of Unemployment

Males (N=80,271)

Model	G^2	d.f	ΔG^2	Δd.f	p-value	rG^2(%)	ID
Baseline	162.66	109			0.0007		5.183
Comparative	162.15	108	0.507	1	0.0006	31	5.183

Females (N=61,252)

Model	G^2	d.f	ΔG^2	Δd.f	p-value	rG^2(%)	ID
Baseline	166.33	102			0.0001		7.534
Comparative	165.31	101	1.013	1	0.0001	61	7.53

The parameter estimates for the comparative model have been presented in Table 8.5 for males. It can be seen that, other things being equal, Americans are less likely than British to be unemployed, with $\beta_{4[COUN(2)]}$=-0.6870 and s.e=0.2968.[20] Chinese are also better placed to

[18]The change in G^2 just gains statistical significance at the 0.05 level. Given a large sample size, this effect is tiny. Therefore, it should not be over interpreted.

[19]To check comparability of education variable, we fit the same model by keeping the American variable of education and converting the British variable. We find that when the interaction effect of ethnicity is added to the mode, the change in G^2 is 0.833 for 1 degree of freedom in the case of males. Therefore we fail to reject the null hypothesis at the 0.05 level. For females, the change in G^2 is 4.53 for 1 degree of freedom. It shows that the interaction effect of ethnicity by country is statistically significant at the 0.05 level. Therefore, the null hypothesis is rejected. However, the interaction effect just attains statistical significance. Given a sample size of 62,592, this effect is hardly considered important. Therefore, we should not over interpret it.

[20] Official statistics show that the national unemployment rate for the U.S. was 5.7% in 1979 and 7.0% in 1980. The average national unemployment rate for Britain from 1983 to 1989 was 10.3%. Both are calculated by dividing the number of unemployed by the

avoid unemployment than non-Chinese, with $\delta_{3[ETHN(2)]}=0.7174$ and s.e=0.2556. However, the fitted log odds of being unemployed versus being in work are the same for Chinese compared to non-Chinese in both countries, with $\delta_{6[ETHN(2)COUN(2)]}=-0.1869$ and s.e=0.2677. The same pattern is also obtained for females with $\delta_{6[ETHN(2)COUN(2)]}=-0.3257$ and s.e=0.3374.

Table 8.5 Risks of Unemployment: Males

	Estimate	s.e.	Parameter
1	-3.263	0.2855	1
2	-0.3388	0.05059	AGE(2)
3	-0.5679	0.05590	AGE(3)
4	-0.6279	0.05925	AGE(4)
5	-0.6413	0.06143	AGE(5)
6	-0.7267	0.06398	AGE(6)
7	-0.6117	0.06551	AGE(7)
8	-0.6695	0.07928	AGE(8)
9	0.1034	0.1817	EDUC(2)
10	0.5653	0.1437	EDUC(3)
11	1.584	0.1400	EDUC(4)
12	0.7174	0.2556	ETHN(2)
13	-0.6870	0.2968	COUN(2)
14	0.7166	0.1894	EDUC(2).COUN(2)
15	0.7927	0.1581	EDUC(3).COUN(2)
16	-0.08195	0.1549	EDUC(4).COUN(2)
17	-0.1869	0.2677	ETHN(2).COUN(2)

number of people in the labour force. The national unemployment rate calculated from our sample is 4.3% for the U.S. and 10.1% for Britain. Therefore there is a certain degree of consistency between official statistics and our results. For references on the U.S., see OCED. *Economic Surveys 1981-1982: United States.* (June, 1982) p.122. For references on Britain, see OECD. *Economic Reviews: United Kingdom* (July, 1987) p.12; OECD. *Economic Reviews: United Kingdom* (1989/1990) p.109.

Table 8.6 Risks of Unemployment: Females

	Estimate	s.e.	Parameter
1	-2.894	0.3518	1
2	-0.2419	0.05601	AGE(2)
3	-0.4606	0.06163	AGE(3)
4	-0.6081	0.06683	AGE(4)
5	-0.6420	0.07132	AGE(5)
6	-0.7208	0.07552	AGE(6)
7	-0.7241	0.08414	AGE(7)
8	-0.5547	0.1046	AGE(8)
9	-0.1596	0.1874	EDUC(2)
10	0.3819	0.1576	EDUC(3)
11	0.7020	0.1567	EDUC(4)
12	0.5747	0.3288	ETHN(2)
13	-0.6393	0.3604	COUN(2)
14	0.7483	0.1968	EDUC(2).COUN(2)
15	0.7768	0.1747	EDUC(3).COUN(2)
16	0.6961	0.1737	EDUC(4).COUN(2)
17	-0.3257	0.3374	ETHN(2).COUN(2)

Conclusions

In this chapter, we tested the comparative hypothesis that the relative level of occupational success of Chinese in Britain is not different from that of Chinese in the U.S.. The hypothesis was derived from previous separate analyses of Chinese occupational attainment relative to majority whites and other major non-white ethnic minorities in each country. Preliminary analysis indicated trends of similarity between foreign-born Chinese in the two countries.

In testing the hypothesis, we ran logistic regressions in which we assumed that the chance of reaching the service class or avoiding unemployment depended on age, education, ethnicity, country, education by country, and ethnicity by country. Seven out of eight tests we conducted showed that in both access to the service class and avoidance of unemployment, country differences in the ethnic advantage of Chinese over non-Chinese disappeared for male and female immigrants, after controlling for other things.

The significance of this finding is that it rejects the common notion that Chinese in Britain have a rather negative occupational profile. By the same token, it refutes the "success story" of Chinese in America, which has been much exaggerated by media coverage and taken as evidence for American exceptionalism. In a broader sense, the negative evidence we have presented in this study points in the same direction as other comparative studies (such as that of social mobility)[21], namely, "the USA does not, or at least, does no longer, stand apart from all the other nations"[22] - specifically, in this case, in the level of relative occupational success achieved by Chinese immigrants. Indeed, as comparative research continues, techniques will be developed to take into consideration more alleged "peculiarities"[23] of the U.S.. In time, genuine comparative research will be conducted from which more convincing evidence will emerge for the evaluation of American "exceptionalism".

As a final note, we have unfortunately not been able to carry on with the comparative analysis of native-born Chinese in both countries. Data on the native-born are already available for the U.S. but not mature for Britain. As a matter of fact, comparative analysis on second and subsequent generations is more effective in bringing out ethnic differences in the occupational attainment process than studying immigrants alone. With regard to Chinese, we speculate that the social and economic entry of the immigrant generation into the host society precedes high levels of formal education for its children. This seems to be the case for American-born Chinese whose relative level of occupational success has been found to supersede that of their parents. We have no evidence so far on the British-born Chinese, due to data limitations. At this stage, the Home Affairs Committee's speculation that the second generation of Chinese is still caught in traditional catering jobs, does not encourage arguments for

---

[21]Robert Erikson and John Goldthorpe, *Constant Flux* (Oxford: Clarendon Press, 1992).

[22] Erikson and Goldthorpe, *European Sociological Review* 1 (1985) p.19.

[23]Robert Erikson and John Goldthorpe, "Are American Social Mobility Rates Exceptionally High? New Evidence on an Old Issue," *American Sociological Review*, 1985, 19.

the greater relative occupational attainment of Chinese descendants in Britain. Such speculation, however, should be examined by rigorous empirical research in the future.

Conclusion

In this thesis, I have compared the relative chances of occupational success between Chinese in Great Britain and in the United States. I became interested in this question as a sociologist of Chinese origin, who is concerned with the well being of growing overseas Chinese communities. The comparative research project itself is inspired by a persistent interest in ethnic stratification, arising from my sociological training first in the United States, and later in Great Britain.

Much of American literature in recent decades has pointed out the occupational success of Asian Americans, including Chinese immigrants and their subsequent generations. Although Chinese achievement in income remains debatable, their success in occupational status (in particular, that attained through the pursuit of high educational qualifications) is generally confirmed by scholars. Such is not the case for Chinese in Britain, as revealed by the British sociological literature. This seems to give support to the idea of American exceptionalism.

I privately suspected that this difference might be more methodological rather than substantive. American Chinese may have integrated into the American occupational structure very well, but this is not in itself sufficient to establish the fact of American exceptionalism. The difference between Chinese minorities in the two countries might not lie in different levels of occupational attainments, so much as in our disparate knowledge of what each of them has achieved. What is lacking in existing British studies is rigorous empirical analysis of nationally representative data. I have adopted this method in the hope of unveiling implicit patterns that may be embodied in micro-level case studies but certainly not readily available from them. First I made separate investigations of British Chinese and American Chinese. Then, I combined the samples and conducted comparative analysis, so that patterns emerging from the previous analysis, or revised hypotheses, were tested.

I started by asking whether, in the context of modern industrialized societies, specifically in the 1980s, the ascribed status of ethnicity is weak in its explanatory power for existing inter-ethnic group occupational disparity. If, as predicted by the "logic of industrialism", ethnic minorities attain similar occupational status as whites, given the same amount of education and labour market experience, we may say that a relatively meritocratic situation has been achieved. If ethnicity contributes to the outcome of occupation, ethnic discrimination is considered to be in existence. Furthermore, I asked, if ethnicity does affect occupational success, whether the effect on occupation differs for people with different educational backgrounds. If the answer is "yes", then I expected the ethnic effect to be weaker among the well educated.

These assumptions form the three major hypotheses of the first part of this study, i.e. when Chinese in Britain and the U.S. are examined separately. As patterns emerge, a similarity between the relative chances of Chinese to succeed occupationally (defined as the fitted log odds of reaching the service class as against not reaching it, or the fitted log odds of being unemployed as against being in work) is revealed for the two countries. Hence, a comparative hypothesis is derived, which, by referring to the ethnic advantage enjoyed by Chinese in both countries, argues for relatively high and nationally comparable occupational success for Chinese on both sides of the Atlantic.

The final question concerns the impact of this investigation. Seven years ago, when the first official report on the Chinese community in Britain was made public, the accuracy of its results was questioned, as many important statistics were based primarily on estimates by local councils.[1] So to what extent does this study help to correct the image of Chinese in this country, especially through comparisons with Chinese in the U.S.? It is hoped that it will be of value to those people involved in Chinese immigration planning and community relations in Britain.

I shall summarize the basic findings, commenting on the explanatory power of the theories used. These theories include meritocracy associated with modernization, occupational returns to human capital, the enclave economy, and American exceptionalism. I shall note how governmental policies towards Chinese in Britain might put these results to use. The summary will be given for Chinese versus other ethnic groups in Britain and the U.S. separately, and for Chinese versus non-Chinese in the two countries combined.

---

[1]Chinese Information and Advice Centre, *Chinese Community in Britain Conference Report* (1985) 21.

Chapter 5 displays occupational disparity caused by ethnic differences. Other things being equal, Chinese male immigrants enjoy an ethnic advantage over South Asians in reaching the service class. Moreover, the ethnic advantage of Chinese is even greater among the qualified than among the unqualified. At all educational levels, however, Chinese male immigrants share similar chances as British-born whites in access to this class. In this respect, ethnic difference is absent between majority whites and Chinese.

Female Chinese immigrants share similar chances as South Asians in access to the service class at all educational levels. At all educational levels, however, female Chinese experience an ethnic penalty in access to the service class compared with majority whites, Irish, and West Indians. Therefore, substantial gender differences are discernible among Chinese immigrants in pursuit of the service class position.

Gender difference in the relative occupational attainments of Chinese immigrants is present in risks of unemployment, too. Other things being equal, Chinese male immigrants seem to have a greater propensity to avoid unemployment than all other ethnic groups. Although Chinese female immigrants enjoy an ethnic advantage over all other non-white minority groups, they reach parity with majority whites and Irish in this respect.

I also tested the hypothesis regarding the ethnic enclave economy for Chinese immigrants. Given the same age and education, working in the wider labour market entails better chances of reaching the service class than working in the enclave economy for both males and females. Moreover, the sector difference remains constant at all educational levels.

These findings have suggested the following:

(1) The effect of ethnicity, which is an ascribed attribute, still plays a part in determining the occupational success. It is therefore important to study culturally distinctive ethnic minorities separately rather than "lumping" them together.

(2) Minority groups may experience ethnic disadvantage in pursuing occupational success in general. But they may have various resources to cope with structural constraints. In the case of Chinese, for instance, a traditional value emphasizing the role of education in occupational mobility, may account for the occupational success of Chinese, particularly, well educated men.

(3) Although the great majority of Chinese in Britain work in the catering industry, the enclave economy does not provide equitable chances of reaching the service class, nor does it reduce risks of unemployment,

compared with the wider labour market. Therefore the ethnic enclave economy does not have a positive effect on occupational success.

(4) We have identified major gender differences in Chinese occupational attainment both in access to the service class and avoidance of unemployment. Therefore, our decision to study male and female immigrants separately is supported. Unfortunately, the small sample size of the native-born Chinese does not allow us to replicate the same analysis on the native-born. Therefore, the question of generational difference in the relative occupational success of Chinese remains unanswered.

On Chinese in the United States

Chapter Seven suggests substantial differences in occupational attainments between Chinese and other ethnic groups. In the case of male immigrants, Chinese display an ethnic advantage over all other ethnic groups, except Japanese and Indians, in reaching the service class. The ethnic advantage of Chinese is even greater among the qualified rather than among the unqualified. Well educated Chinese share similar chances as well educated Japanese and Indians of reaching the service class. But poorly educated Chinese experience an ethnic penalty in doing so compared with poorly educated Japanese and Indians. Moreover, male Chinese immigrants have a greater propensity than all other ethnic groups except Japanese to avoid unemployment. The ethnic advantage of Chinese seems to be greater among the unqualified.

Chinese female immigrants are significantly less successful than majority white women in entering the service class at all educational levels. They also have a lower propensity than black women to reach this class at the highest educational level, although they occupy a relatively advantageous position compared with other Asian Americans. Yet it is among the least qualified that the ethnic penalty is greatest for Chinese. This finding is different from that for unemployment, where the ethnic advantage of Chinese is rather greater among the unqualified.

By testing the same hypothesis on the native-born, I have found that Chinese males have similar chances as Koreans of reaching the service class. They enjoy an ethnic advantage over all other ethnic groups, including majority whites. Chinese males also have similar chances as Koreans and Japanese of avoiding unemployment. They enjoy an ethnic advantage over all other ethnic groups in this regard too. The ethnic advantage of Chinese remains the same at all educational levels.

Native-born Chinese females enjoy an ethnic advantage over all non-white ethnic minorities in access to the service class. At higher educational levels, they share the same chance as whites of reaching it, but at lower

248

educational levels, they have a greater propensity than whites in this respect. With regard to risks of unemployment, Chinese women exhibit an ethnic advantage over only whites, blacks and Hispanics. They have similar chances as all other Asian Americans of avoiding unemployment.

I also tested hypotheses concerning the Chinese ethnic enclave economy. It is found that occupational returns to education are different for people working in the enclave and people working in the wider labour market. Working in the wider labour market entails greater occupational pay-offs only for the well-educated, while the enclave economy provides advantages for the unqualified in both access to the service class and avoidance of unemployment. The same pattern applies to male and female immigrants alike. Moreover, sector seems to make no difference for native-born Chinese males, but working in the wider labour market entails greater occupational returns for native-born Chinese women at all educational levels.

The findings suggest the following:

(1) There are gender and generational differences in the relative level of Chinese occupational attainment. Therefore, our strategy of making separate studies of male immigrants, female immigrants, native-born males, and native-born females is supported.

(2) The ethnic effect on class varies with gender. Compared with that of Chinese male immigrants, the ethnic advantage of Chinese female immigrants is weaker in both access to the service class and risks of unemployment. Good education, in particular, pays off for the occupation of Chinese males at a higher rate than for most other ethnic groups. It does not pay off to the same extent for Chinese women.
This calls for research in the future.

(3) Ethnicity has lingering effects upon occupational success. American-born Chinese display a greater level of relative occupational success than immigrant Chinese. This shows that native-born Chinese have made greater strides into the American occupational structure than their foreign-born parents.

(4) The positive role of the Chinese enclave economy is confirmed only for poorly educated immigrants. For well educated immigrants and native-born Chinese, females in particular, greater occupational success is achieved by working outside the enclave. This finding contributes new evidence to the complex debate of ethnic solidarity.[2]

---

[2]Portes, Nee and Sanders, Zhou and Logan.

Similarity in occupational attainments characterises male and female Chinese in Britain and the U.S. The pattern is found after controls are introduced for structural differences. When disparities in the proportion of service class jobs, unemployment rates, and the educational systems in the two countries are taken into account, no difference is found in the relative chance of reaching the service class or avoiding unemployment for Chinese in comparison with anyone else. Being Chinese in Britain does not entail a greater ethnic penalty than being Chinese in the U.S. with regard to access to the service class.

These findings suggest little difference in relative occupational profile between British and American Chinese. The description of Chinese in the U.S. as a success group may be correct, as my results indicate, but there is little evidence from our study to support the idea that Chinese in this country have a lower occupational profile. Instead, I have found plenty of evidence to the contrary. Therefore the common contrast between Chinese in Britain and the U.S. is refuted. With this knowledge, we may question the idea of American "exceptionalism" in "providing an avenue for immigrants of all sorts to make their way into the higher levels of the American economy in a very few generations".[3] Given the definition of "exceptionalism", we have at least found, in the case of Chinese, that Britain is not less "exceptional" than America.[4] This is not to say that America and Britain have generally become exceptionally meritocratic. Our results indicate that there is a long way to go before "immigrants of 'ALL' sorts" catch up with majority whites and particularly successful ethnic minorities.

On policy implications

Chinese are a success story in Great Britain. In spite of the restrictive immigration rules and practices which apply to all ethnic minorities, Chinese in this country have excelled in occupational attainment, to no less an extent than Chinese have in the United States. It is time that this was made known to make the public, whose opinion has long been dominated by inaccurate knowledge based on poor research results.

---

[3]Peter Temin, "Free Land and Federalism: American Economic Exceptionalism," *Is America Different: A New Look at American Exceptionalism* ed. Byron E. Shafer (Oxford: Clarendon Press, 1991).

[4]The question whether this signifies Chinese exceptionalism is beyond the scope of the present thesis. Our results enable us to reject American exceptionalism in one aspect of social life, but they are not sufficient to establish Chinese exceptionalism.

For those involved in immigration planning and ethnic relations, it is important to note that the traditional point of departure - a view of ethnic minorities as "problems",[5] should be completely changed, in particular in the light of updated research findings.   In the case of Chinese, it is important to realize the positive contribution they have made to British society, be it in business management, in professional skills, and even in enriching the diet of ordinary British people.   It is perhaps sensible for policy makers to direct their discussions to the causes of Chinese occupational success, rather than remain "stuck" with "problem" finding. This is because Chinese could become a role model for other minority groups to emulate, if strong and sufficient emphasis and encouragement were given to those factors conducive to success.   These factors, however, should not include the imposition of selective criteria on immigration, like the "brain drain" in Hong Kong in 1997.   Occupational equality with the dominant group does not have to be achieved by recruiting ethnic minority elites, as the very example of Chinese in Britain has taught us.   The 1997 Hong Kong immigration criteria contradict the liberal idea of meritocracy in an industrial society.

Last, for my fellow Chinese, I hope that my work has provided an up-to-date and accurate picture of their relative occupational position vis-a-vis wider British society, and vis-a-vis Chinese in America.   In the past, this knowledge was denied them by the failure of such organizations as the Commission for Racial Equality to fulfil their obligations.[6]   My study has given solid support, through laborious quantitative analysis, to a positive image of working Chinese in this country.   By realizing the level of occupational success they have already achieved, Chinese in Britain may now be confident that they are not in this country just to be "helped".[7] They themselves have helped this country and its people and will continue to do so.

---

[5]Home Affairs Committee, *The Chinese Community in Britain* 1985, 1.

[6]Chinese Information and Advice Centre, *Chinese Community in Britain Conference Report* 1985, 19.

[7]Home Affairs Committee, *Chinese Community in Britain*, 1985.

Appendices

Appendix 5.1 Access to Service Class: Male Immigrants

	Estimate	s.e.	Parameter
1	1.629	0.5361	1
2	0.5415	0.5189	AGE(2)
3	-0.08146	0.5260	AGE(3)
4	0.5578	0.6736	AGE(4)
5	-0.8758	0.8617	AGE(5)
6	1.413	0.7230	AGE(6)
7	1.562	0.9298	AGE(7)
8	-7.836	41.17	AGE(8)
9	-0.9646	0.5683	EDUC(2)
10	-3.346	0.6564	EDUC(3)
11	-3.138	0.6022	EDUC(4)
12	-4.824	0.6699	EDUC(5)
13	**-1.690**	**0.5907**	**ETHN(2)**
14	**-1.634**	**0.6946**	**ETHN(3)**
15	-1.160	0.7330	ETHN(4)
16	-0.8407	0.6029	ETHN(5)
17	0.3636	0.6459	ETHN(6)
18	-0.03858	0.5564	ETHN(7)

(to be continued)

19	-0.1674	0.5952	AGE(2).ETHN(2)
20	-0.1661	0.7097	AGE(2).ETHN(3)
21	0.1624	0.6935	AGE(2).ETHN(4)
22	-0.4651	0.6003	AGE(2).ETHN(5)
23	-0.4024	0.5954	AGE(2).ETHN(6)
24	-0.01608	0.5314	AGE(2).ETHN(7)
25	0.6323	0.6031	AGE(3).ETHN(2)
26	0.6128	0.7529	AGE(3).ETHN(3)
27	0.5451	0.7284	AGE(3).ETHN(4)
28	0.02574	0.6208	AGE(3).ETHN(5)
29	0.1959	0.5986	AGE(3).ETHN(6)
30	0.9916	0.5375	AGE(3).ETHN(7)
31	0.2352	0.7353	AGE(4).ETHN(2)
32	-0.4080	0.8964	AGE(4).ETHN(3)
33	-0.2552	0.8656	AGE(4).ETHN(4)
34	-1.246	0.8712	AGE(4).ETHN(5)
35	-0.2285	0.7316	AGE(4).ETHN(6)
36	0.4841	0.6840	AGE(4).ETHN(7)
37	1.479	0.9127	AGE(5).ETHN(2)
38	0.6907	1.044	AGE(5).ETHN(3)
39	1.480	1.002	AGE(5).ETHN(4)
40	1.400	0.9847	AGE(5).ETHN(5)
41	1.022	0.9091	AGE(5).ETHN(6)
42	1.863	0.8706	AGE(5).ETHN(7)
43	-0.6727	0.7868	AGE(6).ETHN(2)
44	-1.732	0.9699	AGE(6).ETHN(3)
45	-2.002	0.9491	AGE(6).ETHN(4)
46	-1.962	0.9568	AGE(6).ETHN(5)
47	-1.587	0.7860	AGE(6).ETHN(6)
48	-0.3020	0.7347	AGE(6).ETHN(7)
49	-0.6662	1.004	AGE(7).ETHN(2)
50	-0.04898	1.204	AGE(7).ETHN(3)
51	-1.255	1.130	AGE(7).ETHN(4)
52	-1.301	1.289	AGE(7).ETHN(5)
53	-1.715	0.9839	AGE(7).ETHN(6)
54	-0.3366	0.9402	AGE(7).ETHN(7)
55	8.691	41.17	AGE(8).ETHN(2)
56	1.161	51.27	AGE(8).ETHN(3)
57	7.727	41.18	AGE(8).ETHN(4)
58	8.070	41.20	AGE(8).ETHN(5)
59	7.645	41.17	AGE(8).ETHN(6)
60	8.848	41.17	AGE(8).ETHN(7)

61	0.2676	0.6123	EDUC(2).ETHN(2)
62	-0.3509	0.7101	EDUC(2).ETHN(3)
63	-0.02827	0.7421	EDUC(2).ETHN(4)
64	-0.09343	0.6553	EDUC(2).ETHN(5)
65	-0.6591	0.6592	EDUC(2).ETHN(6)
66	-0.7310	0.5888	EDUC(2).ETHN(7)
67	1.179	0.7086	EDUC(3).ETHN(2)
68	1.059	0.8269	EDUC(3).ETHN(3)
69	1.187	0.8080	EDUC(3).ETHN(4)
70	1.066	0.7290	EDUC(3).ETHN(5)
71	0.5654	0.7346	EDUC(3).ETHN(6)
72	0.6981	0.6722	EDUC(3).ETHN(7)
73	1.042	0.6396	EDUC(4).ETHN(2)
74	0.9323	0.7411	EDUC(4).ETHN(3)
75	-1.090	0.8199	EDUC(4).ETHN(4)
76	0.2753	0.7205	EDUC(4).ETHN(5)
77	-0.6405	0.6869	EDUC(4).ETHN(6)
78	-0.6123	0.6202	EDUC(4).ETHN(7)
79	1.361	0.7223	EDUC(5).ETHN(2)
80	-7.732	15.06	EDUC(5).ETHN(3)
81	0.4828	0.8454	EDUC(5).ETHN(4)
82	1.111	0.8478	EDUC(5).ETHN(5)
83	0.1035	0.7471	EDUC(5).ETHN(6)
84	0.2346	0.6878	EDUC(5).ETHN(7)

Appendix 5.2 Risks of Unemployment: Male Immigrants

	Estimate	s.e.	Parameter
1	-3.213	1.073	1
2	-0.9968	0.8863	AGE(2)
3	-0.4691	0.7852	AGE(3)
4	-0.1316	0.9144	AGE(4)
5	-7.993	18.90	AGE(5)
6	-0.9233	1.158	AGE(6)
7	-0.2028	1.206	AGE(7)
8	1.496	0.9354	AGE(8)
9	-0.1572	1.444	EDUC(2)
10	-6.711	17.46	EDUC(3)
11	2.141	1.104	EDUC(4)
12	0.8669	1.131	EDUC(5)
13	0.8133	1.122	ETHN(2)
14	1.068	1.176	ETHN(3)
15	2.112	1.218	ETHN(4)
16	0.3983	1.205	ETHN(5)
17	1.027	1.159	ETHN(6)
18	0.3151	1.100	ETHN(7)
19	0.6132	0.9336	AGE(2).ETHN(2)
20	1.063	0.9314	AGE(2).ETHN(3)
21	0.2366	0.9460	AGE(2).ETHN(4)
22	-0.05501	1.032	AGE(2).ETHN(5)
23	0.5118	0.9399	AGE(2).ETHN(6)
24	0.5980	0.9001	AGE(2).ETHN(7)
25	0.6643	0.8366	AGE(3).ETHN(2)
26	0.02479	0.8808	AGE(3).ETHN(3)
27	-0.9523	0.8971	AGE(3).ETHN(4)
28	0.2569	0.9089	AGE(3).ETHN(5)
29	-0.2287	0.8398	AGE(3).ETHN(6)
30	-0.1683	0.8007	AGE(3).ETHN(7)

31	-0.001072	0.9636	AGE(4).ETHN(2)
32	0.2355	0.9783	AGE(4).ETHN(3)
33	-1.490	0.9936	AGE(4).ETHN(4)
34	-0.6831	1.205	AGE(4).ETHN(5)
35	-0.2280	0.9579	AGE(4).ETHN(6)
36	-0.5375	0.9299	AGE(4).ETHN(7)
37	7.501	18.91	AGE(5).ETHN(2)
38	8.166	18.91	AGE(5).ETHN(3)
39	6.951	18.91	AGE(5).ETHN(4)
40	7.076	18.92	AGE(5).ETHN(5)
41	6.867	18.91	AGE(5).ETHN(6)
42	6.838	18.91	AGE(5).ETHN(7)
43	0.4055	1.214	AGE(6).ETHN(2)
44	1.447	1.209	AGE(6).ETHN(3)
45	-0.3675	1.209	AGE(6).ETHN(4)
46	1.254	1.267	AGE(6).ETHN(5)
47	-0.1603	1.200	AGE(6).ETHN(6)
48	0.01768	1.174	AGE(6).ETHN(7)
49	0.3713	1.255	AGE(7).ETHN(2)
50	0.4082	1.272	AGE(7).ETHN(3)
51	-1.189	1.269	AGE(7).ETHN(4)
52	1.506	1.438	AGE(7).ETHN(5)
53	-0.5049	1.246	AGE(7).ETHN(6)
54	-0.7175	1.223	AGE(7).ETHN(7)
55	-1.636	1.050	AGE(8).ETHN(2)
56	-0.1822	1.133	AGE(8).ETHN(3)
57	-2.387	1.039	AGE(8).ETHN(4)
58	-0.8619	1.534	AGE(8).ETHN(5)
59	-2.282	0.9973	AGE(8).ETHN(6)
60	-2.492	0.9642	AGE(8).ETHN(7)
61	-0.7672	1.553	EDUC(2).ETHN(2)
62	0.9503	1.541	EDUC(2).ETHN(3)
63	-0.1989	1.615	EDUC(2).ETHN(4)
64	0.03494	1.646	EDUC(2).ETHN(5)
65	-0.6373	1.563	EDUC(2).ETHN(6)
66	0.6348	1.470	EDUC(2).ETHN(7)

67	7.150	17.46	EDUC(3).ETHN(2)
68	6.808	17.47	EDUC(3).ETHN(3)
69	6.582	17.47	EDUC(3).ETHN(4)
70	7.018	17.47	EDUC(3).ETHN(5)
71	7.235	17.46	EDUC(3).ETHN(6)
72	7.090	17.46	EDUC(3).ETHN(7)
73	-1.723	1.152	EDUC(4).ETHN(2)
74	-1.198	1.212	EDUC(4).ETHN(3)
75	-1.495	1.245	EDUC(4).ETHN(4)
76	-0.9350	1.255	EDUC(4).ETHN(5)
77	-1.564	1.185	EDUC(4).ETHN(6)
78	-1.292	1.130	EDUC(4).ETHN(7)
79	0.6317	1.167	EDUC(5).ETHN(2)
80	0.5698	1.218	EDUC(5).ETHN(3)
81	0.1341	1.267	EDUC(5).ETHN(4)
82	0.5240	1.279	EDUC(5).ETHN(5)
83	0.6438	1.202	EDUC(5).ETHN(6)
84	0.8024	1.155	EDUC(5).ETHN(7)

Appendix 5.3 Access to Service Class: Female Immigrants

	Estimate	s.e.	Parameter
1	0.4610	0.4538	1
2	0.3262	0.5080	AGE(2)
3	-0.6576	0.5794	AGE(3)
4	-0.4617	0.7233	AGE(4)
5	0.2765	0.7946	AGE(5)
6	-1.013	1.303	AGE(6)
7	1.412	0.9610	AGE(7)
8	-1.078	0.6035	AGE(8)
9	0.1360	0.4577	EDUC(2)
10	-1.472	0.4605	EDUC(3)
11	-1.898	0.4623	EDUC(4)
12	-2.790	0.4616	EDUC(5)
13	-1.020	0.5347	ETHN(2)
14	-0.1511	0.7649	ETHN(3)
15	-0.3386	0.5237	ETHN(4)
16	**-1.142**	**0.5502**	**ETHN(5)**
17	0.4111	0.5165	ETHN(6)
18	-0.2427	0.4777	ETHN(7)
19	-0.2483	0.6278	AGE(2).ETHN(2)
20	-0.9153	1.002	AGE(2).ETHN(3)
21	0.1906	0.5933	AGE(2).ETHN(4)
22	0.2337	0.6565	AGE(2).ETHN(5)
23	-0.8958	0.5864	AGE(2).ETHN(6)
24	-0.2606	0.5252	AGE(2).ETHN(7)
25	0.4919	0.7099	AGE(3).ETHN(2)
26	0.6780	1.041	AGE(3).ETHN(3)
27	2.061	0.6612	AGE(3).ETHN(4)
28	1.410	0.7319	AGE(3).ETHN(5)
29	0.5103	0.6404	AGE(3).ETHN(6)
30	0.6512	0.5947	AGE(3).ETHN(7)

31	0.8385	0.8217	AGE(4).ETHN(2)
32	0.7965	1.124	AGE(4).ETHN(3)
33	2.014	0.7860	AGE(4).ETHN(4)
34	1.012	0.9018	AGE(4).ETHN(5)
35	0.4149	0.7721	AGE(4).ETHN(6)
36	0.6852	0.7357	AGE(4).ETHN(7)
37	0.002959	0.8940	AGE(5).ETHN(2)
38	-1.596	1.521	AGE(5).ETHN(3)
39	1.043	0.8503	AGE(5).ETHN(4)
40	-0.8047	1.444	AGE(5).ETHN(5)
41	-0.4503	0.8409	AGE(5).ETHN(6)
42	0.01256	0.8076	AGE(5).ETHN(7)
43	1.558	1.384	AGE(6).ETHN(2)
44	-4.819	17.87	AGE(6).ETHN(3)
45	2.396	1.342	AGE(6).ETHN(4)
46	1.241	1.563	AGE(6).ETHN(5)
47	0.9614	1.331	AGE(6).ETHN(6)
48	1.309	1.312	AGE(6).ETHN(7)
49	-1.185	1.172	AGE(7).ETHN(2)
50	-6.834	22.33	AGE(7).ETHN(3)
51	-1.031	1.091	AGE(7).ETHN(4)
52	-0.5672	1.964	AGE(7).ETHN(5)
53	-1.695	1.007	AGE(7).ETHN(6)
54	-1.089	0.9745	AGE(7).ETHN(7)
55	-3.139	26.67	AGE(8).ETHN(2)
56	0.000	aliased	AGE(8).ETHN(3)
57	-5.666	15.17	AGE(8).ETHN(4)
58	0.000	aliased	AGE(8).ETHN(5)
59	0.1745	1.075	AGE(8).ETHN(6)
60	0.000	aliased	AGE(8).ETHN(7)
61	0.01356	0.5145	NEWG(1).NEWE(2)
62	**1.206**	**0.4697**	**NEWG(1).NEWE(3)**
63	0.000	aliased	NEWG(2).NEWE(1)
64	0.000	aliased	NEWG(2).NEWE(2)
65	0.000	aliased	NEWG(2).NEWE(3)

Appendix 5.4.a Parameter Estimates for Model 1: Male Immigrants (N=4019)

Access to Service Class

	Estimate	s.e.
Constant	1.109	0.1963
Age		
25-29	0	
30-34	0.3827*	0.1519
35-39	0.3720*	0.1607
40-44	0.4504*	0.1768
45-49	0.3707*	0.1804
50-54	0.2686	0.2056
55-59	0.6110*	0.2273
60-64	0.4672	0.2986
Education		
Degree	0	
A-level	-0.9046*	0.1408
O-level	-2.130*	0.1453
CSE	-2.814*	0.1456
None	-3.956*	0.1669
Ethnicity		
Briti. w/British Qual.	0	
Chine. w/British Qual.	0.2266 (1.25)	0.3019
Chine. w/Foreign Qual.	0.1297 (1.14)	0.2476
India. w/British Qual.	-0.6616*(0.52)	0.1947
India. w/Foreign Qual.	-0.6025*(0.55)	0.1516
Pakis. w/British Qual.	-1.081* (0.34)	0.2746
Pakis. w/Foreign Qual.	-1.393* (0.25)	0.2396
A.Asi. w/British Qual.	-0.8928*(0.41)	0.2433
A.Asi. w/Foreign Qual.	-0.8871*(0.41)	0.2007
W.Ind. w/British Qual.	-0.1186 (0.89)	0.2048
W.Ind. w/Foreign Qual.	-1.120* (0.33)	0.2275
Irish. w/British Qual.	0.0299 (1.03)	0.1653
Irish. w/Foreign Qual.	0.0000	aliased

G^2=437 d.f=354   * significant at 0.05 level

The number in ( ) is the exponentiated value of the coefficient, i.e. fitted odds.

Appendix 5.4.b Parameter Estimates for Model 1: Male Immigrants
(N=4019)

<u>Risks of Unemployment</u>

	Estimate	s.e.
Constant	-2.276	0.2156
Age		
25-29	0	
30-34	-0.4735*	0.1529
35-39	-0.3832*	0.1662
40-44	-0.4280*	0.1740
45-49	-0.6718*	0.1803
50-54	-0.4834*	0.2029
55-59	-0.5991*	0.2327
60-64	-0.3119	0.2921
Education		
Degree	0	
A-level	-0.1132	0.2680
O-level	0.3781	0.2303
CSE	0.7187*	0.2101
None	1.351*	0.1992
Ethnicity		
Briti. w/British Qual.	0	
Chine. w/British Qual.	-2.3080*(0.10)	0.9389
Chine. w/Foreign Qual.	-0.8205*(0.44)	0.3475
India. w/British Qual.	0.0929 (1.09)	0.2037
India. w/Foreign Qual.	0.0315 (1.03)	0.1584
Pakis. w/British Qual.	0.4421 (1.56)	0.2254
Pakis. w/Foreign Qual.	0.8061*(2.24)	0.1723
A.Asi. w/British Qual.	0.6085*(1.84)	0.2194
A.Asi. w/Foreign Qual.	0.2393 (1.27)	0.1598
W.Ind. w/British Qual.	-0.6948*(0.50)	0.3137
W.Ind. w/Foreign Qual.	-0.1822 (0.83)	0.2451
Irish. w/British Qual.	-0.1089 (0.90)	0.1911
Irish. w/Foreign Qual.	0.0000	aliased

G^2=331 d.f=354   * significant at 0.05 level

The number in ( ) is the exponentiated value of the coefficient, i.e.
fitted odds.

Appendix 5.4.c Parameter Estimates for Model 1: Female Immigrants
(N=2880)
Access to Service Class

	Estimate	s.e.
Constant	.9200	0.2260
Age		
25-29	0	
30-34	0.2117	0.1638
35-39	0.4014*	0.1733
40-44	0.5165*	0.1825
45-49	0.3186	0.1940
50-54	0.4887*	0.2152
55-59	0.3011	0.2684
60-64	0.0000	aliased
Education		
Degree	0	
A-level	-0.2909	0.1780
O-level	-2.082*	0.1849
CSE	-2.564*	0.1942
None	-3.414*	0.1963
Ethnicity		
Briti. w/British Qual.	0	
Chine. w/British Qual.	-0.4384(0.65)	0.3447
Chine. w/Foreign Qual.	-0.3578(0.70)	0.2534
India. w/British Qual.	-1.042*(2.83)	0.2721
India. w/Foreign Qual.	-1.302*(0.27)	0.1994
Pakis. w/British Qual.	0.0197(1.02)	0.5107
Pakis. w/Foreign Qual.	-1.188*(0.30)	0.4506
A.Asi. w/British Qual.	-0.0329(0.97)	0.1864
A.Asi. w/Foreign Qual.	0.852*(2.34)	0.1552
W.Ind. w/British Qual.	-0.3010(0.74)	0.2608
W.Ind. w/Foreign Qual.	-1.376*(0.25)	0.2752
Irish. w/British Qual.	0.2570(1.29)	0.1628
Irish. w/Foreign Qual.	0.0000	aliased

$G^2=330$ d.f=272   * significant at 0.05 level

The number in ( ) is the exponentiated value of the coefficient, i.e. fitted odds.

Appendix 5.4.d Parameter Estimates for Model 1: Female Immigrants
(N=2880)

<u>Risks of Unemployment</u>

	Estimate	s.e.
Constant	-2.427	0.3285
Age		
25-29	0	
30-34	-0.1628	0.1825
35-39	-0.5305*	0.2039
40-44	-0.7989*	0.2314
45-49	-1.210*	0.2810
50-54	-1.119*	0.3247
55-59	-0.5348	0.3538
60-64	0.0000	aliased
Education		
Degree	0	
A-level	-0.0115	0.3052
O-level	0.4057	0.2871
CSE	0.8058*	0.2790
None	0.8279*	0.2685
Ethnicity		
Briti. w/British Qual.	0	
Chine. w/British Qual.	-0.4109 (0.66)	0.6303
Chine. w/Foreign Qual.	-0.3784 (0.68)	0.4249
India. w/British Qual.	0.2975 (1.35)	0.3016
India. w/Foreign Qual.	0.5803*(1.79)	0.2168
Pakis. w/British Qual.	0.2026 (1.22)	0.6504
Pakis. w/Foreign Qual.	0.9017*(2.46)	0.3979
A.Asi. w/British Qual.	0.4456 (1.56)	0.2443
A.Asi. w/Foreign Qual.	0.0615 (1.06)	0.2413
W.Ind. w/British Qual.	0.1827 (1.20)	0.3396
W.Ind. w/Foreign Qual.	0.4311 (1.54)	0.2841
Irish. w/British Qual.	-0.2003 (0.82)	0.2641
Irish. w/Foreign Qual.	0.0000	aliased

G^2=269 d.f=272   * significant at 0.05 level

The number in ( ) is the exponentiated value of the coefficient, i.e. fitted odds.

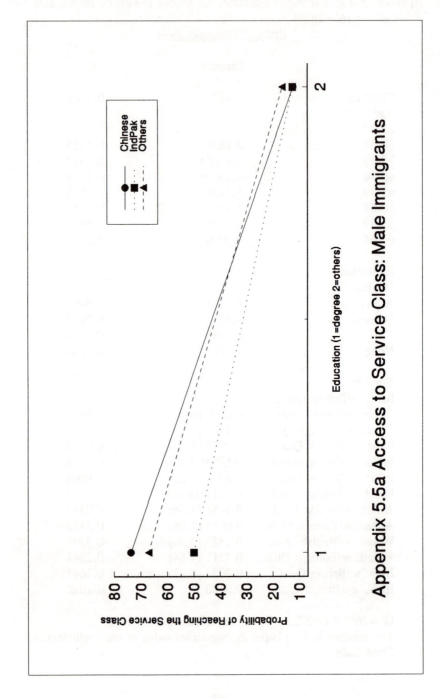

Appendix 5.5a Access to Service Class: Male Immigrants

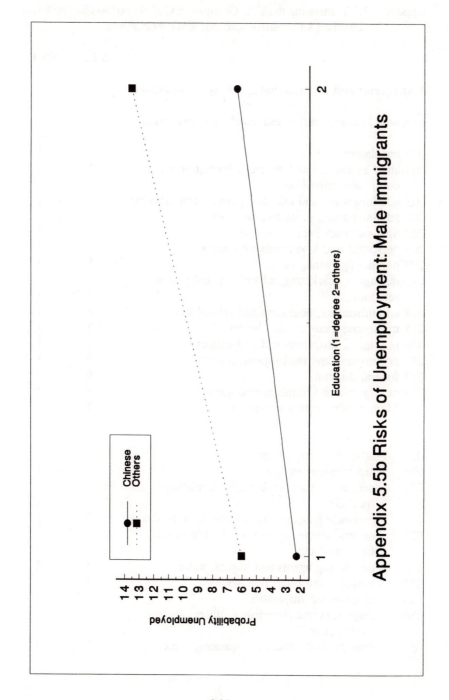

Appendix 5.5b Risks of Unemployment: Male Immigrants

Appendix 7.1 Translating the U.S. Occupation Codes into Goldthorpe Class Schema (S.E. = self-employed; EMP = employee)

		S.E.	EMP.

Managerial and professional specialty occupations

Executive, administrative and managerial occupations

		S.E.	EMP.
003	legislators	5	1
004	chief executives and general administrators, public administration	5	1
	public administration	5	1
005	administrators and officials, public administration	5	1
006	administrators, protective services	5	1
007	financial managers	5	1
008	personnel and labour relations managers	5	1
009	purchasing managers	5	1
013	managers, marketing, advertising and public relations		
	relations	5	1
014	administrators, education and related fields	5	1
015	managers, medicine and health	5	1
016	managers, properties and real estates	5	1
017	postmasters and mail superintendents	5	1
018	funeral directors	6	8
019	managers and administrators, n.e.c.	5	1
	Management related occupations	5	1
023	accountants and auditors	5	1
024	underwriters	5	1
025	other financial officers	5	1
026	management analyst	5	1
027	personnel, training and labour relations specialists		
	specialists	5	1
028	purchasing agents, buyers and farm products	5	1
029	buyers, wholesale and retail trade except farm products		
	farm products	5	1
033	purchasing agents and buyers, n.e.c.	5	1
034	business and protection agents	5	1
035	construction inspectors	5	1
036	inspectors and compliance officers, except construction		
	construction	5	1
037	management related occupations, n.e.c.	5	1

Engineers, architects and surveyors
043	architects	1	1
	Engineers	1	1
044	aerospace	1	1
045	metallurgical and materials	1	1
046	mining	1	1
047	petroleum	1	1
048	chemical	1	1
049	nuclear	1	1
053	civil	1	1
054	agricultural	1	1
055	electrical and electronic	1	1
056	industrial	1	1
057	mechanical	1	1
058	marine and naval architects	1	1
059	engineers, n.e.c.	1	1
063	surveyors and mapping scientists	1	1
	Mathematical and computer scientists	1	1
064	computer systems analysts and scientists	1	1
065	operations and systems researchers and analysts	1	1
066	actuaries	1	1
067	statisticians	1	1
068	mathematical scientists, n.e.c.	1	1
	Natural scientists	1	1
069	physicists and astronomers	1	1
073	chemists except biochemists	1	1
074	atmospheric and space scientists	1	1
075	geologists and geodesists	1	1
076	physical scientists, n.e.c.	1	1
077	agricultural and food scientists	1	1
078	biological and life scientists	1	1
079	forestry and conservation scientists	1	1
083	medical scientists	1	1

Heath diagnosing occupations
084	physicians	1	1
085	dentists	1	1
086	veterinarians	1	1
086	optometrists	1	1

087	podiatrists	1	1
088	health diagnosing practitioners, n.e.c.	1	1

Health assessment and treating occupations

095	registered nurses	1	1
096	pharmacists	1	1
097	dietitians	1	1

therapists

098	inhalation therapists	1	1
099	occupational therapists	1	1
103	physical therapists	1	1
104	speech therapists	1	1
105	therapists, n.e.c.	1	1
106	physicians assistants	1	3

Teachers, postsecondary

113	earth, environmental, and marine science teachers	1	1
		1	1
114	biological science teachers	1	1
115	chemistry teachers	1	1
116	physics teachers	1	1
117	natural science teachers, n.e.c.	1	1
118	psychology teachers	1	1
119	economics teachers	1	1
123	history teachers	1	1
124	political science teachers	1	1
125	sociology teachers	1	1
126	social science teachers, n.e.c.	1	1
127	engineering teachers	1	1
128	mathematical science teachers	1	1
129	computer science teachers	1	1
133	medical science teachers	1	1
134	health specialties teachers	1	1
135	business, commerce and marketing teachers	1	1
136	agriculture and forestry teachers	1	1
137	art, drama and music teachers	1	1
138	physical education teachers	1	1
139	education teachers	1	1
143	English teachers	1	1
144	foreign languages teachers	1	1
145	law teachers	1	1

146	social work teachers	1	1
147	theology teachers	1	1
148	trade and industrial teachers	1	1
149	home economics teachers	1	1
153	teachers, postsecondary, n.e.c.	1	1
154	postsecondary teachers, subjects not specified	1	1

Teachers except postsecondary

155	teachers, prekindergarten and kindergarten	1	1
156	teachers, elementary school	1	1
157	teachers, secondary school	1	1
158	teachers, special education	1	1
159	teachers, n.e.c.	1	1

163	Counsellors, educational and vocation	1	1

Librarians, archivists and curators | 1 | 1

164	librarians	1	1
165	archivists and curators	1	1

Social scientists and urban planners

166	economists	1	1
167	psychologists	1	1
168	sociologists	1	1
169	social scientists, n.e.c.	1	1
173	urban planners	1	1

Social recreation and religious workers

174	social workers	1	1
175	recreation workers	1	1
176	clergy	1	1
177	religious workers, n.e.c.	1	1

Lawyers and judges

178	lawyers	1	1
179	judges	1	1

Writers, artists, entertainers and athletes

183	authors	1	1
184	technical writers	1	1
185	designers	1	1
186	musical and composers	1	1

187	actors and directors	1	1
188	painters, sculptors, craft artists and artist print makers	1	1
189	photographers	1	8
193	dancers	1	4
194	artists, performers and related workers, n.e.c.	1	1
195	editors and reporters	1	1
197	public relations specialists	1	1
198	announcers	1	1
199	athletes	1	8

Technical, sales, and administrative support occupations

Technicians and related support occupations

Health technologists and technicians

203	clinical laboratory technologists and technicians	5	1
204	dental hygienists	5	1
205	health record technologists and technicians	5	1
206	radiologic technicians	5	1
207	licensed practical nurses	5	3
208	health technologists and technicians	5	1

Technologists and technicians, except health

Engineering and related technologists and technicians

213	electrical and electronic technicians	5	1
214	industrial engineering technicians	5	1
215	mechanical engineering technicians	5	1
216	engineering technicians, n.e.c.	5	1
217	drafting occupations	5	1
218	surveying and mapping technicians	5	1

Science technicians

223	biological technicians	5	1
224	chemical technicians	5	1
225	science technicians, n.e.c.	5	1

Technicians, except health, engineering and science

| 226 | airplane pilot and navigators | 5 | 1 |

227	air traffic controllers	5	1
228	broadcast equipment operators	5	1
229	computer programmers	5	1
233	tool programmers, numerical control	5	1
234	legal assistants	5	1
235	technicians, n.e.c.	5	1

Sales occupations

243	supervisors and proprietors, sales occupations	5	1
253	insurance sales occupations	5	3
254	real estate sales occupations	5	1
245	securities and financial services sales occupations	5	1

Sales representatives, fiance and business services

256	advertising and related sales occupations	5	3
257	sales occupations, other business services	5	3

Sales representatives, commodities except retail

258	sales engineers	5	3
259	sales representatives, mining, manufacturing, and wholesale	5	3

Sales workers, retail and personal services

263	sales workers, motor vehicles and boats	5	3
264	sales workers, apparel	5	3
265	sales workers, shoes	5	3
266	sales workers, furniture and home furnishings	5	3
267	sales workers, radio, TV, hi-fi and appliances	5	3
268	sales workers, hardware and building supplies	5	3
269	sales workers, parts	5	3
274	sales workers, other commodities	5	5
275	sales counter clerks	5	4
276	cashiers	5	4
277	street and door-to-door sales workers	6	10
278	news vendors	6	10

Sale related occupations

283	demonstrators, operators and models, sales	5	3

284	auctioneers	5	3
285	sales support occupations, n.e.c.	5	3

Administrative supportive occupations

Administrative support occupations

303	supervisors, general office	5	1
304	supervisors, computer equipment operators	5	1
305	supervisors, financial record processing	5	1
306	chief communication operators	5	1
307	supervisors, distribution, scheduling and adjusting clerks	5	1

Computer equipment operators

308	computer operators	5	3
309	peripheral equipment operators	5	3

Secretaries, stenographers and typists

313	secretaries	5	3
314	stenographers	5	3
315	typists	5	3

Information clerks

316	interviewers	5	3
317	hotel clerks	5	3
318	transportation ticket and reservation agents	5	3
319	receptionist	5	3
323	information clerks, n.e.c.	5	3

Record processing occupations, except financial

325	classified-ad clerks	5	3
326	correspondence clerks	5	3
327	order clerks	5	3
328	personnel clerks, except payroll and timekeeping	5	3
329	library clerks	5	3
335	file clerks	5	3
336	record clerks	5	3

Financial records processing occupations

337	bookkeeping, accounting and auditing clerks	5	3
338	payroll and timekeeping clerks	5	3

339	billing clerks	5	3
343	cost and rate clerks	5	3
344	billing, posting and calculating machine operators	5	3

Duplicating, mail and other office machine operators

345	duplicating machine operators	5	3
346	mail preparing and paper handling machine operators	5	3
347	office machine operators, n.e.c.	5	3

Communication equipment operators

348	telephone operators	5	3
349	telegraphers	5	3
353	communications equipment operators, n.e.c.	5	3

Mail and message distributing occupations

354	postal clerks, exc. mail carriers	6	10
355	mail carrier, postal service	6	10
356	mail clerks, exc. postal service	6	10
357	messengers	6	10

Material recording, scheduling and distributing clerks, n.e.c.

359	dispatchers	5	3
363	production coordinators	5	1
364	traffic, shipping and receiving clerks	5	3
365	stock and inventory clerks	5	3
366	master readers	5	3
368	weigher, measurers and checkers	5	3
369	samplers	5	3
373	expediters	5	3
374	material recording, scheduling, and distributing clerks, n.e.c.	5	3

Adjustors and investigators

375	insurance adjusters, examiners and investigators	5	3
376	investigators and adjusters, except insurance	5	3
377	eligibility clerks, social welfare	5	3
378	bill and account collectors	5	3

Miscellaneous administrative support occupations

379	general office clerks	5	3
383	bank tellers	5	3
384	proof readers	5	3
385	data-entry keyers	5	3
	miscellaneous administrative support occupation	5	3
386	statistical clerks		
387	teacher's aides	6	10
389	administrative support occupations, n.e.c.	5	3

Service occupations

Private household occupations

403	launders and ironers	6	10
404	cooks, private household	6	4
405	housekeepers and butlers	6	4
406	child care workers, private household	6	10
407	private household cleaners and servants	6	10

Protective service occupations
supervisors, protective service occupations

413	supervisors, firefighting and fire prevention occupations	5	8
414	supervisors, police and detectives	5	2
415	supervisors, guards	5	8

Fire fighting and fire prevention occupations

416	fire inspection and fire prevention occupations	5	8
417	fire fighting occupations	5	8

Police and detectives

418	police and detectives, public service		2
423	sheriffs, bailiffs and other law enforcement officers	5	8
424	correctional institution officers	5	8

Guards

425	crossing guards	6	10
426	guards and police etc. public service	6	10
427	protective service occupations, n.e.c.	6	10

Service occupations, except protective and household
food preparation and service occupations

433	supervisors, food preparation and service occupations	5	8
434	bar tenders	6	10
435	waiters and waitresses	6	10
436	cooks, except short order	6	9
437	short order cooks	6	9
438	food counter, fountain and related occupations	6	10
439	kitchen workers, food preparation	6	10
443	waiters and waitresses' assistants	6	10
444	miscellaneous food preparation occupations	6	10

Health service occupations

445	dental assistants	6	10
446	health aides except nursing	6	10
447	nursing aides, orderlies and attendants	6	10

Cleaning and building service occupations, except household

448	supervisors, cleaning and building service workers	5	8
449	maids and housemen	6	10
453	janitors and cleaners	6	10
454	elevator operators	6	10
455	pest control occupations	6	10

Personal service occupations

456	supervisors, personnel service occupations	5	8
457	barbers	6	9
458	hairdressers and cosmetologists	6	9
459	attendants, amusement and recreation facilities	6	10
463	guides	5	4
464	ushers	6	10
465	public transportation attendants	6	10
466	baggage porters and bellhops	6	10
467	welfare service aides	6	10
468	child care workers except private household	5	3
469	personal service occupations, n.e.c.	6	10

Farming, forestry and fishing occupations

Farm operators and managers

473	farmers, except horticultural	7	7
474	horticultural specialty farmers	7	7
475	managers, farms, except horticulture	7	7
476	managers, horticultural farms	7	7

Farm occupations, except managerial

477	supervisors, farm workers	7	11
479	farm workers	7	11
483	marine life cultivation workers	7	11
484	nursery workers	7	11

Related agricultural occupations

485	supervisors, related agricultural occupations	6	8
486	groundkeepers and gardeners, except farm	6	10
487	animal caretakers, except farm	6	10
488	graders and sorters, agricultural products	6	10
489	inspectors, agricultural products	6	10

Forestry and logging occupations

494	supervisors, forestry and lodging workers	7	11
495	forestry workers, except lodging	7	11
496	timber cutting and logging occupations	7	11

Fishers, hunters and trappers

497	captains and other officers	5	2
498	fishers	6	10
499	hunters and trappers	7	11

Precision production, craft and repair occupations

Mechanics and repairers

503	supervisors, mechanics and repairers, mechanics, repairers, except supervisors vehicle and mobile equipment repairers	5	8
505	automobile mechanics, except apprentices	6	9
506	automobile mechanics apprentices	6	9
507	bus, truck and stationary engine mechanics	6	9
508	aircraft engine mechanics	6	9
509	small engine repairers	6	9
514	automobile body and related repairers	6	9
515	aircraft mechanics, except engine	6	9

516	heavy equipment mechanics	6	9
517	farm equipment mechanics	6	9
518	industrial machinery repairers	6	9
519	machinery maintenance occupations	6	9
	electrical and electronic equipment repairers	6	9
523	electronic repairers, communications and industrial equipment	6	9
525	data processing equipment repairers	6	9
526	household appliances and power tool repairers	6	9
527	telephone line installers and repairers	5	8
529	telephone installers and repairers	5	8
533	miscellaneous electrical and electronic equipment repairers	6	9
534	heating, air conditioning, and refrigeration mechanics	6	9
	miscellaneous mechanics and repairers	6	9
535	camera, watch and musical instrument mechanics	6	9
536	locksmiths and safe repairers	6	9
538	office machine repairers	6	9
539	mechanical controls and valve repairers	6	9
543	elevator installers and repairers	6	9
544	millwrights	6	9
547	specified mechanics and repairers, n.e.c.	6	9
549	not specified mechanics and repairers	6	9

Construction trades
Supervisors, construction occupations

553	supervisors, brickmasons, stonemasons, and tile setters	5	8
554	supervisors, carpenters and related workers	5	8
555	supervisors, electricians and power transmission installers	5	8
556	supervisors, painters, paperhangers and plasterers	5	8
557	supervisors, plumbers, pipefitters and steamfitters	5	8
558	supervisors, n.e.c.	5	8

Construction trades, except supervisors
563   brickmasons, and stonemasons, except

	apprentices	6	9
564	brickmason and stonemason apprentices	6	9
565	tile setters, hard and soft	6	9
566	carpet installers	6	9
567	carpenters, except apprentices	6	9
569	carpenter apprentices	6	9
573	drywall installers	6	9
575	electricians, except apprentices	6	9
576	electrician apprentices	6	9
577	electrical power installers and repairers	6	9
579	painters, construction and maintenance	6	9
583	paperhangers	6	9
584	plasterers	6	9
585	plumbers, pipefitters and steamfitters, except apprentices	6	9
587	plumber, pipefitter, and steamfitter apprentices	6	9
588	concrete and terrazzo finishers	6	10
589	glaziers	6	10
593	insulation workers	6	10
594	paving, surfacing and tamping equipment operators	6	10
595	roofers	6	10
596	sheetmetal duct installers	6	10
597	structural metal workers	6	10
598	drillers, earth	6	10
599	construction trades, n.e.c.	6	10

Extractive occupations

613	supervisors, extractive occupations	5	8
614	drillers, oil well	5	10
615	explosives workers	5	10
616	mining machine operators	5	10
617	mining occupations, n.e.c.	5	10

Precision production occupations

633	supervisors, production occupations precision metal working occupations	5	8
634	tool and die makers, except apprentices	6	9
635	tool and die maker apprentices	6	9
636	precision assemblers, metal	6	10
637	machinists, except apprentices	6	10

278

639	machinist apprentices	6	10
643	boilermakers	6	9
644	precision grinder, fitters and tool sharpeners	6	10
645	pattern makers and model makers, metal	6	9
646	layout workers	6	10
647	precious stones and metals workers (jewellers)	6	9
649	engravers, metal	6	10
653	sheet metal workers, except apprentices	6	9
654	sheet metal worker apprentices	6	9
655	miscellaneous precision metal workers	6	10

precision woodworking occupations

656	pattern makers and model makers, wood	6	9
657	cabinet makers and bench carpenters	6	9
658	furniture and wood finishers	6	9
659	miscellaneous precision woodmakers	6	9

precision, textile, apparel and furnishings machine workers

666	dressmakers	6	9
667	tailors	6	9
668	upholsterers	6	9
669	shoe repairers	6	9
673	apparel and fabric pattern makers	6	9
674	miscellaneous precision apparel and fabric workers	6	9

precision workers, assorted materials | | 6 | 9 |

675	hand moulders and shapers, except jewellers	6	9
676	pattern makers, layout workers and cutters	6	9
677	optical good workers	6	9
678	dental laboratory and medical appliance technicians	6	9
679	bookbinders	6	9
683	electrical and electronic equipment assemblers	6	9
684	miscellaneous precision workers, n.e.c.	6	9

precision food production occupations | | 6 | 9 |

686	butchers and meat cutters	6	9
687	bakers	6	9
688	foodbatch makers	6	9

	precision inspectors, tasters and related workers		
689	inspectors, tasters and graders	6	9
693	adjusters and calibrators	6	9
	plant and system operators		
694	water and sewage treatment plant operators	6	9
695	power plant operators	6	9
696	stationary engineers	6	9
699	miscellaneous plant and system operators	6	9

Operators, fabricators and labourers

Machine operators, assemblers and inspectors
Machine operators and tenders, except precision

	metal working and plastic working machine operators		
703	lathe and turning machine set-up operators	6	9
704	lathe and turning machine operators	6	10
705	milling and planing machine operators	6	10
706	punching and stamping press machine operators	6	10
707	rolling machine operators	6	10
708	drilling and boring machine operators	6	10
709	grinding, abrading, buffing and polishing machine operators	6	10
713	forging machine operators	6	10
714	numerical control machine operators	6	10
715	miscellaneous metal, plastic, stone, and glass working machine operators	6	10
717	fabricating machine operators, n.e.c.	6	10

	Metal and plastic processing machine operators		
719	moulding and casting machine operators	6	10
723	metal plating machine operators	6	10
724	heat treating equipment operators	6	10
725	miscellaneous metal and plastic processing machine operators	6	10

	Woodworking machine operators		
726	wood lathe, routing and planing machine operators	6	9
727	sawing machine operators	6	9

728	shaping and joining machine operators	6	9
729	nailing and tacking machine operators	6	9
733	miscellaneous woodworking machine operators	6	9

Printing machine operators

734	printing machine operators	6	9
735	photoengravers and lithographers	6	9
736	type setters and compositors	6	9
737	miscellaneous printing machine operators	6	9

Textile, apparel and furnishing machine operators

738	winding and twisting machine operators	6	10
739	knitting, looping, taping and weaving machine operators	6	10
743	textile cutting machine operators	6	10
744	textile sewing machine operators	6	10
745	show machine operators	6	10
747	pressing machine operators	6	10
748	launderer and dry cleaning machine operators	6	10
749	miscellaneous textile machine operators	6	10

Machine operators, assorted materials

753	cementing and gluing machine operators	6	10
754	packaging and filling machine operators	6	10
755	extruding and forming machine operators	6	10
756	mixing and blending machine operators	6	10
757	separating, filtering and clarifying machine operators	6	10
758	compressing and compacting machine operators	6	10
759	painting and paint spraying machine operators	6	10
763	roasting and baking machine operators, food	6	10
764	washing, cleaning and picking machine operators	6	10
765	folding machine operators	6	10
766	furnace, kiln and oven operators, exc. food	6	10
768	crushing and grinding machine operators	6	10
769	slicing and cutting machine operators	6	10
773	motion picture projectionists	5	8
774	photographic process machine operators		

	miscellaneous and not specified machine operators	5	8
777	miscellaneous and not specified machine operators	6	10
779	machine operators, n.e.c.	6	10

Fabricators, assemblers and hand working occupations

783	welders and cutters	6	9
784	solderers and blazers	6	9
785	assemblers	6	10
786	hand cutting and trimming occupations	6	10
787	hand moulding, casting and forming occupations	6	9
789	hand painting, coating and decorating occupations	6	10
793	hand engraving and printing occupations	6	9
794	hand grinding and polishing occupations	6	10
795	miscellaneous hand working occupations	6	10

Production inspectors, tasters and samplers and weighers

796	production inspectors, checkers and examiners	6	10
797	production testers	6	10
798	production samplers and weighers	6	10
799	graders and sorters, exc. agricultural	6	10

Transportation and material moving occupations

Motor vehicle operators

803	supervisors, motor vehicle operators	5	8
804	truck drivers, heavy	6	10
805	truck drivers, light	6	10
806	driver-sales workers	6	10
808	bus drivers	6	10
809	taxi cab drivers and chauffeurs	6	10
813	parking lot attendants	6	10
814	motor transportation occupations, n.e.c.	6	10

Transportation occupations, except motor vehicles
rail transportation occupations

| 823 | railroad conductors and yardmasters | 6 | 9 |

824	locomotive operating occupations	6	9
825	railroad brake, signal and switch operators	6	9
826	rail vehicle operators, n.e.c.	6	9
	water transportation occupations		
828	ship captains and mates, except fishing boats	5	1
829	sailors and deckhands	6	10
833	marine engineers	5	1
834	bridge, lock, and light house tenders	6	10

Material moving equipment operators

843	supervisors, material moving equipment operators	5	8
844	operating engineers	6	10
845	longshore equipment operators	6	9
848	hoist and winch operators	6	9
849	crane and tower operators	6	9
853	excavating and loading machine operators	6	9
855	grader, dozer and scraper operators	6	9
856	industrial truck or tractor equipment operators	6	9
859	miscellaneous material moving equipment operators	6	9

Handlers equipment cleaners, helpers and labourers

863	supervisors, handlers, equipment cleaners and labourers	5	8
864	helpers, mechanics and repairers	6	10
	helpers, construction and extractive occupations	6	10
865	helpers, construction trades	6	10
866	helpers, surveyor	6	10
867	helpers, extractive occupations	6	10
869	construction labourers	6	10
873	production helpers	6	10
	freight, stock and material handlers	6	10
875	garbage collectors	6	10
876	stevedores	6	10
877	stockhandlers and baggers	6	10
878	machine feeders and offbearers	6	10

883	freights, stock and material handlers	6	10
885	garage and serving station related occupations	6	10
887	vehicle washers and equipment cleaners	6	10
888	hand packers and packagers	6	10
889	labourer, except construction	6	10

905 unemployed, last worked in armed forces since 1975
909 unemployed, last worked in 1974 or earlier

Appendix 7.2 SPSSX Procedure for Translating American Occupation into
Goldthorpe's Class Schema

```
$ sel uscensus
$ work 50000
$ assign sys$scratch spsiowfi
$ assign sys$scratch spsiowfo
$ spssx/output=census.lis
file handle=a/name='[cheng.uscensus]asian.sys'
get file=a
file handle=b/name='[cheng.uscensus]us1pc.sys'
add files file=*/file=b

do if (any(class,1,2,3,4,7))

compute jgclass=0
if (any(occup,3,4,5,6,7,8,9,13,14,15,16,17,19,23,24,25,
            26,27,28,29,33,34,35,36,37,43,44,45,46,
            47,48,49,53,54,55,56,57,58,59,63,64,65,66,
            67,68,69,73,74,75,76,77,78,79,83,84,85,86,87,
            88,89,95,96,97,98,99,103,104,105,113,114,115,
            116,117,118,119,123,124,125,126,127,128,129,
            133,134,135,136,137,138,139,143,144,
            145,146,147,148,149,153,154,156,157,158,159,
            163,164,165,166,167,168,169,173,174,175,176,
            177,178,179,183,184,185,186,187,188,
            194,195,197,198,203,204,205,206,208,
            213,214,215,216,217,218,223,224,225,
            226,227,228,229,233,234,235,243,254,255,
            303,304,305,306,307,363,414,418,497,828,833))
            jgclass=1

if (any(occup,106,155,207,253,256,257,258,259,
            263,264,265,266,267,26,269,274,
            283,284,285,308,309,313,314,315,316,
            317,318,323,325,326,327,328,329,335,336,337,
            338,339,343,344,345,346,347,348,349,353,359,
            364,365,366,368,369,373,374,375,376,377,
            378,379,383,384,385,386,389,468))
            jgclass=3
```

```
if (any(occup,193,275,276,319,404,405,463))
        jgclass=4

if (any(occup,473,474,475,476))
        jgclass=7

if (any(occup,18,189,199,413,415,416,417,423,424,
        433,448,456,485,503,527,529,
        553,554,555,556,557,558,613,633,678,773,
        774,803,843,863))
        jgclass=8

if(any(occup,436,437,457,458,505,506,507,508,
        509,514,515,516,517,518,519,
        523,525,526,533,534,535,536,538,539,
        543,544,547,549,563,564,565,566,567,569,573,
        575,576,577,579,583,584,585,587,
        634,635,643,645,647,653,654,656,657,658,
        659,666,667,668,669,673,674,675,676,677,679,
        683,684,686,687,688,689,693,694,695,696,699,
        703,726,727,728,729,733,734,735,736,737,
        783,784,787,793,823,824,825,826,845,848,849,
        853,855,856,859))
        jgclass=9

if (any(occup,277,278,354,355,356,357,387,403,406,407,
        425,426,427,434,435,438,439,443,444,445,
        446,447,449,453,454,455,459,464,465,
        466,467,469,486,487,488,489,498,588,589,
        593,594,595,596,597,598,599,614,615,616,
        617,636,637,639,644,646,649,655,704,
        705,706,707,708,709,713,714,715,717,719,
        723,724,725,738,739,743,744,745,747,
        748,749,753,754,755,756,757,758,759,763,
        764,765,766,768,769,777,779,785,786,
        789,794,795,796,797,798,799,804,805,806,808,
        809,813,814,829,834,844,864,865,866,
        867,869,873,875,876,877,878,883,
        885,887,888,889))
        jgclass=10
```

```
if (any(occup,477,479,483,484,494,495,496,499))
          jgclass=11

else if (any(class,5,6))
compute jgclass=0
if (any(occup,43,44,45,46,47,48,49,53,54,55,56,57,58,59,
          63,64,65,66,67,68,69,73,74,75,76,77,78,79,
          83,84,85,86,87,88,89,95,96,97,98,99,
          103,104,105,106,113,114,115,116,117,118,119,
          123,124,125,126,127,128,129,133,134,
          135,136,137,138,139,143,144,145,146,
          147,148,149,153,154,155,156,157,158,159,
          163,164,165,166,167,168,169,173,174,175,
          176,177,178,179,183,184,185,186,187,188,
          189,193,194,195,197,198,199))
          jgclass=1

if (any(occup,3,4,5,6,7,8,9,13,14,15,16,17,18,19,
          23,24,25,26,27,28,29,33,34,35,36,37,
          203,204,205,206,207,208,213,214,
          215,216,217,218,223,224,225,226,227,228,
          229,233,234,235,243,253,254,255,256,257,
          258,259,263,264,265,266,267,268,269,
          274,275,276,283,284,285,303,304,305,
          306,307,308,309,313,314,315,316,317,
          318,319,323,325,326,327,328,329,335,
          336,337,338,339,343,344,345,346,347,348,349,
          353,359,363,364,365,366,368,369,373,374,375,
          376,377,378,379,383,384,385,386,389,413,
          414,415,416,417,418,423,424,
          433,448,456,463,468,497,503,527,529,
          553,554,555,556,557,558,613,614,615,616,617,
          633,678,773,774,803,828,833,843,863))
          jgclass=5

if (any(occup,277,278,354,355,356,357,387,403,404,
          405,406,407,425,426,427,434,435,436,437,
          438,439,443,444,445,446,447,449,453,
          454,455,457,458,459,464,465,466,467,
          469,485,486,487,488,489,498,505,506,
          507,508,509,514,515,516,517,518,
          519,523,525,526,533,534,535,536,538,
```

```
                    539,543,544,547,549,563,564,565,566,567,569,
                    573,575,576,577,579,583,584,585,
                    587,588,589,593,594,595,596,597,598,599,
                    634,635,636,637,639,643,644,645,646,647,649,
                    653,654,655,656,657,658,659,666,667,668,669,
                    673,674,675,676,677,679,683,684,
                    686,687,688,689,693,694,695,696,699,703,
                    704,705,706,707,708,709,713,714,715,717,
                    719,723,724,725,726,727,728,729,
                    733,734,735,736,737,738,739,743,744,
                    745,747,748,749,753,754,755,756,757,758,
                    759,763,764,765,766,768,769,777,
                    779,783,784,785, 786,787,789,793,794,795,
                    796,797,798,799,804,805,806,808,
                    809,813,814,823,824,825,826,
                    829,834,844,845,848,849,853,855,856,
                    859,864,865,866,867,869,873,875,876,877,878,
                    883,885,887,888,889))
                    jgclass=6

if (any(occup,473,474,475,476,477,479,483,
            484,494,495,496,499))
            jgclass=7
end if
value labels jgclass 1 'I+II'
                    3 'IIIa'
                    4 'IIIb'
                    5 'IVa'
                    6 'IVb'
                    7 'IVc'
                    8 'V'
                    9 'VI'
                   10 'VIIa'
                   11 'VIIb'

save outfile='census.sys'

finish
```

Appendix 7.3. Goldthorpe Class Distribution for All

Class	Frequency	Percent	Cumulative Percent
I&II	60,672	27.9	27.9
IIIa	43,223	19.8	47.7
IIIb	6,387	2.9	50.6
IVa	8,087	3.7	54.4
IVb	4,961	2.3	56.6
IVc	2,186	1.0	57.6
V	6,591	3.0	60.7
VI	22,289	10.2	70.9
VIa	60,862	27.9	98.8
VIb	2,523	1.2	100.0
Total	217,781	100.0	100.0

Appendix 7.4 Goldthorpe Class Distribution for Males

Class	Frequency	Percent	Cumulative Percent
I&II	35,295	30.8	30.8
IIIa	10,881	9.5	40.3
IIIb	1,113	1.0	41.3
IVa	5,541	4.8	46.1
IVb	3,756	3.3	49.4
IVc	1,858	1.6	51.0
V	5,331	4.7	55.6
VI	17,272	15.1	70.7
VIIa	31,767	27.7	98.4
VIIb	1,826	1.6	100.0
Total	114,640	100.0	100.0

Appendix 7.5 Goldthorpe Class Distribution for Females

Class	Frequency	Percent	Cumulative
I&II	25,377	24.6	24.6
IIIa	32,342	31.4	56.0
IIIb	5,274	5.1	61.1
IVa	2,546	2.5	63.5
IVb	1,205	1.2	64.7
IVc	328	.3	65.0
V	1,260	1.2	66.3
VI	5,017	4.9	71.1
VIIa	29,095	28.2	99.3
VIIb	697	.7	100.0
Total	103,141	100.0	100.0

Appendix 7.6 Male Immigrants: Access to the Service Class

	Estimate	s.e.	Parameter
1	1.580	0.09118	1
2	0.06851	0.1090	AGE(2)
3	0.1852	0.1213	AGE(3)
4	0.1379	0.1254	AGE(4)
5	0.05886	0.1381	AGE(5)
6	0.06321	0.1626	AGE(6)
7	-0.1211	0.1712	AGE(7)
8	-0.2741	0.2068	AGE(8)
9	-1.868	0.08944	EDUC(2)
10	-3.739	0.1307	EDUC(3)
11	-4.202	0.1672	EDUC(4)
12	-0.3502	0.1899	ETHN(2)
13	**-1.132**	**0.1371**	**ETHN(3)**
14	**-0.5526**	**0.1878**	**ETHN(4)**
15	-0.2156	0.1229	ETHN(5)
16	**-0.8708**	**0.1966**	**ETHN(6)**
17	**-0.9150**	**0.1717**	**ETHN(7)**
18	**-0.6682**	**0.2055**	**ETHN(8)**
19	**-0.4744**	**0.09552**	**ETHN(9)**
20	0.09783	0.08007	AGE(2).EDUC(2)
21	-0.002088	0.1060	AGE(2).EDUC(3)
22	-0.1465	0.1730	AGE(2).EDUC(4)
23	-0.1133	0.08657	AGE(3).EDUC(2)
24	-0.03338	0.1099	AGE(3).EDUC(3)
25	-0.2019	0.1670	AGE(3).EDUC(4)
26	-0.1719	0.09454	AGE(4).EDUC(2)
27	0.05536	0.1159	AGE(4).EDUC(3)
28	-0.3686	0.1719	AGE(4).EDUC(4)
29	-0.03986	0.1039	AGE(5).EDUC(2)
30	0.1817	0.1228	AGE(5).EDUC(3)
31	-0.4786	0.1802	AGE(5).EDUC(4)
32	-0.1922	0.1186	AGE(6).EDUC(2)
33	0.09170	0.1347	AGE(6).EDUC(3)
34	-0.2772	0.1758	AGE(6).EDUC(4)
35	-0.04850	0.1327	AGE(7).EDUC(2)
36	0.3103	0.1452	AGE(7).EDUC(3)
37	0.006561	0.1843	AGE(7).EDUC(4)

38	0.1099	0.1625	AGE(8).EDUC(2)
39	0.3999	0.1765	AGE(8).EDUC(3)
40	-0.2542	0.2209	AGE(8).EDUC(4)
41	0.2757	0.1761	AGE(2).ETHN(2)
42	0.2549	0.1526	AGE(2).ETHN(3)
43	0.09538	0.2001	AGE(2).ETHN(4)
44	0.08562	0.1439	AGE(2).ETHN(5)
45	-0.06632	0.1937	AGE(2).ETHN(6)
46	0.05533	0.1755	AGE(2).ETHN(7)
47	-0.04412	0.1836	AGE(2).ETHN(8)
48	0.1308	0.1070	AGE(2).ETHN(9)
49	0.7118	0.2003	AGE(3).ETHN(2)
50	0.3564	0.1624	AGE(3).ETHN(3)
51	0.05636	0.2056	AGE(3).ETHN(4)
52	0.3375	0.1566	AGE(3).ETHN(5)
53	0.2251	0.2173	AGE(3).ETHN(6)
54	0.3602	0.1913	AGE(3).ETHN(7)
55	0.2625	0.1992	AGE(3).ETHN(8)
56	0.3162	0.1213	AGE(3).ETHN(9)
57	0.9420	0.2256	AGE(4).ETHN(2)
58	0.6165	0.1678	AGE(4).ETHN(3)
59	0.05558	0.2069	AGE(4).ETHN(4)
60	0.4699	0.1664	AGE(4).ETHN(5)
61	0.6546	0.2286	AGE(4).ETHN(6)
62	0.3050	0.1985	AGE(4).ETHN(7)
63	0.1045	0.2206	AGE(4).ETHN(8)
64	0.3991	0.1227	AGE(4).ETHN(9)
65	1.027	0.2491	AGE(5).ETHN(2)
66	0.2397	0.1839	AGE(5).ETHN(3)
67	0.09559	0.2259	AGE(5).ETHN(4)
68	0.1620	0.1914	AGE(5).ETHN(5)
69	-0.1360	0.2727	AGE(5).ETHN(6)
70	0.5548	0.2177	AGE(5).ETHN(7)
71	0.2255	0.2388	AGE(5).ETHN(8)
72	0.4684	0.1301	AGE(5).ETHN(9)
73	-0.01836	0.2971	AGE(6).ETHN(2)
74	0.1986	0.2043	AGE(6).ETHN(3)
75	-0.06208	0.2744	AGE(6).ETHN(4)
76	0.3219	0.2365	AGE(6).ETHN(5)
77	0.4721	0.3337	AGE(6).ETHN(6)
78	0.5152	0.2421	AGE(6).ETHN(7)
79	0.4748	0.2461	AGE(6).ETHN(8)

80	0.6662	0.1465	AGE(6).ETHN(9)
81	0.5188	0.3715	AGE(7).ETHN(2)
82	0.01939	0.2405	AGE(7).ETHN(3)
83	0.1224	0.3281	AGE(7).ETHN(4)
84	0.2718	0.3113	AGE(7).ETHN(5)
85	-0.1966	0.3962	AGE(7).ETHN(6)
86	0.2846	0.2752	AGE(7).ETHN(7)
87	0.2549	0.2817	AGE(7).ETHN(8)
88	0.5492	0.1526	AGE(7).ETHN(9)
89	-0.4069	0.4903	AGE(8).ETHN(2)
90	-0.3098	0.3049	AGE(8).ETHN(3)
91	-0.3681	0.4711	AGE(8).ETHN(4)
92	0.3437	0.4344	AGE(8).ETHN(5)
93	0.09501	0.5751	AGE(8).ETHN(6)
94	0.2205	0.3559	AGE(8).ETHN(7)
95	0.8193	0.3303	AGE(8).ETHN(8)
96	0.5555	0.1868	AGE(8).ETHN(9)
97	**0.6472**	**0.1667**	**EDUC(2).ETHN(2)**
98	**0.4349**	**0.1047**	**EDUC(2).ETHN(3)**
99	-0.1090	0.1286	EDUC(2).ETHN(4)
100	0.1175	0.1067	EDUC(2).ETHN(5)
101	0.3569	0.1808	EDUC(2).ETHN(6)
102	0.2341	0.1493	EDUC(2).ETHN(7)
103	-0.05649	0.1918	EDUC(2).ETHN(8)
104	**0.2020**	**0.08230**	**EDUC(2).ETHN(9)**
105	**0.8785**	**0.2165**	**EDUC(3).ETHN(2)**
106	**0.5871**	**0.1882**	**EDUC(3).ETHN(3)**
107	0.2659	0.2028	EDUC(3).ETHN(4)
108	**0.6506**	**0.1798**	**EDUC(3).ETHN(5)**
109	0.3427	0.2607	EDUC(3).ETHN(6)
110	**0.5472**	**0.1949**	**EDUC(3).ETHN(7)**
111	0.1779	0.2203	EDUC(3).ETHN(8)
112	**0.5379**	**0.1172**	**EDUC(3).ETHN(9)**
113	**0.7221**	**0.3438**	**EDUC(4).ETHN(2)**
114	**0.5284**	**0.2382**	**EDUC(4).ETHN(3)**
115	**1.267**	**0.2653**	**EDUC(4).ETHN(4)**
116	**0.8235**	**0.2076**	**EDUC(4).ETHN(5)**
117	**0.8516**	**0.2869**	**EDUC(4).ETHN(6)**
118	**0.5454**	**0.2067**	**EDUC(4).ETHN(7)**
119	-0.007207	0.2495	EDUC(4).ETHN(8)
120	**0.3113**	**0.1356**	**EDUC(4).ETHN(9)**

Appendix 7.7 Male Immigrants: Risks of Unemployment

	Estimate	s.e.	Parameter
1	-4.453	0.2608	1
2	-0.6073	0.2731	AGE(2)
3	-0.1916	0.2750	AGE(3)
4	-0.5384	0.2926	AGE(4)
5	-0.1167	0.2616	AGE(5)
6	-0.2871	0.2976	AGE(6)
7	-0.1079	0.2899	AGE(7)
8	0.08728	0.3194	AGE(8)
9	1.193	0.2558	EDUC(2)
10	1.329	0.2742	EDUC(3)
11	1.418	0.2583	EDUC(4)
12	**1.726**	**0.4725**	**ETHN(2)**
13	**0.9640**	**0.3716**	**ETHN(3)**
14	-0.7081	0.6075	ETHN(4)
15	**1.028**	**0.3236**	**ETHN(5)**
16	0.8663	0.4865	ETHN(6)
17	0.6316	0.5054	ETHN(7)
18	**1.619**	**0.4734**	**ETHN(8)**
19	**0.7973**	**0.2865**	**ETHN(9)**
20	-0.8981	0.5273	AGE(2).ETHN(2)
21	0.5879	0.3621	AGE(2).ETHN(3)
22	1.363	0.4959	AGE(2).ETHN(4)
23	0.09725	0.3573	AGE(2).ETHN(5)
24	0.7857	0.4090	AGE(2).ETHN(6)
25	0.1226	0.3551	AGE(2).ETHN(7)
26	0.1923	0.3200	AGE(2).ETHN(8)
27	0.2713	0.2842	AGE(2).ETHN(9)
28	-1.509	0.6232	AGE(3).ETHN(2)
29	-0.4828	0.3993	AGE(3).ETHN(3)
30	0.3922	0.5260	AGE(3).ETHN(4)
31	-0.5973	0.3758	AGE(3).ETHN(5)
32	0.5090	0.4351	AGE(3).ETHN(6)
33	0.05630	0.3539	AGE(3).ETHN(7)
34	-0.6246	0.3418	AGE(3).ETHN(8)

35	-0.4656	0.2895	AGE(3).ETHN(9)
36	-1.359	0.8069	AGE(4).ETHN(2)
37	-0.3766	0.4429	AGE(4).ETHN(3)
38	0.6326	0.5380	AGE(4).ETHN(4)
39	-0.1671	0.4043	AGE(4).ETHN(5)
40	0.6580	0.4834	AGE(4).ETHN(6)
41	-0.2829	0.4074	AGE(4).ETHN(7)
42	-0.4092	0.3670	AGE(4).ETHN(8)
43	-0.1709	0.3078	AGE(4).ETHN(9)
44	-1.114	0.6858	AGE(5).ETHN(2)
45	-0.3113	0.4169	AGE(5).ETHN(3)
46	0.5767	0.5340	AGE(5).ETHN(4)
47	0.1324	0.3817	AGE(5).ETHN(5)
48	0.7287	0.4415	AGE(5).ETHN(6)
49	-0.5787	0.4029	AGE(5).ETHN(7)
50	-0.5582	0.3400	AGE(5).ETHN(8)
51	-0.7121	0.2801	AGE(5).ETHN(9)
52	-0.9568	0.8248	AGE(6).ETHN(2)
53	-0.4052	0.4623	AGE(6).ETHN(3)
54	0.5618	0.6528	AGE(6).ETHN(4)
55	0.1985	0.4614	AGE(6).ETHN(5)
56	0.8121	0.5367	AGE(6).ETHN(6)
57	-0.6835	0.4611	AGE(6).ETHN(7)
58	-0.5324	0.3727	AGE(6).ETHN(8)
59	-0.6439	0.3139	AGE(6).ETHN(9)
60	-1.232	1.097	AGE(7).ETHN(2)
61	-0.3159	0.4556	AGE(7).ETHN(3)
62	-0.6957	1.108	AGE(7).ETHN(4)
63	0.2733	0.5223	AGE(7).ETHN(5)
64	1.019	0.5373	AGE(7).ETHN(6)
65	0.1029	0.4106	AGE(7).ETHN(7)
66	-0.9867	0.3933	AGE(7).ETHN(8)
67	-0.6590	0.3059	AGE(7).ETHN(9)
68	-6.342	8.721	AGE(8).ETHN(2)
69	-0.6096	0.5354	AGE(8).ETHN(3)
70	1.267	0.7163	AGE(8).ETHN(4)
71	-0.3138	0.8148	AGE(8).ETHN(5)
72	-0.6922	1.088	AGE(8).ETHN(6)
73	-0.6300	0.5465	AGE(8).ETHN(7)
74	-1.291	0.4724	AGE(8).ETHN(8)
75	-0.8789	0.3398	AGE(8).ETHN(9)

76	**-1.447**	**0.4875**	**EDUC(2).ETHN(2)**
77	**-0.9151**	**0.3495**	**EDUC(2).ETHN(3)**
78	0.2448	0.5073	EDUC(2).ETHN(4)
79	-0.4104	0.3191	EDUC(2).ETHN(5)
80	-0.7490	0.4718	EDUC(2).ETHN(6)
81	-0.06127	0.5079	EDUC(2).ETHN(7)
82	-0.6073	0.4822	EDUC(2).ETHN(8)
83	-0.5500	0.2834	EDUC(2).ETHN(9)
84	**-2.188**	**0.6718**	**EDUC(3).ETHN(2)**
85	-0.3886	0.3852	EDUC(3).ETHN(3)
86	0.5225	0.5339	EDUC(3).ETHN(4)
87	-0.2667	0.3748	EDUC(3).ETHN(5)
88	-0.8925	0.5065	EDUC(3).ETHN(6)
89	-0.1334	0.5212	EDUC(3).ETHN(7)
90	-0.3277	0.4833	EDUC(3).ETHN(8)
91	-0.1584	0.2984	EDUC(3).ETHN(9)
92	-0.3381	0.6113	EDUC(4).ETHN(2)
93	-0.6156	0.3817	EDUC(4).ETHN(3)
94	0.05510	0.6231	EDUC(4).ETHN(4)
95	-0.1581	0.3532	EDUC(4).ETHN(5)
96	-0.4882	0.4848	EDUC(4).ETHN(6)
97	0.2557	0.4983	EDUC(4).ETHN(7)
98	-0.03559	0.4738	EDUC(4).ETHN(8)
99	0.3908	0.2850	EDUC(4).ETHN(9)

Appendix 7.8 Female Immigrants: Access to Service Class

	Estimate	s.e.	Parameter
1	0.8808	0.09276	1
2	0.2707	0.1029	AGE(2)
3	0.2069	0.1179	AGE(3)
4	0.1199	0.1287	AGE(4)
5	-0.03414	0.1580	AGE(5)
6	-0.1782	0.1761	AGE(6)
7	-0.4170	0.2120	AGE(7)
8	-0.2057	0.2728	AGE(8)
9	-1.517	0.08686	EDUC(2)
10	-3.098	0.1254	EDUC(3)
11	-4.583	0.1782	EDUC(4)
12	-0.05678	0.2297	ETHN(2)
13	-0.1600	0.1221	ETHN(3)
14	-0.2141	0.2122	ETHN(4)
15	-0.1047	0.1501	ETHN(5)
16	-0.3871	0.2808	ETHN(6)
17	-0.2974	0.1811	ETHN(7)
18	0.3962	0.2088	ETHN(8)
19	**0.5926**	**0.1099**	**ETHN(9)**
20	-0.3848	0.2390	AGE(2).ETHN(2)
21	0.1360	0.1353	AGE(2).ETHN(3)
22	-0.1973	0.1914	AGE(2).ETHN(4)
23	-0.03588	0.1669	AGE(2).ETHN(5)
24	0.02978	0.2322	AGE(2).ETHN(6)
25	-0.1662	0.1857	AGE(2).ETHN(7)
26	-0.007455	0.1670	AGE(2).ETHN(8)
27	-0.1902	0.1144	AGE(2).ETHN(9)
28	-0.04834	0.2609	AGE(3).ETHN(2)
29	0.3020	0.1499	AGE(3).ETHN(3)
30	-0.1843	0.2085	AGE(3).ETHN(4)
31	0.2318	0.1863	AGE(3).ETHN(5)
32	-0.02835	0.2687	AGE(3).ETHN(6)
33	0.02778	0.2013	AGE(3).ETHN(7)

34	-0.007657	0.1888	AGE(3).ETHN(8)
35	-0.08737	0.1295	AGE(3).ETHN(9)
36	-0.1988	0.2631	AGE(4).ETHN(2)
37	0.1986	0.1646	AGE(4).ETHN(3)
38	-0.2390	0.2243	AGE(4).ETHN(4)
39	0.4648	0.2176	AGE(4).ETHN(5)
40	-0.3006	0.3413	AGE(4).ETHN(6)
41	0.3543	0.2190	AGE(4).ETHN(7)
42	-0.02883	0.2132	AGE(4).ETHN(8)
43	0.03398	0.1408	AGE(4).ETHN(9)
44	0.01088	0.2625	AGE(5).ETHN(2)
45	0.2571	0.1989	AGE(5).ETHN(3)
46	-0.01846	0.2721	AGE(5).ETHN(4)
47	0.1783	0.2827	AGE(5).ETHN(5)
48	-0.02576	0.4403	AGE(5).ETHN(6)
49	-0.03718	0.2732	AGE(5).ETHN(7)
50	0.2884	0.2368	AGE(5).ETHN(8)
51	0.1622	0.1691	AGE(5).ETHN(9)
52	0.04496	0.2852	AGE(6).ETHN(2)
53	0.1171	0.2346	AGE(6).ETHN(3)
54	0.01122	0.3886	AGE(6).ETHN(4)
55	0.3081	0.3667	AGE(6).ETHN(5)
56	-0.2538	0.6076	AGE(6).ETHN(6)
57	0.3903	0.2920	AGE(6).ETHN(7)
58	0.3682	0.2642	AGE(6).ETHN(8)
59	0.3247	0.1861	AGE(6).ETHN(9)
60	0.05190	0.4163	AGE(7).ETHN(2)
61	0.3182	0.2775	AGE(7).ETHN(3)
62	-0.02961	0.6503	AGE(7).ETHN(4)
63	1.263	0.5121	AGE(7).ETHN(5)
64	-0.2080	0.8646	AGE(7).ETHN(6)
65	0.6720	0.3490	AGE(7).ETHN(7)
66	0.7706	0.3017	AGE(7).ETHN(8)
67	0.4844	0.2218	AGE(7).ETHN(9)
68	-0.006698	0.6386	AGE(8).ETHN(2)
69	0.1962	0.3792	AGE(8).ETHN(3)
70	-6.322	10.55	AGE(8).ETHN(4)
71	0.8684	0.8915	AGE(8).ETHN(5)
72	-5.469	13.93	AGE(8).ETHN(6)
73	-0.5907	0.5887	AGE(8).ETHN(7)
74	0.09180	0.3916	AGE(8).ETHN(8)
75	0.1015	0.2845	AGE(8).ETHN(9)

76	-0.3409	0.2072	EDUC(2).ETHN(2)
77	-0.06721	0.1093	EDUC(2).ETHN(3)
78	-0.002937	0.1862	EDUC(2).ETHN(4)
79	-0.04142	0.1405	EDUC(2).ETHN(5)
80	-0.1422	0.2739	EDUC(2).ETHN(6)
81	0.002192	0.1667	EDUC(2).ETHN(7)
82	**-0.4685**	**0.2004**	**EDUC(2).ETHN(8)**
83	**-0.3306**	**0.1036**	**EDUC(2).ETHN(9)**
84	-0.4104	0.2502	EDUC(3).ETHN(2)
85	-0.2877	0.1956	EDUC(3).ETHN(3)
86	**-0.5448**	**0.2417**	**EDUC(3).ETHN(4)**
87	**0.5792**	**0.2024**	**EDUC(3).ETHN(5)**
88	0.1636	0.3157	EDUC(3).ETHN(6)
89	0.2665	0.2121	EDUC(3).ETHN(7)
90	-0.3010	0.2247	EDUC(3).ETHN(8)
91	-0.1780	0.1384	EDUC(3).ETHN(9)
92	**0.8801**	**0.3496**	**EDUC(4).ETHN(2)**
93	**0.5867**	**0.2451**	**EDUC(4).ETHN(3)**
94	0.4435	0.3285	EDUC(4).ETHN(4)
95	**1.195**	**0.2726**	**EDUC(4).ETHN(5)**
96	**0.9138**	**0.3784**	**EDUC(4).ETHN(6)**
97	0.4795	0.2904	EDUC(4).ETHN(7)
98	0.05297	0.2860	EDUC(4).ETHN(8)
99	**0.4434**	**0.1961**	**EDUC(4).ETHN(9)**

Appendix 7.9   Female Immigrants: Risks of Unemployment

	Estimate	s.e.	Parameter
1	-3.286	0.2209	1
2	-0.4189	0.2256	AGE(2)
3	-0.3619	0.2487	AGE(3)
4	-0.3101	0.2448	AGE(4)
5	-0.7408	0.2962	AGE(5)
6	-0.6457	0.2930	AGE(6)
7	-0.02439	0.2734	AGE(7)
8	-0.05297	0.3333	AGE(8)
9	0.1435	0.2350	EDUC(2)
10	0.1602	0.2634	EDUC(3)
11	0.8352	0.2283	EDUC(4)
12	-1.267	1.040	ETHN(2)
13	**-1.068**	**0.3448**	**ETHN(3)**
14	0.2333	0.5235	ETHN(4)
15	**0.8884**	**0.2946**	**ETHN(5)**
16	0.8017	0.5362	ETHN(6)
17	-0.2442	0.4451	ETHN(7)
18	-0.1842	0.5590	ETHN(8)
19	-0.3323	0.2672	ETHN(9)
20	-0.3540	0.4517	AGE(2).ETHN(2)
21	0.4909	0.3165	AGE(2).ETHN(3)
22	-0.2506	0.3260	AGE(2).ETHN(4)
23	0.09380	0.3036	AGE(2).ETHN(5)
24	0.02617	0.3690	AGE(2).ETHN(6)
25	0.05823	0.3418	AGE(2).ETHN(7)
26	-0.09019	0.2936	AGE(2).ETHN(8)
27	0.2909	0.2460	AGE(2).ETHN(9)
28	-0.4126	0.4766	AGE(3).ETHN(2)
29	0.03780	0.3572	AGE(3).ETHN(3)
30	-0.3033	0.3461	AGE(3).ETHN(4)
31	-0.5982	0.3625	AGE(3).ETHN(5)
32	-0.3969	0.4592	AGE(3).ETHN(6)
33	0.3082	0.3548	AGE(3).ETHN(7)
34	-0.1519	0.3181	AGE(3).ETHN(8)
35	-0.1275	0.2729	AGE(3).ETHN(9)

36	-0.6755	0.4603	AGE(4).ETHN(2)
37	0.1953	0.3573	AGE(4).ETHN(3)
38	-0.9614	0.3953	AGE(4).ETHN(4)
39	-0.2670	0.3772	AGE(4).ETHN(5)
40	0.1614	0.4478	AGE(4).ETHN(6)
41	0.006235	0.3784	AGE(4).ETHN(7)
42	-0.7619	0.3507	AGE(4).ETHN(8)
43	-0.2039	0.2717	AGE(4).ETHN(9)
44	-0.2705	0.4553	AGE(5).ETHN(2)
45	0.9985	0.3997	AGE(5).ETHN(3)
46	-0.07524	0.4449	AGE(5).ETHN(4)
47	0.4556	0.4510	AGE(5).ETHN(5)
48	1.049	0.5126	AGE(5).ETHN(6)
49	0.8246	0.4133	AGE(5).ETHN(7)
50	-0.3335	0.3957	AGE(5).ETHN(8)
51	0.1464	0.3212	AGE(5).ETHN(9)
52	-0.3327	0.4695	AGE(6).ETHN(2)
53	0.5685	0.4265	AGE(6).ETHN(3)
54	0.1040	0.5363	AGE(6).ETHN(4)
55	0.1178	0.5731	AGE(6).ETHN(5)
56	0.3080	0.6899	AGE(6).ETHN(6)
57	0.8439	0.4092	AGE(6).ETHN(7)
58	-0.4435	0.4021	AGE(6).ETHN(8)
59	0.09923	0.3165	AGE(6).ETHN(9)
60	-1.367	0.6965	AGE(7).ETHN(2)
61	-0.1213	0.4486	AGE(7).ETHN(3)
62	0.1385	0.5397	AGE(7).ETHN(4)
63	-0.7095	0.8024	AGE(7).ETHN(5)
64	-0.1706	0.8099	AGE(7).ETHN(6)
65	0.1610	0.4505	AGE(7).ETHN(7)
66	-1.251	0.4046	AGE(7).ETHN(8)
67	-0.8206	0.3064	AGE(7).ETHN(9)
68	-0.9873	1.103	AGE(8).ETHN(2)
69	0.9263	0.4638	AGE(8).ETHN(3)
70	0.3438	0.6563	AGE(8).ETHN(4)
71	-6.212	10.84	AGE(8).ETHN(5)
72	0.3928	1.127	AGE(8).ETHN(6)
73	0.4531	0.5191	AGE(8).ETHN(7)
74	-1.771	0.5500	AGE(8).ETHN(8)
75	-0.6081	0.3670	AGE(8).ETHN(9)

76	1.870	1.049	EDUC(2).ETHN(2)
77	0.5837	0.3412	EDUC(2).ETHN(3)
78	0.1545	0.5396	EDUC(2).ETHN(4)
79	-0.07390	0.3160	EDUC(2).ETHN(5)
80	0.1012	0.5530	EDUC(2).ETHN(6)
81	0.4819	0.4565	EDUC(2).ETHN(7)
82	0.7370	0.5770	EDUC(2).ETHN(8)
83	0.2611	0.2821	EDUC(2).ETHN(9)
84	**2.133**	**1.055**	**EDUC(3).ETHN(2)**
85	**0.9836**	**0.3964**	**EDUC(3).ETHN(3)**
86	0.6698	0.5411	EDUC(3).ETHN(4)
87	0.2833	0.3584	EDUC(3).ETHN(5)
88	-0.3214	0.5768	EDUC(3).ETHN(6)
89	0.6873	0.4720	EDUC(3).ETHN(7)
90	**1.172**	**0.5801**	**EDUC(3).ETHN(8)**
91	**0.7363**	**0.3029**	**EDUC(3).ETHN(9)**
92	1.362	1.076	EDUC(4).ETHN(2)
93	**1.071**	**0.3425**	**EDUC(4).ETHN(3)**
94	0.2263	0.5306	EDUC(4).ETHN(4)
95	-0.004648	0.3258	EDUC(4).ETHN(5)
96	-0.8447	0.5543	EDUC(4).ETHN(6)
97	0.4773	0.4422	EDUC(4).ETHN(7)
98	**1.282**	**0.5649**	**EDUC(4).ETHN(8)**
99	**0.6457**	**0.2775**	**EDUC(4).ETHN(9)**

Appendix 7.10 Native-born Females: Access to Service Class

	Estimate	s.e.	Parameter
1	1.537	0.1324	1
2	0.1114	0.03932	AGE(2)
3	0.1699	0.04290	AGE(3)
4	0.1589	0.04639	AGE(4)
5	0.1732	0.04817	AGE(5)
6	0.1574	0.04907	AGE(6)
7	0.07058	0.05288	AGE(7)
8	-0.08123	0.06753	AGE(8)
9	-1.976	0.1493	EDUC(2)
10	-2.988	0.1794	EDUC(3)
11	-3.553	0.3362	EDUC(4)
12	-0.1700	0.1572	ETHN(2)
13	-0.3890	0.3411	ETHN(3)
14	**-0.9482**	**0.4091**	**ETHN(4)**
15	-0.6955	0.3530	ETHN(5)
16	-1.580	1.009	ETHN(6)
17	**-0.9192**	**0.1790**	**ETHN(7)**
18	-0.2075	0.2129	ETHN(8)
19	-0.08389	0.1408	ETHN(9)

20	0.0005997	0.1788	EDUC(2).ETHN(2)
21	0.1303	0.3711	EDUC(2).ETHN(3)
22	0.5088	0.5038	EDUC(2).ETHN(4)
23	0.7700	0.4155	EDUC(2).ETHN(5)
24	1.948	1.301	EDUC(2).ETHN(6)
25	**0.4594**	**0.2057**	**EDUC(2).ETHN(7)**
26	-0.006270	0.2337	EDUC(2).ETHN(8)
27	0.1286	0.1596	EDUC(2).ETHN(9)
28	-0.2830	0.2097	EDUC(3).ETHN(2)
29	-0.1964	0.3959	EDUC(3).ETHN(3)
30	0.9547	0.5450	EDUC(3).ETHN(4)
31	0.1938	0.4476	EDUC(3).ETHN(5)
32	1.114	1.484	EDUC(3).ETHN(6)
33	0.1757	0.2471	EDUC(3).ETHN(7)
34	-0.4083	0.2585	EDUC(3).ETHN(8)
35	-0.2901	0.1882	EDUC(3).ETHN(9)
36	-0.3731	0.3943	EDUC(4).ETHN(2)
37	0.07792	0.5594	EDUC(4).ETHN(3)
38	**1.522**	**0.7615**	**EDUC(4).ETHN(4)**
39	0.2475	0.6137	EDUC(4).ETHN(5)
40	**4.237**	**1.366**	**EDUC(4).ETHN(6)**
41	-0.5577	0.4058	EDUC(4).ETHN(7)
42	**-0.9592**	**0.4019**	**EDUC(4).ETHN(8)**
43	-0.5875	0.3454	EDUC(4).ETHN(9)

Appendix 7.11 Chinese Male Immigrants: Access to Service Class

	Estimate	s.e.	Parameter
1	0.7049	0.1600	1
2	0.2961	0.1518	AGE(2)
3	0.7554	0.1629	AGE(3)
4	0.7198	0.1558	AGE(4)
5	0.9174	0.1550	AGE(5)
6	0.7035	0.1650	AGE(6)
7	0.9081	0.1524	AGE(7)
8	-1.183	0.1465	EDUC(2)
9	-2.115	0.1506	EDUC(3)
10	-2.720	0.1486	EDUC(4)
11	**1.328**	**0.1936**	**ENCL(2)**
12	-0.01639	0.1961	AGE(2).ENCL(2)
13	-0.3010	0.2183	AGE(3).ENCL(2)
14	-0.08545	0.2156	AGE(4).ENCL(2)
15	-0.2767	0.2240	AGE(5).ENCL(2)
16	-0.2435	0.2488	AGE(6).ENCL(2)
17	-0.5711	0.2204	AGE(7).ENCL(2)
18	**-0.5925**	**0.1772**	**EDUC(2).ENCL(2)**
19	**-1.261**	**0.2080**	**EDUC(3).ENCL(2)**
20	**-1.103**	**0.2141**	**EDUC(4).ENCL(2)**

Appendix 7.12 Chinese Male Immigrants: Risks of Unemployment

	Estimate	s.e.	Parameter
1	-3.410	0.3724	1
2	-0.5992	0.2733	AGE(2)
3	-0.2060	0.2755	AGE(3)
4	-0.5515	0.2929	AGE(4)
5	-0.1161	0.2620	AGE(5)
6	-0.2793	0.2980	AGE(6)
7	-0.02635	0.2490	AGE(7)
8	0.1743	0.4027	EDUC(2)
9	0.2139	0.3994	EDUC(3)
10	0.3237	0.3755	EDUC(4)
11	-1.410	0.4378	ENCL(2)
12	1.372	0.5194	EDUC(2).ENCL(2)
13	1.618	0.5561	EDUC(3).ENCL(2)
14	1.622	0.5250	EDUC(4).ENCL(2)

Appendix 7.13 Chinese Female Immigrants: Access to Service Class

	Estimate	s.e.	Parameter
1	0.1715	0.1774	1
2	0.3738	0.09829	AGE(2)
3	0.3598	0.1115	AGE(3)
4	0.4633	0.1167	AGE(4)
5	0.3820	0.1334	AGE(5)
6	0.3595	0.1402	AGE(6)
7	0.03137	0.1423	AGE(7)
8	-1.102	0.1956	EDUC(2)
9	-1.747	0.1978	EDUC(3)
10	-2.567	0.1938	EDUC(4)
11	**0.9197**	**0.1876**	**ENCL(2)**
12	-0.3706	0.2204	EDUC(2).ENCL(2)
13	**-1.053**	**0.2441**	**EDUC(3).ENCL(2)**
14	**-1.004**	**0.2705**	**EDUC(4).ENCL(2)**

Appendix 7.14 Chinese Female Immigrants: Risks of Unemployment

	Estimate	s.e.	Parameter
1	-2.764	0.4935	1
2	-0.6535	0.4513	AGE(2)
3	-0.9126	0.5754	AGE(3)
4	-1.199	0.7637	AGE(4)
5	-10.11	52.72	AGE(5)
6	-0.4388	1.054	AGE(6)
7	-9.809	54.29	AGE(7)
8	-0.4652	0.5938	EDUC(2)
9	-1.629	0.8024	EDUC(3)
10	0.1298	0.5798	EDUC(4)
11	-0.2214	0.5032	ENCL(2)
12	0.2847	0.5930	AGE(2).EDUC(2)
13	1.201	0.8461	AGE(2).EDUC(3)
14	-0.02567	0.6258	AGE(2).EDUC(4)
15	0.8899	0.7079	AGE(3).EDUC(2)
16	2.010	0.9068	AGE(3).EDUC(3)
17	-0.06728	0.7661	AGE(3).EDUC(4)
18	1.108	0.9005	AGE(4).EDUC(2)
19	1.809	1.065	AGE(4).EDUC(3)
20	0.8709	0.8560	AGE(4).EDUC(4)
21	10.44	52.72	AGE(5).EDUC(2)
22	10.53	52.72	AGE(5).EDUC(3)
23	9.029	52.72	AGE(5).EDUC(4)
24	-9.791	54.84	AGE(6).EDUC(2)
25	1.677	1.276	AGE(6).EDUC(3)
26	-0.4846	1.134	AGE(6).EDUC(4)
27	9.799	54.30	AGE(7).EDUC(2)
28	9.842	54.30	AGE(7).EDUC(3)
29	9.850	54.29	AGE(7).EDUC(4)
30	0.1782	0.5919	EDUC(2).ENCL(2)
31	0.8651	0.6245	EDUC(3).ENCL(2)
32	1.242	0.5482	EDUC(4).ENCL(2)

Appendix 8.1 Goodness of Fit: Access to the Service Class

Males (N=82,482)[1]

Model	G^2	d.f	ΔG^2	Δd.f	p-value	$rG^2(\%)$	ID
Baseline	258.2	93			0.0000		1.984
Comparative	243.87	92	14.36	1	0.0000	5.6	1.946

Female (N=62,592)

Model	G^2	d.f	ΔG^2	Δd.f	p-value	$rG^2(\%)$	ID
Baseline	141.06	84			0.0001		1.468
Comparative	141.02	83	0.037	1	0.0001	0.03	1.468

---

[1]The samples of both males and females used for the U.S. coding are slightly bigger than the samples used for the British coding. This is because, for British only, the variable of the "highest qualification" was used for the British coding and the "age terminating continuous fulltime education" was used for the U.S. coding to check the results. There are fewer missing values for the latter variable than for the former variable. Therefore, in checking the results based on British coding, we cannot claim to use exactly the same sample.

308

Appendix 8.2 Access to the Service Class: Males

	Estimate	s.e.	Parameter
1	-0.9545	0.1570	1
2	0.2967	0.02781	AGE(2)
3	0.5125	0.02921	AGE(3)
4	0.4803	0.03115	AGE(4)
5	0.4192	0.03339	AGE(5)
6	0.4394	0.03581	AGE(6)
7	0.3784	0.03926	AGE(7)
8	0.2660	0.04845	AGE(8)
9	-1.864	0.05189	EDUC(2)
10	-3.844	1.006	EDUC(3)
11	-6.237	11.43	EDUC(4)
12	0.2843	0.1575	ETHN(2)
13	1.295	0.1587	COUN(2)
14	-0.2607	0.05570	EDUC(2).COUN(2)
15	0.4356	1.008	EDUC(3).COUN(2)
16	1.411	11.48	EDUC(4).COUN(2)
17	-0.5828	0.1603	ETHN(2).COUN(2)

Appendix 8.3 Access to the Service Class: Females

	Estimate	s.e.	Parameter
1	-1.931	0.2758	1
2	**0.1697**	**0.03209**	**AGE(2)**
3	**0.2012**	**0.03450**	**AGE(3)**
4	**0.1684**	**0.03745**	**AGE(4)**
5	0.08943	0.04149	AGE(5)
6	**0.1002**	**0.04462**	**AGE(6)**
7	**0.1069**	**0.05051**	**AGE(7)**
8	-0.01091	0.06715	AGE(8)
9	**-1.681**	**0.09620**	**EDUC(2)**
10	-7.579	10.60	EDUC(3)
11	-6.940	43.95	EDUC(4)
12	0.1353	0.2777	ETHN(2)
13	**1.890**	**0.2774**	**COUN(2)**
14	**-0.3861**	**0.09888**	**EDUC(2).COUN(2)**
15	4.119	10.60	EDUC(3).COUN(2)
16	4.038	43.96	EDUC(4).COUN(2)
17	-0.05316	0.2802	ETHN(2).COUN(2)

Appendix 8.4 Goodness of Fit: Risks of Unemployment

Males (N=82,482)

	G^2	d.f	ΔG^2	Δd.f	p-value	$rG^2(\%)$	ID
Baseline	108.74	93			0.1264		4.092
Comparative	107.91	92	0.833	1	0.1230	0.76	4.109

Females (N=62,592)

	G^2	d.f	ΔG^2	Δd.f	p-value	$rG^2(\%)$	ID
Baseline	119.15	84			0.0071		5.332
Comparative	114.63	83	4.53	1	0.0123	3.8	5.239

Appendix 8.5 Risks of Unemployment: Males

	Estimate	s.e.	Parameter
1	-2.989	0.2494	1
2	-0.3415	0.04873	AGE(2)
3	-0.5828	0.05350	AGE(3)
4	-0.6267	0.05674	AGE(4)
5	-0.6009	0.05809	AGE(5)
6	-0.6518	0.06209	AGE(6)
7	-0.5709	0.06463	AGE(7)
8	-0.6336	0.07913	AGE(8)
9	0.6716	0.08738	EDUC(2)
10	2.206	0.2790	EDUC(3)
11	2.834	1.417	EDUC(4)
12	0.7716	0.2405	ETHN(2)
13	-0.7778	0.2616	COUN(2)
14	0.1158	0.09803	EDUC(2).COUN(2)
15	-0.9630	0.2844	EDUC(3).COUN(2)
16	-1.054	1.458	EDUC(4).COUN(2)
17	-0.2261	0.2538	ETHN(2).COUN(2)

Appendix 8.6 Risks of Unemployment: Females

	Estimate	s.e.	Parameter
1	-2.906	0.3209	1
2	**-0.2409**	**0.05463**	**AGE(2)**
3	**-0.4914**	**0.06025**	**AGE(3)**
4	**-0.6000**	**0.06436**	**AGE(4)**
5	**-0.6466**	**0.06872**	**AGE(5)**
6	**-0.6808**	**0.07418**	**AGE(6)**
7	**-0.7211**	**0.08364**	**AGE(7)**
8	**-0.5825**	**0.1109**	**AGE(8)**
9	0.2120	0.1085	EDUC(2)
10	**1.120**	**0.4631**	**EDUC(3)**
11	-4.238	16.18	EDUC(4)
12	**0.8205**	**0.3116**	**ETHN(2)**
13	-0.4396	0.3294	COUN(2)
14	**0.4125**	**0.1191**	**EDUC(2).COUN(2)**
15	0.05937	0.4675	EDUC(3).COUN(2)
16	5.805	16.19	EDUC(4).COUN(2)
17	-0.6299	0.3211	ETHN(2).COUN(2)

313

Bibliography

Anwar, Muhammad (1979), *The Myth of Return: Pakistanis in Britain*,London, Heinemann.

Anwar, Muhammad (1990), "The Participation of Asians in the British Political System", in Clarke,C., Peach, C. and Vertovec, S. (ed.), *South Asians Overseas: Migration and Ethnicity*, Cambridge, Cambridge University Press.

Ballard, Roger E. and Holden, B.M. (1975), "The Employment of Coloured Graduates in Britain", *New Community*, IV.

Barringer, H.R., Takeuchi, D.T. and Xenos, P. (1990), "Education, Occupational Prestige and Income of Asian Americans", *Sociology of Education*, 63, pp. 27-43.

Baxter, S.C.C. (1988), *A Political Economy of the Ethnic Chinese Catering Industry*. Unpublished Ph.D Thesis, University of Aston.

Baxter, S.C.C. and Raw, G. (1988), "Fast Food, Fettered Work: Chinese Women in the Ethnic Catering Industry", in Westwood, S. and Bhachu, P. (ed.), *Enterprising Women: Ethnicity, Economy and Gender Relations*. London: Routledge, 1988.

Becker, G. (1964), *Human Capital*, New York, Columbia University Press.

Blalock, H.M.. (1956), "Economic Discrimination and Negro Increase", *American Sociological Review*, 21, pp. 584-588.

Blalock, H.M. (1957), "Percent Nonwhite and Discrimination in the South," *American Sociological Review*, 22, pp. 677-682.

Blalock, H. M. (1979), *Social Statistics*, Tokyo: McGraw-Hill Kogakusha, Ltd.

Blau, P. M. and Duncan, O.D. (1967), *The American Occupational Structure*, New York, John Wiley and Sons, Inc.

Blau, P. M and Ruan, D. (1990), "Inequality of Opportunity in Urban China and America", *Research in Social Stratification and Mobility*, 9, pp.3-32.

Boissevain, J. et al. (1990), "Ethnic Entrepreneurs and Ethnic Strategies", in Waldinger, R., Aldrich, H., Ward, R. and Associates (ed.), *Ethnic Entrepreneurs: Immigrant Business in Industrial Societies*, Sage Series Race and Ethnic Relations, I.

Brennan, J. and McGeevor, P. (1987), *Employment of Graduates from Ethnic Minorities: A Report by the Council for National Academic Awards for the Commission for Racial Equality*. London, The Commission for Racial Equality.

Brennan, J. and McGeevor, P. (1990), *Ethnic Minorities and the Graduate Labour Market: A Report by the Council for National Academic Awards for the Commission for Racial Equality*, London, The Commission for Racial Equality.

Brown, C. (1985), *Black and White Britain: The Third PSI Survey*, Gower, Policy Studies Institute.

Brown, D. L. and Fuguitt, G. (1972), "Percent Nonwhite and Racial Disparity in Nonmetropolitan Cities in the South", *Social Science Quarterly*, 53, pp. 573-582.

Cabezas, A. Y. (1979), "Disadvantaged Employment Status of Asian and Pacific Americans", *Civil Rights Issues of Asian and Pacific Americans: Myths and Realities: A Consultation Sponsored by the United States Commission for Civil Rights*, Washington, The United States Commission for Civil Rights, pp. 441-442.

Castles, S. and Kosack, G. (1985), *Immigrant Workers and Class Structure in Western Europe*, London, Oxford University Press.

Chan, A. (1986), *Employment Prospect of Chinese Youth in Britain* London, Commission for Racial Equality.

Chan, H. S. and Chan, Y. (1989), "Origin and Destination: the Case of Taiwan", in Hsiao, H.H. et al (ed.), *Taiwan: A Newly Industrialised State*, Taipei, National Taipei University.

Cheng, Y., Dai, J. Z. and Goldthorpe, J. (1992), "Social Mobility in Urban and Rural China", Paper presented at ISA RC28 Social Stratification Committee, Trento, May.

Cheung, C. W. (1975), *The Chinese Way: A Social Study of the HK Chinese Community in a Yorkshire City*, Thesis from University of York.

Chow, Y. T. (1966), *Social Mobility in China: Status Careers Among the Gentry in a Chinese Community*, New York, Atherton Press.

Chinese Information and Advice Centre, *"Chinese Community in Britain" Conference Report*. London, March.

Chiswick, B. R. (1983), "An Analysis of the Earnings and the Employment of Asian American Men", *Journal of Labour Economics*, 1, pp. 197-214.

Coleman, D. (1983), "The Demography of Ethnic Minorities", *Journal of Biosocial Science Supplement*, 8, pp. 43-87.

Commission for Racial Equality, (1983), *Vietnamese Refugees in Britain*, London, Commission for Racial Equality.

Craig, L. (1988), *The Residential Dispersal and Social Isolation of Chinese in Greater Manchester*, Oxford, Oriel College, Unpublished B.A. Thesis.

Dale, A. (1986), "The Role of Theories of Labour Market Segmentation in Understanding the Position of Women in the Occupational Structure", University of Surrey: Occasional Papers in Sociology.

Dale, A., Arber, S. and Procter, M. (1988), *Doing Secondary Analysis*. London: Unwin Hyman.

Dale, A. and Glover, J. (1990), "An analysis of Women's Employment Patterns in the U.K., France and the U.S.A.: The Value of Survey Based Comparison", Department of Employment: Research Paper No.75.

Davis, R. B. (1991), "Sample Enumeration Methods for Model Interpretation," Paper presented at the International Conference of Statistical Analysis in Utrech.

de Tocqueville, A. (1990), *Democracy in America*, New York, Vintage Books.

Duleep, H. (1988), *The Economic Status of Americans of Asian Descent: An Exploratory Investigation*. Washington: The United States Commission for Civil Rights, 1988.

Duncan, O. D. (1968), "Inheritance of Poverty or Inheritance of Race", in Daniel Patrick Moynihan (ed.), *Understanding Poverty*, New York, Basic Books, pp. 85-110.

Economist. (28 April 1990), "The Chinese in Britain: A Chequered History", *Economist*.

Embree, A. T. (1988), *Encyclopedia of Asian History*. New York: Charles Scribner's Sons, 1988.

Erikson, R. and Goldthorpe, J. (1985), "Are American Rates of Social Mobility Exceptionally High? New Evidences on An Old Issue", *European Sociological Review*, 1, pp. 1-22.

Erikson, R. and Goldthorpe, J. (1992), *Constant Flux: A Study of Class Mobility in Industrial Societies*, Oxford, Clarendon Press.

ESRC Data Archive, *ESRC Data Archive Catalogue: Guide and Index*, Cambridge, Chadwyck-Healey.

316

ESRC Data Archive, Complete Documents on Labour Force Survey from 1983 to 1989.

Fienberg, S. E. (1980), *The Analysis of Cross-Classified Categorical Data*, Cambridge, MIT Press.

Freeborne, J. D. M. (1980), *The Chinese Communities in Britain: With Special Reference to Housing and Education*, Unpublished Ph.D Thesis, University of London.

Frisbie, W. P. and L. Neidert. "Inequality and the Relative Size of Minority Populations: A Comparative Analysis", *American Journal of Sociology*, 82, pp. 1007-1030.

Fujii, E.T. and J. Mak. (1983), "The Determinants of Income of Native and Foreign-born Men in a Multiracial Society", *Applied Economics*,15, pp. 759-776.

Garvey, A. and Jackson, B. (1975), *Chinese Children in Britain: Research and Action Project into the Needs of Chinese Children*, Cambridge, National Education Research and Development Trust.

GLIM Working Party of the Royal Statistical Society, *The Generalised Linear Interactive Modelling System (Release 3.77)*, Oxford, Nag.

Goldthorpe, J.H. (1983), *Revised Class Schema 1983: Based on OPCS Classification of Occupations 1983*, Provided by John Goldthorpe.

Goldthorpe, J. H. (1987), *Social Mobility and Class Structure in Modern Britain (Second Edition)*, Oxford, Clarendon Press.

Gordon, M. (1964), *Assimilation in American Life: The Role of Race, Religion and National Origin*, New York, Oxford University Press.

Granovetter, M. (1981), "Toward a Sociological Theory of Income Differences", in Berg, I. (ed.), *Sociological Perspectives on Labour Market*, New York, Academic Press, pp. 11-43.

Han, S. F. (1975), *The Chinese in Sabah East Malaysia*, The Chinese Association for Folklore.

Haralambos, M. (1985), *Sociology: New Directions*, Causeway Books.

Hayes, J. (1977), *The Hong Kong Region 1850-1911: Institutions and Leadership in Town and Countryside*, Folkstone, Wm Dawson and Sons, Ltd.

Heath, A. (1981), *Social Mobility*, Fontana Paperbacks.

Heath, A. and Ridge, J. (1983), "Social Mobility of Ethnic Minorities", *Journal of Biosocial Science, Suppl.*, 8, pp. 169-184.

Heath, A., Mills, C. and Roberts, J. (1991), "Towards Meritocracy? Recent Evidence on An Old Problem", SCPR Working Paper No.3.

Hicks, J.R. (1964), *The Theory of Wages*, New York, St. Martin's.

Hirschman, C. (1983), "America's Melting Pot Reconsidered", *Annual Reviews of Sociology*, 9, pp. 397-423.

Hirschman, C. (1983), "America's Melting Pot Reconsidered", *Annual Reviews of Sociology*, 9, pp. 397-423.

Hirschman, C. and Wong, M. G. (1986), "The Extraordinary Educational Achievement of Asian Americans: A Search for Historical Evidence and Explanations", *Social Forces*, 65, pp. 1-27.

Hirschman, C. and Wong, M. G. (1981), "Trends in Socio-economic Achievement Among Immigrant and Native-born Americans: 1960 1976", *Sociological Quarterly*, 22, pp. 485-514.

Ho, P. T. (1962), *The Ladder of Success in Imperial China: Aspects of Social Mobility, 1368-1911*, New York, Columbia University Press.

Home Affairs Committee. (1985), *Chinese Community in Britain*. ICPSR. (1990), *Guide to Resources and Services 1989-1990*, Ann Arbor, ICPSR.

Jarvie, I.C. and Agassi, J. (1969), *Hong Kong: A Society in Transition: Contributions to the Study of Hong Kong Society*, London, Routledgeand Kegan Paul.

Jiobu, R. M. (1976), "Earning Differentials Between Whites and Ethnic Minorities: the Case of Asian Americans, Blacks and Chicanos", *Sociology and Social Research*, 61, pp. 24-38.

Jiobu, R. M. (1988), *Ethnicity and Assimilation: Blacks, Chinese, Filipinos, Japanese, Koreans, Mexicans, Vietnamese and Whites*. Albany: State University of New York Press, 1988.

Jones, P. (1982), "Vietnamese Refugees: A Study of Their Reception and Resettlement in the U.K.", Home Office Research and Planning U n i t Paper 13.

Kerckhoff, A.C., R.T. Campbell and I. Windfield-Laird (1985), "Social Mobility in Great Britain and the United States", *American Journal of Sociology*, 90, pp. 281-308.

Kerr, C. (1964), *Industrialism and Industrial Man*, New York, Oxford University Press.

Kim, H. C. (1980), "Koreans," in Stephen Thernstorm (ed.), *Harvard Encyclopedia of American Ethnic Groups*, Cambridge, The Belknap Press of Harvard University Press.

Knoke, D. and Burke, P.J. (1980), *Loglinear Models Series: Quantitative Applications in the Social Sciences*, Beverley Hill, Sage Publications.

Kuo, W.H. and Lin, N. (1977), "Assimilation Among Chines Americans in Washington D.C.", *Sociological Quarterly*, 18, 340-352.

Lai, Y. L. L. (1975), *Chinese Families in London: A Study into Their Social Needs*, M.A. Thesis from Brunell University.

Lee, O.N. (1991), *Education and Social Changes in Japan, Singapore and Hong Kong*, London, MacMillan.

Lieberson, S. (1980), *A Piece of the Pie: Black and White Immigrants Since 1880*, Berkeley, University of California Press.

Lieberson, S. and Waters, M. (1988), *From Many Strands: Ethnic and Racial Groups in Contemporary America*, New York, Russel Sage Foundation.

Light, I. and Bonacich, E. (1988), *Immigrant Entrepreneurs*, Berkeley, University of California Press.

Lin, N. and Bian, Y.J. (1991), "Getting Ahead in China," *American Journal of Sociology*, 97, pp. 657-688.

Lipset, S. "Changing Social Status and Prejudice: The Race Relations Theories of a Pioneering American Sociologist", *Commentary*, 9, pp.475-479.

Lobo, P. (1992), "Status of Asians and Latinos in the U.S. in the 1980", Paper presented at ISA RC28 Social Stratification Conference Trento, May.

Lyman, S. (1968), "The Race Relations Cycle of Robert Park", *Pacific Sociological Review*, 2, pp. 16-22.

Lyman, S. (1974), Chinese Americans, New School for Social Research.

Madood, T. (1991), "Establishing the Numbers of Ethnic Minority in Degree or Equivalent Courses to Aid Graduate Recruiters", London, Commission for Racial Equality.

Marsh, R. M. (1963) "Values, Demands and Social Mobility", *American Sociological Review*, 28, pp. 565-575.

Marsh, R. M. (1961), *The Mandarins: The Circulation of Elites in China, 1600-1900*, New York, The Free Press of Glencoe.

Massey, D. and Denton, N. (1988), "Trends in the Residential Segregation of Blacks, Hispanics and Asians: 1970-1980", *American Sociological Review*, 52, pp. 802-825.

McMahon, D. (forthcoming), "The Integration of the Irish in Britain", *International Migration Review*.

McNabb, R. and Psacharopoulos, G. (1980), *Racial Earning Differentials in the U.K.*, London School of Economics, Centre for Labour Economics.

Mitchell, R. E. (1972), *Family Life in Urban Hong Kong*.

Mitchell, R. E. (1972), *Pupil, Parent and School: A Hong Kong Study*, Taipei, The Oriental Cultural Service.

Model, S. (1986), "A Comparative Perspective on the Ethnic Enclave", *International Migration Review*, XIX, pp. 64-81.

Montero, D. (1981), "The Japanese Americans: Changing Patterns of Assimilation Over Three Generations", *American Sociological Review*, 46, pp. 829-839.

319

Montero, D. and Tsukashima, R. (1977), "Assimilation and Educational Attainments: The Case of the Second Generation Japanese American", Sociological Quarterly, 18, pp. 490-503.

Nam, C. B. and Philliber, S. G. (1984), *Population: A Basic Orientation*, Englewood Cliff, Prentice Hall.

Nee, V. (1989), "A Theory of Market Transition: From Redistribution to Markets in State Socialism", *American Sociological Review*, 54, pp. 267-282.

Newsweek. (21 June 1971), "Success Story: Outwhiting the Whites", *Newsweek*, 24.

Ng, K. C. (1968), *The Chinese in London*, London, Oxford University Press.

OECD (1980), *OECD Economic Surveys: United States*.

OECD (1987), *OECD Economic Surveys: United Kingdom*.

OECD (1988/1989), *OECD Economic Surveys: United Kingdom*.

Office for Official Publications of the European Communities, *Labour Force Sample Survey*, Luxumberg, Office for Official Publications of the European Community.

Office of Population Censuses and Surveys (1980), *Classification of Occupations and Coding Index*, London, Her Majesty's Stationary Services.

Osgood, C. (1975), *The Chinese: A Study of a Hong Kong Community*, Tuscon, The University of Arizona Press.

Payne, C., Payne, J. and Heath, A. (1993), "Modelling Trends in Multiway Tables," in R. Davis and Dale, A. (ed.), *Analyzing Social and Political Change: A Case Book of Methods*, London, Sage.

Park, R. and Burgess, E. (1924), *Introduction to the Science of Sociology*, Chicago, The University of Chicago Press.

Parsons, T. (1968), "The Social Class as a Social System: Some of Its Functions in American Society", *Harvard Educational Review*, 1, pp. 69-90.

Peach, C. (1968), *West Indian Migration to Britain: A Social Geography*, London, Oxford University Press.

Peach, C. (1983), "Factors Affecting the Distribution of West Indians in Great Britain", *Journal of Biosocial Science Supplement*, 8, pp. 151-163.

Peach, C. (1991), "The Caribbeans in Europe: Contrasting Patterns of Migration and Settlement in Britain, France and Netherlands", ESRC Research Paper, 15.

Peach, C., Robinson, V., Maxted, J. and Chance, J. (1988), "Immigration and Ethnicity", in Halsey, A.H. (ed.), *British Social Trend Since 1900: A Guide to the Changing Social Structure of Britain*, London, The Macmillan Press.

Peterson, W. (1971), *Japanese Americans*, New York, Random House.

Peterson, W. (9 January 1966), "Success Story: Japanese American Style", *New York Times Magazine*, p.38.

Phizacklea, A. (1988), "Entrepreneurship, Ethnicity and Gender", in Westwood, S. and Bhachu, P. (ed.), *Enterprising Women: Ethnicity, Economy and Gender Relations*, London, Routledge.

Piore, M.J. (1980), "Economic Fluctuation, Job Security and Labour Market Duality in France, Italy and the United States", *Politics and Society*, 9, pp. 379-407.

Plewis, I. (1988), "Assessing and Understanding the Educational Progress of Children from Different Ethnic Groups", *Journal of the Royal Statistical Society, Series A*, 151, pp. 316-326.

Pong, S. and Post, D. (1991), "Trends in Gender and Family Background Effects on School Attainments: the Case of Hong Kong", *British Journal of Sociology*, 42, pp. 249-271.

Portes, A. and Stepick, A. (1985), "Unwelcomed Immigrants: The Labour Market Experiences of 1980 (Mariel) Cuban and Haitian Refugees in South Florida", *American Sociological Review*, 50, pp. 493-514.

Portes, A. and Rumbaut, R.G. (1990), *Immigrant America: A Portrait*, Berkeley, University of California Press.

The Republic of China Ministry of Education, *Educational Statistics of the Republic of China*, Taipei.

Richmond, A. (1990), "Race Relations and Immigration: A Comparative Perspective", *International Journal of Comparative Sociology*, XXXI, pp. 156-176.

Robinson, V. (1986), *Transients, Settlers and Refugees*, Oxford, Clarendon Press.

Robinson, V. (1990), "Boom and Gloom: the Success and Failure of South Asians in Britain" in Clarke, C., Peach, C. and Vertovec, S. (ed.), *South Asians Overseas: Migration and Ethnicity*, Cambridge, Cambridge University Press.

Roizen, J. and Jepson, M. (1985), *Degrees for Jobs: Employer Expectations of Higher Education*, Guilford, Neilson.

Runnymede Trust. (1985), "The Chinese Community in Britain Background Paper", *Runnymede Trust Bulletin*, 178, pp. 8-15.

Runnymede Trust. (1986), *The Chinese Community in Britain: The Home Affairs Committee Report in Context*, London, The Runnymede Trust.

Schmid, C. and Nobbe, C. (1965), "Socioeconomic Differentials Among Nonwhite Races", *American Sociological Review*, pp. 909-922.

Sewell, W. and Hauser, R. (1975), *Education, Occupation and Earnings*, New York, Academic Press.

Shafer, B. E. (1991), *Is America Different? A New Look at American Exceptionalism*, Oxford, Clarendon Press.

Shang, A. (1984), The Chinese in Britain, London, Batsford Academic and Educational.

Shavit, Y. and Blossfeld, H. (1992), *Persistent Inequality: Changing Educational Stratification in Thirteen Centuries*, Boulder, Co., West View Press.

Steinberg, S. (1981), *The Ethnic Myth: Race, Ethnicity and Class in America*, Boston, Beacon Press.

Shultz, T.W. (1961), "Investment in Human Capital", *American Economic Review*, 51, pp. 1-17.

SPSS Inc. (1988), *SPSS-X User's Manual: 3rd Edition*, Chicago, SPSS Inc.

Stewart, M. B. (1982), "Racial Discrimination and Occupational Attainments in Britain", London School of Economics, Institute of Labour Economics.

Sung, B. L. (1967), *The Story of the Chinese in America*, New York, MacMillan Co.

Sung, B.L. (1975), *Chinese American Manpower and Employment*, Washington, U.S. Department of Labour, Manpower Administration.

Suzuki, B. H. (1988), "Asian Americans in Higher Education: Impact of Changing Demographics and Other Social Forces", A paper presented for a national Symposium on the Changing Demographics of Higher Education, New York City.

Sweeting, A. (1983), "Hong Kong", in Postlethwaite, T.N. (ed.), *Schooling in East Asia*, Oxford, Pergamon.

Tanna, K. (1987), *The Experience of South Asian University Students in the British Educational System and in Their Search for Work*, Ph.D Thesis, University of Aston.

Temin, P. (1991), "Free Land and Federalism: American Economic Exceptionalism", in Shafer. B. E. (ed.), *Is America Different: A New Look at American Excpetionalism*, Oxford, Claredon Press.

Trow, M. (1991), "American Higher Education: Exceptional or Just Different?" in Shafer, B. E. (ed.), *Is America Different: A New Look at American Exceptionalism*, Oxford, Clarendon Press.

Tsai, S. S. H. (1986), *The Chinese Experience in America*, Blommington and Indianapolis, Indiana University Press.

Tsai, S. L., Gates, Hill and Chiu, H. Y. (1992), "Schooling Taiwan's Women: Educational Attainments in the Mid-Twentieth Century", Paper presented at ISA RC28 Social Stratification Conference, Trento, May.

UNESCO. (1990), *Statistical Yearbook*.

UNIRAS A/S. (1991), *UNIGRAPH+2000 User's Manual*, Soborg, Denmark, UNIRAS A/S.

U.S. Bureau of the Census. (1973), "Racial and Ethnic Composition", *The Method and Materials of Demography*, Washington, U.S. Bureau of the Census.

U.S. Commission on Civil Rights. (1980), *Success of Asian Americans: Fact or Fiction?* Washington, Clearing House Publication, 64.

U.S. Commission on Civil Rights (1989), *Voices Across America: Roundtable Discussions of Asian Civil Rights Issues: Summary and Transcript of Roundtable Conferences in Houston, New York City and San Francisco*, Washington, U.S. Commission on Civil Rights.

U.S. Department of Commerce, Bureau of the Census. (1984), *Census of Population Housing, 1980 (United States): Public Use Microdata Samples*, Ann Arbor, ICPSR.

U.S. News and World Report. (26 December 1966), "Success Story of One Minority Group in U.S.", pp. 73-76.

Varon, B. F. (1967), "The Japanese Americans: Comparative Occupational Status", *Demography*, 3, p. 811.

Waldinger, R. (1983), *Ethnic Enterprise and Industrial Change: A Case Study of the New York Garment Industry*, Ph.D. Thesis, University of Harvard.

Waldinger, R. (1984), "immigrant Enterprise and the Structure of the labour Market", in Finnegan, R. and Gallie, D. (ed.), *New Approaches to Economic Life*, Manchester, Manchester University Press.

Watson, J. L. (1974), "Restaurants and Remittances: Chinese Immigrant Workers in London", in Foster, M. and Kemper, R. (ed.), *Anthropologists in Cities*, Boston, Little, Brown and Co..

Watson, J. L. (1975), *Emigration and the Chinese Lineage: The Mans in Hong Kong and London*, Berkeley, University of California Press.

Watson, J. L. (1976/1977), "Chinese Emigrant Ties to the Home Community", *New Community*, 5.

Watson, J. L. (1977), "The Chinese: Hong Kong Villagers in the British Catering Trade," in Watson, J.L. (ed.), *Between Two Cultures: Migrants and Minorities in Britain*, Oxford, Basil Blackwell.

Wilson, K. L. and Portes, A. (1980), "Immigrant Enclaves: An Analysis of the Labour Market Experiences of Cubans in Miami", *American Journal of Sociology*, 86, pp. 295-319.

Wong, H. H. (1980), *The Relative Economic Status of Chinese, Japanese, Black and White Men in California*, Unpublished Ph.D. Thesis, University of California at Berkeley.

Wong, S. L. (1985), "The Chinese Family Firm: A Model", *British Journal of Sociology*, 36, 58-80.

Zhou, M. and Logan, J. (1989), "Returns on Human Capital in Ethnic Enclaves: New York City's Chinatown", *American Sociological Review*, 54, pp. 809-820.

Index

215, 216-218, 223-226, 229, 230, 232, 234-239, 243, 246-250, 252, 258, 260, 262, 291, 297, 303, 305, 306, 308-310

sex 6, 7, 21, 39, 40, 42, 53, 55, 64-68, 70, 93, 115-117, 120-122, 155, 164-166, 178, 181, 195, 202

Shafer, B. 322

Shang, A. 322

social mobility 6, 19, 34, 41, 94-96, 106, 108, 192, 193, 227, 243, 315, 317-319

Southeast Asia 15, 19, 110, 111, 122

status attainment 22-24

Stewart, M. 322

Taiwan 15, 55, 57, 74, 96, 106, 107, 110, 122, 159, 315, 322

unemployment 16, 46, 68, 90, 195, 196, 199, 200, 202, 203, 205, 207, 209, 210, 212, 213, 214-218, 223-226, 229, 230, 232, 234, 239-243, 247-250, 255, 261, 263, 294, 300, 306, 307, 311-313

United States Census of Population and Housing 6, 36

Vietnamese 5, 7, 17, 18, 27, 39, 43, 53, 59, 61, 64, 67, 69, 90, 113, 117, 155-157, 161, 162, 164-166, 172, 175, 177-179, 181, 185, 187, 195, 208, 210, 212, 230, 232, 316, 318

Waldinger, R. 315, 323

Watson, J 323

West Indian 30, 43, 57, 61, 67-69, 77, 90, 232, 320

Whites 3-7, 10-12, 19, 22, 24-28, 38, 39, 53, 55, 57, 58, 65-67, 69, 70, 74, 77, 84, 86, 110, 111, 113, 116, 117, 155-157, 165, 166, 172, 173, 176-179, 181, 182, 186, 187, 199, 200, 209, 210, 212, 229-232, 242, 246-248, 249, 250, 318, 320

Zhou, M. 324